T0247856

FINAL VERDICT

Also by Tobias Buck

*After the Fall: Crisis, Recovery and the
Making of a New Spain*

FINAL VERDICT

The Holocaust on Trial in the 21st Century

Tobias Buck

 hachette
BOOKS

NEW YORK

Hachette Books
Hachette Book Group
1290 Avenue of the Americas
New York, NY 10104
HachetteBooks.com
Twitter.com/HachetteBooks
Instagram.com/HachetteBooks

First Hachette Books Edition: April 2024
Published in the UK 2024 by Weidenfeld & Nicolson.

Published by Hachette Books, an imprint of Hachette Book Group, Inc. The Hachette Books name and logo is a trademark of the Hachette Book Group.

The Hachette Speakers Bureau provides a wide range of authors for speaking events. To find out more, go to hachettespeakersbureau.com or email HachetteSpeakers@hbgusa.com.

Books by Hachette Books may be purchased in bulk for business, educational, or promotional use. For information, please contact your local bookseller or Hachette Book Group Special Markets Department at: special.markets@hbgusa.com.

The publisher is not responsible for websites (or their content) that are not owned by the publisher.

Library of Congress Control Number: 2024931063

ISBNs: 9780306832307 (hardcover), 9780306832321 (ebook)

Printed in the United States of America

LSC-C

Printing 1, 2024

To Ana and Tom

Contents

CHAPTER ONE

The man behind the red folder

The wooden door swings open, and an old man in a wheelchair enters the courtroom. His face is hidden behind a red cardboard folder, which he holds up with a single steady hand. For additional camouflage, he wears a pair of black sunglasses and a dark, wide-brimmed hat. All eyes in the room have turned toward him but he has no intention of returning their gaze. The old man sits in silence, flanked by his daughter and his lawyer, still hiding from the camera clicking away in front of him. As the seconds tick by, nervous anticipation fills the room.

Moments later, the judge orders the photographer and cameraman to leave, allowing the old man to lower the red folder and show his face. Sitting at the far end of the courtroom, I crane my neck to catch a first glimpse of the accused. He looks younger than his ninety-three years, alert, with dark eyes and neatly cropped white hair. In the row in front of me, an old woman starts crying, her slight frame shaking with silent sobs. The old man in the dock is her husband.

Turning to the accused, Anne Meier-Göring, the presiding judge, starts proceedings with a few simple questions.

"Can you hear me?"

"Yes," the old man says.

"Are you Bruno Dey?"

"Yes."[1]

1

It is October 17, 2019, the opening day of a trial in Hamburg's imposing criminal justice building. The trial is historic in more ways than one. Bruno Dey is accused of being involved in a crime that took place more than seven decades ago: the murder of at least 5,230 prisoners at Stutthof, a Nazi concentration camp in present-day Poland. He was only seventeen when he arrived at the camp, and became a member of the SS unit charged with guarding the site and ensuring that none of the desperate prisoners could flee. Dey has admitted that he served as a guard at Stutthof from August 1944 to April 1945, but he denies the accusation that he had any role in the murders, even as a subordinate, or accessory.

It is his name that appears on the charge sheet, but everyone in the courtroom knows that Dey will not be judged alone. As with all trials that examine the crimes of the Nazi regime, the Hamburg case raises questions—difficult, uncomfortable questions—that go far beyond the criminal culpability of any individual. They are questions that have weighed on the world since the first images of the camps and their victims emerged after the war. They cut especially deeply for Germans like myself but today seem profoundly relevant to all nations: how could this happen? Who is guilty? And what would I have done?

In many ways, Bruno Dey was the perfect foil to examine these questions. He had little in common with the Nazi leaders convicted at the Nuremberg trials or the thuggish murderers who later stood trial in German courts for their deeds at Auschwitz, Sobibor, and Treblinka. He was different, too, from the sinister desk perpetrators like Adolf Eichmann, tried and hanged in Israel for his pivotal role in the planning and execution of the Holocaust. Dey was not pivotal to anything, not even at Stutthof. He was a simple guard, who looked down from his watchtower,

2

and who in the midst of war, death and untold suffering never once saw the need to fire his gun. He was the smallest of small cogs, in a machine whose murderous intent he claims he never fully understood. That claim would face intense scrutiny over the course of the trial but no one ever doubted that the defendant occupied one of the lowest rungs of the camp hierarchy.

As I sat and listened to the opening exchanges, I found myself transfixed. I realized that it was precisely Dey's historical insignificance that interested and unsettled me. Like most sane human beings, I could not imagine myself as a murderer, or the commandant of a concentration camp or a senior officer in an organization of brutes like the SS. Surely, even in a dictatorship, in a time of war, my moral compass would not have failed me so badly. When we look at black-and-white images of the defendants at Nuremberg we feel revulsion, but we also feel the consolation of distance. We can tell ourselves with confidence that we would never have acted like them. On this October morning in Hamburg, however, as I looked across the courtroom at the impassive figure of Dey, I was not sure I could say the same thing about him. Would I, as a seventeen-year-old in Nazi Germany, have acted differently? Would I have had the moral courage to climb down from that watchtower, hand over my rifle and say: "No more"? And if I could not be sure, could anyone in this courtroom? Would the black-robed lawyers who represented Stutthof survivors have said "No"? Would the calm, confident figure of Meier-Göring, the presiding judge, have said "No"? And if she could not be sure, could the court still convict?

I had come to Hamburg to file a short story on the opening of the trial for my newspaper, but I resolved to return to the hearings as often as I could. I wanted to see how this drama played out. I wanted to see how the court wrestled with the moral and legal dilemmas thrown up by the case, but also how

Dey himself understood his role and his responsibility. Surely he sensed that for him, as for everyone else in the courtroom, this was a trial of last opportunities: a last opportunity for survivors to tell their story in a court of law, a last opportunity for an old man to confront his guilt and his conscience in front of a judge, and a last opportunity for Germany and its legal system to show that justice would be done, no matter how late.

For me, too, this was something of a last opportunity. The Holocaust had held a grip on me since my early teenage years in Germany, when I developed a sudden and deep curiosity about the Nazi period, and specifically the murder of Europe's Jews. Aged fourteen, I joined an evening class in my hometown to study antisemitism and the origins of the Holocaust. In 1990, with the Iron Curtain only just broken, I went to southern Poland to visit Auschwitz, part of a trip organized by survivors of the camp that left an indelible impression. I sought out and interviewed Holocaust survivors, including in my hometown of Darmstadt, a small university town close to Frankfurt. I wrote about my experience in Auschwitz in painfully earnest prose for my school newspaper, and eventually submitted a long, handwritten piece for an essay competition organized by the Israeli Ministry of Education. I remember winning a surprisingly large amount of money, along with a heavy bronze medal adorned with Hebrew lettering and the silhouette of Jerusalem. The medal still sat on a shelf in my old bedroom back in Darmstadt, as did dozens of faded copies of the monthly newsletter issued by the Auschwitz survivors' society, which I joined around the same time. Like most youthful obsessions, this one faded in the years that followed. I left Germany in my mid-twenties to become a journalist, returning many years later to cover my home country as a foreign correspondent.

Back in Berlin, I wrote stories about politics and business, defense policy and the environment, art, society and football—but also, every so often, about German history, and how that history wove itself into the present. And I wrote, once again, about the Holocaust, about survivors and perpetrators, and about a past that has never come to rest. I was driven by a curiosity common to all journalists in pursuit of a good story, but also by a sense of urgency. I knew that, with every month that passed, the voices of the victims and the guilty were falling silent. My German grandparents had died many years ago, and until now it had never occurred to me that I could—or should—try to find out what they knew and what they did during the war. The more I thought about this, the more striking this omission appeared. I had heard plenty of stories of their suffering at the end of the war, when my grandfather became a prisoner of war in the Soviet Union and, with the Red Army closing in on her hometown, my grandmother made a desperate escape in the depths of winter. But my understanding of what they did and didn't do before the collapse—during those twelve terrible years of Nazi rule—was hazy at best.

For Britons and Americans, who look back at the defeat of Nazi Germany as a defining triumph in each nation's history, such reticence must seem strange. In Germany, however, it was far from unusual—even many decades after the war. Now, the last members of the *Kriegsgeneration*, the war generation, were in their eighties and nineties. There were not many left who could talk, and fewer still who wanted to—especially if their memories involved wearing the uniform of the SS. But Dey would talk. He had to talk. And I wanted to hear what he had to say.

Bruno Johannes Dey was born on August 28, 1926, in Obersommerkau, a village less than 30 kilometers inland from the Hanseatic port city of Danzig. Neither place name appears on a map these days. At the time of Dey's birth, both Obersommerkau and Danzig were part of a German enclave, bordering the Baltic Sea to the north and surrounded on land by the state of Poland. After the war, Danzig and its hinterland became Polish. The few Germans who had clung on to their homes despite the advance of Stalin's Red Army were expelled to the West. Dey's birthplace today goes by the name of Ząbrsko Górne, while Danzig became Gdańsk.

The basic facts of Dey's life leading up to his day in court were described in the official indictment in sober prose that ran to barely four pages. His father was a farmer who worked the family's 39 acres of land in an area known as the Danzig heights. A young widower, he married Dey's mother when she was twenty-three (his first wife was her sister). The couple had seven children, though one of Dey's sisters died at birth, and another at the age of fourteen. Five survived the war: Dey along with two sisters and two brothers. The indictment noted that the defendant started school in 1932, after Easter, as was customary in Germany at the time.

It was, even by the standards of Germany's fraught and bloody twentieth century, a fateful year: in February, Adolf Hitler obtained German citizenship, allowing the Austrian-born leader of the National Socialists to stand as a candidate for the highest office in the land, the Reich presidency. Dey's first year in school was spent mostly under the auspices of the Weimar Republic, Germany's ill-fated excursion in democracy. But the menacing pull of Hitler and his Brownshirts was growing stronger with every week. In the federal elections on July 31, 1932, the National Socialists won almost 40 percent of the vote, emerging as the largest party in the Reichstag for the first time. A second ballot was held in November, in which the fascists lost strength but managed to retain their position as the dominant force in parliament. The Weimar Republic was dead before Dey completed his first year in school: the Reichstag burned down in February 1933, followed by the first wave of repression and persecution of political opponents.

The Nazis triumphed in the federal elections of March 1933, a vote scarred by repression, violence, and voter intimidation, and Hitler proclaimed the Third Reich a few days later.

At about the same time, in a sleepy suburb north of Munich, an abandoned munitions factory was being readied to house political prisoners, starting with Social Democrat and Communist leaders. Formally opened on March 15, 1933, Dachau would become the first Nazi concentration camp, a place of fear, humiliation, torture, and murder that remained in operation almost until the bitter end. By the time American soldiers arrived at its gates in April 1945, more than 32,000 men, women, and children had met their death there.

Dey left school in 1940, aged fourteen. "I enjoyed the learning, but not the company of the classmates. I became a loner… I didn't connect with anyone and I didn't trust anyone," he would later tell the court. Dey was friendless and bullied by his classmates, who beat him and stole the apples he used to take to school for his lunch breaks. Instead of supporting him, his parents blamed Dey for getting into trouble. As soon as he arrived home he would be put to work on the farm, fetching the cows to be milked, picking up stones from the field, weeding, planting potatoes. "Was there anything positive you remember from your childhood, something you thought was especially nice?" the judge would ask him in one of the later trial hearings. "Nice? Was there anything nice?" Dey responded. "There wasn't much that was nice."

His school years came to an end just as the Wehrmacht prepared its lightning strike on France. Poland—the country that once surrounded his home region—had been conquered and dismembered the previous year, and subjected to brutal occupation by Nazi Germany in the west and Stalin's

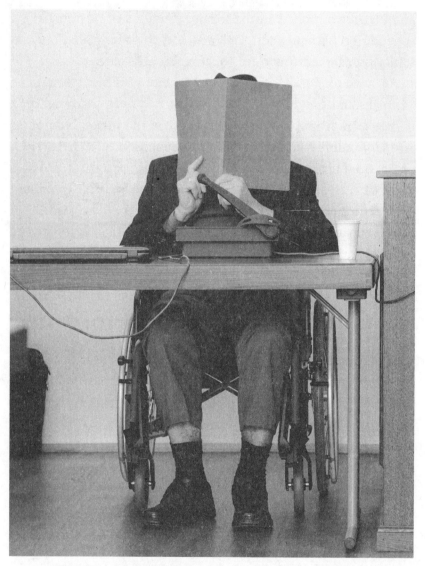

"For more than seventy years, no one in Germany was interested in a simple guard." Bruno Dey in court.

Soviet Union in the east. Too young to join the fighting, Dey embarked on a two-year apprenticeship as a baker, as safe and as peaceful a profession as one might imagine, under the circumstances. He had dreamed of a career driving or working with motorcars, but his father dispatched him to the bakery regardless. By his own account, he had already learned the importance of keeping his head down, and the risks of taking a political stand. Dey's father was a member of the Zentrumspartei, a conservative political movement closely aligned with the Roman Catholic Church. The Zentrum's deputies had backed Hitler's claim for sweeping extra-legal powers in 1933, but the party was disbanded and its politicians persecuted all the same. Dey's father, too, suffered harassment, after he was heard making critical remarks over the handling of the war. As Dey recalled, his father was warned he could end up in Stutthof, the nearby concentration camp that would become so familiar to his son a few years later. Dey himself initially resisted joining the Hitler Youth, despite pressure from his schoolmates, but ultimately signed up. He claimed he only ever attended a couple of the group's meetings. His excuse was that, as a baker's apprentice, he got up too early to take part in *Hitlerjugend* activities.

In 1943, with the tide of war already turned and the mass killing of Jews and other enemies of the Reich already well under way, Dey underwent his *Musterung*, the official medical inspection prior to commencing military service. The doctors found a heart problem that meant he was certified to do duty only inside barracks, but not on the front line—a medical assessment that would emerge as a significant theme of the trial. Despite the increasingly dire need for new soldiers, his military service was deferred by a year. Sometime around Easter 1944, Dey was finally called up to join the Wehrmacht, and was posted to an infantry battalion in nearby Stettin (now Szczecin). In early June, still only seventeen, he was sent to Stutthof for the first time, to perform guard duties along with other soldiers from his battalion. Dey fell sick with diphtheria, forcing him to spend some time in a hospital in Danzig, but he returned to Stutthof in early August, when he was formally inducted into the first company of the *SS-Totenkopfsturmbann Stutthof*, one of the notorious "skull" units of the SS. Named after the skull-and-crossbones insignia on their uniform, the members of this unit were responsible for guarding the Nazi concentration camps. This was the beginning of his eight-month tour of guard duty at the concentration camp—a fraction of his lifetime, but the only period of interest to the judges in Hamburg. Dey insisted that he never volunteered to join the SS, or indeed to serve at Stutthof. The idea that there might be some alternative course of action—for example volunteering to serve on the Eastern Front—never crossed his mind.

In January 1945, with the Red Army closing in on Danzig, the SS decided to abandon Stutthof, but the evacuation of personnel and prisoners dragged on until April. Thousands of inmates lost their lives on death marches west. Dey himself left the camp in April 1945, making his way to Schleswig-Holstein, the northern German region bordering Denmark, where he was taken prisoner first by the Americans and later by British authorities. Released in December 1945, he initially worked as a baker and farmer in return for food and a roof over his head. The indictment noted that Dey met his future wife—the white-haired woman now sobbing in front of me inside the courtroom—in October 1952. The two became engaged just two months later, on Christmas Eve. He went on to work as a lorry driver, a janitor, and a shipping clerk, built a house on the outskirts of Hamburg, and retired in 1988. He had two daughters, four grandchildren, and four great-grandchildren. The indictment added just one more line to his personal details: "He has no criminal record, nor has he ever come into conflict with the law."

*

Over the course of the next nine months, the defendant would take his seat inside courtroom 200 after the inevitable opening ritual. Each day of the trial, Dey would enter the court together with his lawyer and daughter, shielding his face from the photographer and cameraman during the first minutes.[2] As soon as they left, he would lower the cardboard file and wait for the judge to start proceedings. Anne Meier-Göring sat to his left, on an elevated wooden podium, flanked by two junior judges and two lay judges. Across from him stood the desk occupied by the chief prosecutor Lars Mahnke and a colleague. To his right, facing the judge, sat the lawyers representing survivors of Stutthof and their descendants, several dozen of whom had been granted admission to the trial as so-called "private accessory prosecutors," or co-plaintiffs. This meant they had the right to question witnesses and plead in court along with the state prosecutor. Sitting behind them was Dey's family, and, further back still, journalists and spectators. It was, even by the standards of a big-city murder trial, a large crowd. Dey's white-haired wife was in court on most days, usually accompanied by other members of the family, including his grandchildren. They did not speak to any of the journalists, but the message they sent was clear: they were present to show their support for the defendant, and to ensure he did not feel alone. None did so with more commitment than his daughter, who sat by his side at the front of the courtroom every day, often dressed in a matching blouse and headscarf (she had married a Muslim and followed the Islamic dress code). Dey's lawyer told me later that she had worked hard to support the defense; she studied the case files in depth, and read legal textbooks to prepare herself for the hearings. In court, she watched over her father with a perpetual look of pity and concern.

The courtroom itself exuded a sense of late-nineteenth-century grandeur, with slender Corinthian pillars protruding from the walls and a richly stuccoed coffered ceiling above. A bank of large windows overlooking the square below flooded the room with light, even on gray winter mornings. It was the largest and most ornate in Hamburg's criminal justice building.

These surroundings would become deeply familiar to Dey, as would the key protagonists who shared this stage with him. The most important was Meier-Göring, the presiding judge. It was largely coincidence that had put her in charge of this historic trial: because Dey was only seventeen or eighteen at the time of the alleged crime, by law he had to be treated as a juvenile offender, despite his advanced age at the time of the trial. As the presiding judge of one of three divisions dedicated to youth criminals, it had simply been Meier-Göring's turn to take on his case. However, she had been keen to do so, she later told me. Born in 1968, she had, like most Germans of her generation, been fascinated and troubled by Germany's Nazi past from a young age, and had followed the academic and political debate about how to prosecute and punish Nazi criminals closely. One reason for her early interest, she admitted, was undoubtedly linked to her name: Meier-Göring had no family connection to Hermann Göring, the Nazi leader, but the fact that they shared a name had often prompted questions, especially when she was living and studying abroad. "My name is Göring, so from a very early age I concerned myself with the question of whether my family had anything to do with Hermann Göring. Thank God that wasn't the case," she told me. Long before she became a judge, Meier-Göring had also reflected on broader questions of guilt and responsibility. "I thought a lot about collective guilt, and I also felt it. I could not say—like many people do—that this was only a matter of individual guilt. I always felt a part of German society, and as such felt a certain degree of guilt."

Meier-Göring would face difficult moments over the course of the trial, and an exceedingly difficult decision at the end of it. But her skill at steering these complex hearings was never in doubt: she showed compassion and sensitivity toward the elderly survivors of Stutthof who came to testify in court, but also found a way to relate to the defendant himself. She kept Dey talking and remembering and, on rare occasions, pushed the defendant to question himself. At times, Meier-Göring would speak harshly to the accused, and there were moments when she exposed his evasions with cold, forensic scrutiny. But she seemed to understand that the trial—and the defendant—had to be approached with humanity, and a degree of humility. Dey looked up to her, in more ways than one.

For Meier-Göring, the case of Bruno Dey was the first involving Nazi-era crimes in her twenty years as a judge. Lars Mahnke, the prosecutor, had been investigating suspects like Dey for years but for him, too, this was the first opportunity to bring a case to court, and ultimately to a verdict. A soft-spoken Hamburg native, Mahnke told me had studied law in part due to a "deep-rooted sense of justice," and in part inspired by American courtroom dramas. Before becoming a public prosecutor, he had served as a legal expert in the city's building and planning authority but decided that a job in government administration was too boring. He had worked on the Dey case since 2016, and had spent long hours questioning the defendant about his past. His own interrogations, spanning eight intense sessions at the headquarters of the Hamburg police, had foreshadowed many of the debates that also proved decisive during the trial. Mahnke knew the case, and the man at the center of the case, better than almost anyone in the courtroom. His familiarity with the horrors of Stutthof, too, was second to none. Covering two walls in his large but spartan corner office was a sprawling timeline detailing thousands of individually documented killings at the camp, broken down by method and year.

From the first moment of the trial, there was a striking gulf between the ordinariness of Dey's biography and the magnitude of the alleged crime. This is not unusual in criminal trials, of course, even—or perhaps especially—in trials involving the Holocaust. In Dey's case, however, the contrast between the man and the alleged deed felt especially stark. Facing the court in October 2019 was a frail old man in a wheelchair, who had lost the menace of youth, and arrived each day in court accompanied by a medical team that monitored him carefully throughout the proceedings. His voice was weak, his words often hard to understand. Dey seemed unthreatening, helpless even.

Among the people who sat with me in the press section of courtroom 200 on the opening day was a prominent visitor from Israel: Efraim Zuroff, the director of the Simon Wiesenthal Center in Jerusalem, who had spent long years researching the Holocaust and tracking down Nazi perpetrators. He did not mind being called a "Nazi hunter," and on this day he had come to Hamburg to inspect a rare prey. When I asked Zuroff for his view on the Dey trial, he advised me to look beyond the frail old man sitting in the dock. "These are the last people on earth who deserve any sympathy. Because they had no sympathy for their victims, some of whom were even older than they are today," Zuroff told me in the lobby of the court building, where lawyers, journalists, and observers mingled before and after the hearing. "You look at them and they are trying to look as sick and as out-of-it as possible. But don't see an old frail person—think of someone who was in their physical prime, out there murdering innocent men, women, and children." Zuroff, whose organization has spent decades compiling lists of the most wanted Nazi criminals still at large, insisted that "the passage of time in no way diminishes the guilt of the killers." Old age should not protect people who committed such crimes, he said, if only to help give victims and their families a chance of closure: "We owe it to the victims to try and bring these killers to justice."

I nodded as he spoke to me. He was right, of course. This trial was about the victims as much as it was about the perpetrator. Dozens of Stutthof survivors and their descendants had formally joined the case for the prosecution, hoping that their stories and memories would finally be heard in the one place that really mattered: a court of law. Their testimony would provide some of the most poignant moments in the trial, made more powerful still by the knowledge that such voices would not be heard much longer.

It was Dey, however, who drew me to the trial. My hope was that he could help me understand the incomprehensible, or at least a facet of the incomprehensible. Why did the Holocaust happen? Since the end of the war, there had been no shortage of attempts to answer that question; they filled entire libraries and occupied the minds of legions of historians. The approaches and avenues they took were innumerable, and all started in different places. There were historical explanations, sociological explanations, political and military explanations, and psychological explanations. One school of thought argued that Hitler and leading Nazis had always intended to eliminate Europe's Jews (and many millions more non-Jews in central and eastern Europe). Others believed the Nazi genocide came about in a more haphazard way, and only after an earlier plan to expel all

Jews under German rule to the east failed as a result of German military defeat.

These debates interested me greatly but I had nothing to contribute to them. What I did have was a rare chance to hear and observe an old man, accused of helping murder thousands of people in a Nazi concentration camp, at the end of his life, with little left to lose and with an incentive, perhaps, to come clean after all those years. The charges brought by the prosecution alleged that Bruno Dey played a part—albeit a small part—in a great evil. If he was found guilty, his guilt would be minuscule in comparison to that of Hitler and the Nazi leadership. But Hitler and the Nazi leadership could not have made the Holocaust a reality if it had not been for the hundreds of thousands of Germans who helped. They compiled the deportation lists, shipped the poison gas, rolled out the barbed wire, steered the trains, cooked the executioners' meals, kept the books, and guarded the perimeters of Stutthof, Auschwitz, and Treblinka. What made them say yes? Or more precisely: what stopped them from saying no?

CHAPTER TWO

The second disgrace

Stefan Waterkamp is an ascetic-looking man, tall and stick-thin, with close-cropped hair and long, gangly limbs. In court, Dey's lawyer towered over his client, but he showed little inclination to dominate the proceedings. Over the course of the first weeks and months, he would remain silent for long stretches of the trial, intervening only to request short breaks for the defendant to rest and regain his strength. Waterkamp's defense strategy—much like his manner—was quietly understated. Neither he nor his client seemed to desire an all-out legal battle. When he spoke, he spoke softly. When his client wanted to speak, he let him speak—even if Dey's interventions were not always advantageous to his own defense. Waterkamp's readiness to allow the trial to unfold, and for Dey's story to be told in court, would be tested later on. On the opening day of the trial, however, he focused his argument on a simple question: why now?

His client, Waterkamp said, when he rose to make his first statement, simply could not understand why he found himself in court. Dey had never made a secret of his time in Stutthof. The police had investigated his role in 1975, and concluded there was no case. In 1982, he gave testimony about Stutthof as a witness in another criminal trial. Once again, no one seemed to think he had done anything wrong. The truth, Waterkamp said, was this:

"For more than seventy years no one in Germany was interested in a simple guard who never committed any killings himself."

His statement rang true—and it carried a double rebuke. The first rebuke seemed directed at Germany's legal system today—at the court in Hamburg, at Mahnke, the prosecutor, and at the phalanx of black-robed lawyers who were there to support the prosecution on behalf of Stutthof victims and their descendants. The challenge Waterkamp threw at all of them was this: why prosecute and punish an old man who had only a few more years to live, more than seven decades after the alleged crime took place? Why seek the conviction of a defendant who was a nobody in the camp hierarchy, when so many of the men above him—including those who killed with their own hands, and those whose commands sent thousands to the gas chamber—escaped punishment?

The second rebuke, and perhaps the more resonant, pointed at an earlier generation of German prosecutors, judges, and criminal lawyers, for their historic failure to bring Nazi perpetrators to justice. Indeed, it was not just "simple guards" like Dey who never had to stand trial, but tens of thousands—maybe hundreds of thousands—of potential culprits who orchestrated, led, implemented, and helped bring about the most terrible crime in human history.

For much of the post-war period, Nazi perpetrators had less to fear from the country's prosecutors and judges than common thieves. Historians estimate that as many as a quarter of a million Germans were implicated in the Holocaust.[1] Some of the worst offenders were dealt with by Allied courts between 1945 and 1949, most notably during the Nuremberg trials. Others were turned over to countries in eastern Europe; among them Rudolf Höss, the commandant of Auschwitz, who was convicted and hanged in Poland in 1947. The bulk of cases and culprits, however, were left to West Germany to prosecute. It failed miserably at the task: in total, West German prosecutors launched investigations into some 170,000 suspects in the years after 1945, but only 6,700 were found guilty and sentenced.[2] The vast majority of those convicted—more than 5,100—received prison sentences of less than two years, or were simply fined.[3] Of the 6,000 SS men who served in Auschwitz and survived the war, only 800 were ever put on trial, most of them in front of Polish courts.[4] Over the course of more than seven decades, German judges sentenced no more than fifty SS members who served in Auschwitz.[5] The picture was little different for Stutthof, where some three thousand SS personnel did duty. Just seventy-eight of them were put on trial—most of them in Poland.[6]

That failure was all the more remarkable in the context of Germany's broader approach toward historical memory. In the decades since the end of the war, Germany won admiration around the world for the way it faced up to its past, a collective struggle that gave rise to an entire new vocabulary of heavy German compound nouns: *Vergangenheitsbewältigung*, for example, meaning the process of coming to terms with the past. Or *Erinnerungskultur*, memory culture. Or *Wiedergutmachung*, which literally means "making good again," but can also be translated as "reparation." What ultimately flowed from this struggle was unflinching recognition of the terrible deeds done by Germans in Germany's name between 1933 and 1945, and an unwavering commitment to keep alive the memory of the Holocaust, and to accept Germany's sole and permanent responsibility for the murder of six million Jews.

For much of the recent past, these have not been controversial views to hold. Today, despite the persistent menace of the far right, mainstream German politicians and public figures know that to question the country's guilt means banishment to the margins of society. In a very practical sense, that collective feeling of guilt and responsibility is almost impossible to ignore. The crimes of the Nazis are taught at school, referenced in political speeches, and immortalized in monuments up and down the country. So complete is Germany's commitment to Holocaust remembrance that even recent migrants—whose grandparents and parents were raised thousands of miles from the bloodlands of central and eastern Europe—are taught to embrace it. This expectation to internalize Germany's special guilt and responsibility even extended to the latest generation of refugees, who arrived from Syria, Iraq, and Afghanistan in the hundreds of thousands after 2015. One of the more peculiar political debates triggered by their arrival was whether to make a visit to the site of a former concentration camp compulsory for all recent migrants.[7] While that did not happen, many refugees were indeed taken on tours of Dachau, Buchenwald, and Oranienburg as part of their induction courses into life in Germany. Strange as it may sound, assuming German guilt seemed like an integral part of becoming German.

Perhaps the most striking symbol of Germany's commitment to remember its crimes can be found right in the heart of Berlin, in a vast field of undulating concrete steles just south of the Brandenburg Gate. Here, within sight of the national parliament, reunified Germany built a memorial to its victims on a gargantuan scale. Extending across a site large enough to accommodate three football pitches, the 2,711 slabs of dark gray concrete are arranged in symmetrical rows but the uneven ground and differing height create a maze-like sense of displacement and unease. The fact that it occupies some of the most iconic real estate in the capital is reflective of the central space that the Holocaust occupies in the country's collective conscience.

The Nazi genocide has defined modern, democratic Germany like no other event. It helps explain many of the country's post-war idiosyncrasies. The staunch pacifism and intricate constitution, the aversion to flag-waving and patriotic rhetoric, and the deep mistrust of charismatic leadership—these and a thousand other habits, customs and conventions of modern Germany can be traced back to the Holocaust. The Federal Republic of Germany defined itself—had to define itself—against that stain. If there was any chance of national redemption after the murder of six million Jews (and the death of more than fifty million soldiers and civilians as a result of Hitler's war of aggression), the new Germany would have to prove that it was different. That imperative helped foster a moral absolutism encapsulated in appeals like the one made by the philosopher Theodor W. Adorno, a towering figure in post-war intellectual life. Returning from U.S. exile in 1949, he famously commanded his compatriots to forsake poetry. "To write a poem after Auschwitz is barbaric," he wrote in an essay.[8] The appeal itself was universally ignored; the underlying message of penance and rupture was not. The Holocaust left Germany with two simple commandments: never forget, never repeat.

That moral rigor took time to find broad acceptance, and was in short supply in the years immediately after the war. In the courtroom, it remained an exception for almost the entire history of the Federal Republic. The low number of convictions after 1949, when Germany regained full sovereignty, tells one part of the story. For every perpetrator who was found guilty, thousands escaped without punishment. Yet even those who were brought to trial were often treated with unfathomable leniency, as prosecutors and judges went out of their way to minimize the guilt of the defendants.

The site of the Stutthof concentration camp today.

A case in point is the 1955 trial of Paul-Werner Hoppe, the man in charge of Stutthof at the time when Dey served as a guard, and one of the few concentration camp commandants ever to face justice in a West German court. Born in Berlin in 1910, Hoppe joined the Nazi Party in June 1932 and became a member of the SS the following year. Committed and ambitious, he was selected for SS leadership training, went on to serve as an SS officer in the camps at Dachau and Lichtenburg, and married the daughter of the Lichtenburg camp commander in 1936. Hoppe was wounded during fighting on the Eastern Front in 1942 and appointed to oversee Stutthof the same year. Arrested by the British in 1946, he managed to escape to Switzerland before the authorities could hand him over to Poland (where he would have faced a certain death sentence). He returned to Germany in 1952, but was arrested again and put on trial in the city of Bochum, together with another SS man from Stutthof, Otto Karl Knott. The indictment charged Hoppe with overseeing the murder of hundreds of Jews in a railway car that had been converted into a gas chamber. Prosecutors also charged him for his involvement in the killing of camp prisoners through shots in the back of the neck and through injections of petrol into the heart. In truth, Hoppe was responsible for killing tens of thousands of inmates at Stutthof between 1942 and 1945. But the approach taken by prosecutors and judges at the time—and for many decades to follow—was to limit the number of victims for the purpose of building a solid criminal case, and to focus only on those killings that could be precisely and concretely attributed to the defendant. As it turned out, that was not the only problem when the court handed down its verdict on December 16, 1955. The judges ruled that both Hoppe, the commandant, and Knott, who had thrown the deadly Zyklon B pellets into the gas chamber with his own hands, had acted only as accessories to murder. In the court's view, the two men were only "small figures" in a larger system who had been "led astray and seduced" by the Nazi leadership. Their wrongdoing had been "relatively minor when set against the immense guilt of those who were ultimately responsible."[9] The commandant of Stutthof, the man who had ordered and overseen the murder of tens of thousands of innocent men, women, and children, was sentenced to just five years and three months in prison. Had he been convicted not as an accessory but as a perpetrator—even of just a single murder—he would have faced a mandatory sentence of a lifetime in prison. Knott was sentenced to three years and three months in prison.

The verdict was eventually overturned on appeal and Hoppe's sentence lengthened to nine years. But the federal court of appeal did not call into question the key finding of the lower court—that Hoppe and Knott had acted only as helpers. The former commandant was released from prison in 1960—just three years after the longer sentence was handed down—and went on to live a quiet life in Bochum until his death in 1974.

The leniency shown to Dey's commanding officer was far from unusual. German courts proved to be especially reluctant to convict the so-called *Schreibtischtäter*, or "desk perpetrators," the bureaucrats and officials whose murderous contribution to the Holocaust took place far from the camps but was crucial nonetheless. A good example of this is the case of Benno Martin, a senior SS officer and the chief of police in the city of Nuremberg from 1934 until the end of the war. As a prominent Nazi and veteran SS member, Martin was part of the select audience invited to listen to the notorious first Posen speech made by Heinrich Himmler, the head of the SS, in October 1943. This was the first known instance in which a Nazi leader spoke openly about the extermination of the Jewish people. Himmler went on to praise the SS men responsible for the mass murder in bizarre and chilling words: "Most of you here know what it means when 100 corpses lie next to each other, when there are 500 or when there are 1,000," he said. "To have endured this and at the same time to have remained decent—with exceptions due to human weaknesses—that is what has made us tough, and it is a glorious chapter that has not, and never will be, spoken of."

Martin himself was responsible for the deportation of at least a thousand Jews from Nuremberg and the surrounding region of Franconia in November 1941. The city's once-thriving Jewish community, which traced its roots back to the twelfth century, was all but wiped out under his command. Martin was arrested and interned after the war but despite repeated attempts by local prosecutors to bring his case to trial they failed to secure a conviction—not even as an accessory. In fact, the verdict handed down in 1953 by a court in Nuremberg praised Martin for his commitment to "upholding the rule of law and order in his area of responsibility" and his efforts to "facilitate the situation of the Jewish population and protect them against attacks."[10] The judges went on to argue that "as far as the Jewish question was concerned, Dr. [Martin] was of the opinion that this could only be addressed within the rule of law and while recognizing the demand for humanity."[11] The court also noted approvingly that Martin had tried to ensure that "the Franconian Jews were spared humiliations, insults and mistreatment during the evacuation, and were dealt with in a correct, humane manner."[12] He was acquitted. The ruling reportedly sparked applause and jubilation among members of the public who had attended the trial.

The Nuremberg ruling is shocking for many reasons, not least for its unthinking embrace of Nazi terminology and thought. It refers to the "Jewish question" as if the question—whether Jews should be allowed to live in Germany—was at any point legitimate. The term was pure Nazi propaganda and should have had no place in a courtroom in post-war democratic Germany. The same might be said of the word "evacuation," which is normally held to mean the transfer of people to a place of greater safety. In the jargon of the Nazi state, of course, it meant packing vast numbers of Jews in rail carriages and sending them to their death. Then there is the court's reference to Martin's "humanity" in organizing the practicalities of the deportation, suggesting that his culpability in driving Jews toward the gas chamber was somehow lessened by the fact that the first part of their journey took place without wanton cruelty and public humiliation.

For all their differences, the cases of Paul-Werner Hoppe and Benno Martin highlighted several common features of Germany's post-war approach toward prosecuting Nazi crimes. The first was a general tendency by courts to place most, if not all, of the blame on Hitler and a handful of other senior Nazi leaders—and to treat the entire chain of command below either as mere aides, or as completely innocent. As one German law professor remarked sarcastically at the time: "One perpetrator and sixty million accessories, or: the German people, a people of accessories."[13]

In many ways, this approach reflected the broader sentiment in Germany in the years after the war, when millions of ordinary citizens were suddenly faced with the challenge of justifying their own behavior—and indeed their own crimes—under Nazi rule. For many, this meant casting themselves in the role of the seduced—gullible perhaps but ultimately innocent, too patriotic and too naive to see through Hitler's lies. Alongside such personal myths sat the idea that certain groups—notably the officers and soldiers of the Wehrmacht, but also German bureaucrats, judges and lawyers—had only done their duty. Unlike the SS and Gestapo, for instance, these loyal servants had "stayed clean." Indeed, the notion of the "clean Wehrmacht" remained broadly intact until the mid-1990s, when a fiercely controversial exhibition documented the crimes of Germany's armed forces during the Second World War—and their complicity in the Holocaust.

The only category of Nazi criminals that German courts seemed genuinely comfortable taking on were the violent brutes. Also known as "excess perpetrators," these were the men (and women) who acted with such uncommon sadism and cruelty that they stood out even among the ranks of the SS. Hermine Braunsteiner, for example, was an especially feared guard at the Majdanek death camp, who met and married an American military officer after the war, and moved with him to the U.S. She was identified and eventually extradited to Germany only in 1973, and put on trial in the city of Düsseldorf. The court found her guilty of aiding the gassing of more than a hundred children at Majdanek. What stood out to those who followed her trial, however, was less her specific role at the camp than the tales of her excessive brutality: kicking prisoners with her steel-capped boots, for example, or seizing children by the hair and tossing them on trucks to take them to the gas chamber, and whipping women to death.[14] Her nickname, according to survivors, was the "Stomping Mare."

Another case of excessive brutality came to court in Bayreuth in 1957. This one concerned the SS officer Martin Sommer, who was sentenced to a lifetime in prison for the mistreatment and murder of inmates at the Buchenwald concentration camp. Known as the "Hangman of Buchenwald," Sommer was described by the prosecution as the man responsible for "probably the most hideous group of sadistic atrocities unearthed since the war."[15] He beat and tortured his victims to death, killed inmates out of pure bloodlust and murdered a priest by dousing him with water and leaving him tied outside in the cold, where he froze to death overnight.[16]

In both cases, the courts undoubtedly arrived at the correct verdict (both Braunsteiner and Sommer would likely have faced the death sentence had their trials taken place before 1949). At the same time, it is hard to escape the conclusion that Germany's post-war judiciary was missing the bigger picture. The uncomfortable truth is that the repugnant deeds of Braunsteiner and Sommer were not just excessive but also exceptional. The overwhelming majority of Holocaust victims did not die as a result of individual sadism or wanton acts of cruelty by camp guards. They died because of a murderous system that worked—and killed—regardless of whether or not the individuals involved were sadists or not, whether they had qualms about their role or not, whether they liked what they saw or not, whether they intended to be murderers or not.

More often than not, the men and women at the grim end of that murderous chain, the Braunsteiners and Sommers, were entirely replaceable. They had the opportunity to live out their sadistic impulses only because people more senior, more powerful, and more intelligent than them had built a system that allowed them to. Yet those senior and powerful people often escaped with far lighter sentences—if they faced prosecution and trial at all. As Hans-Christian Jasch and Wolf Kaiser write in their book on the Holocaust in German courts: "The focus of the criminal prosecution in the Federal Republic was placed on sadistic intensive perpetrators who formed part of the camp personnel or the *Kapos* [prisoners turned guards] who collaborated with them. The mostly bourgeois and university-educated *Schreibtischtäter*, who were typically already well integrated into post-war society, were mostly let off the hook."[17]

The quintessential *Schreibtischtäter*, of course, were the fifteen men who attended the Wannsee Conference, the notorious meeting on January 20, 1944, that was called to discuss and find a "final solution of the Jewish question." A select group of top officials and officers that included Reinhard Heydrich, the head of the Nazi state security apparatus, as well as Adolf Eichmann, met in a palatial villa overlooking the Wannsee lake on the outskirts of Berlin. Though it lasted little more than ninety minutes, the conference was a landmark event in the history of the Holocaust—the moment when all the key branches of the Nazi state came together to discuss and coordinate the murder of European Jewry. The fact that those mass killings were already under way—notably in the form of the "Holocaust of bullets" in occupied Russia—does not dim the significance of the event. According to the historian Peter Longerich, "the Wannsee Conference set a course that determined the when, the how and the where of the 'final solution.' The destruction of the European Jews became a project that would no longer be completed to a large extent only after the war, but during the war."[18] The protocol itself remains a most disturbing document. Drafted by Eichmann, its fifteen pages oscillate between precision and evasion: precision when it came to defining the different graduations of Jewish ancestry that would decide over life and death; evasion when it came to spelling out the fate that awaited the millions of Jews now at Hitler's mercy. The document spoke of "evacuation to the east" and "elimination by natural causes" before cautioning that the more resilient "remaining stock" of the Jewish population would have to be "treated accordingly." For all the verbal obfuscation, the meaning of those words was perfectly clear to the men present.

Aside from Eichmann and Heydrich, the conference was attended by high-ranking members of the justice, interior, and foreign ministries, the police and SS, the party, and the authority charged with overseeing occupied Poland. The involvement of so many branches of the Nazi state and security apparatus was no coincidence. Heydrich wanted co-ordination but he also wanted complicity. No part of the Nazi hierarchy would be able to say that it did not know about the murderous plan. All would have their names on the key document. All would be guilty.

All were guilty. But not all of the fifteen participants paid a price. Five of the men who attended the Wannsee Conference died before the end of the war, while two were tried and executed in the immediate post-war years. Justice also caught up with Adolf Eichmann. The remaining seven, however, were either never charged, or escaped with minor punishment. Among them was Otto Hofmann, a powerful SS general and the head of the SS Race and Settlement Main Office. He was part of the Nazi old guard, having joined the party in 1923, a full decade before Hitler came to power. A fierce antisemite, Hofmann was considered an expert on the matter of "mixed-breed Jews," whose mass sterilization he argued for at Wannsee. Captured after the war, he was sentenced to twenty-five years in prison by an Allied court in 1948, but was pardoned and released just six years later. He lived a quiet life in south-western Germany until his death in 1982.

Gerhard Klopfer fared even better. Another high-ranking SS member, he attended the conference in his function as state secretary of the Nazi Party Chancellery. Klopfer briefly went into hiding after Germany's defeat in 1945, but was captured by Allied forces and held in several internment camps before acting as a witness—and only as a witness—during the Nuremberg trials.[19] No charges were ever brought against him. His only punishment came through the so-called "denazification" procedure, which saw civilian tribunals review the records of millions of Germans after the war and classify them according to their degree of involvement in the Nazi state. Klopfer was deemed to be only *minderbelastet*, a lesser offender. Even though his role at the Wannsee Conference was known at the time, Klopfer's only sanction was a fine of 2,000 Deutschmarks and a three-year probation period during which he was banned from high-profile professions.[20] He eventually settled in the Swabian city of Ulm, opened a law firm, and lived out his life undisturbed, a respected member of the local community once again. At the time of his death in 1987 he was the oldest surviving participant of the Wannsee Conference. Not that you would have known from reading the family tribute in the local paper at the time, which declared simply that Klopfer had passed away "after a fulfilled life that served the well-being of all who were in his sphere of influence."[21]

The reluctance to punish the greatest crime in human history can be partly explained by practical considerations. By 2019, defendants like Dey were few and far between, but in 1950 there were hundreds of thousands like him. Prosecuting each and every German implicated in the Holocaust would have stretched the country's justice system to breaking point and beyond. It would almost certainly have made the mammoth task of establishing and securing democracy in post-war Germany harder than it already was. But there was also, with few exceptions, no real willingness to try: traumatized by war, the vast majority of Germans wanted to move on as quickly as possible. If there was guilt to apportion, they thought that it should fall on Hitler and the immediate Nazi leadership, not on the millions of ordinary Germans who had supported and served his regime for years. Far from accepting their own guilt and complicity in his rise, a large majority of Germans saw themselves as victims of the Nazi regime. Had their cities not been destroyed? Had they not lost fathers, brothers, and sons in the war? Had millions of ethnic Germans not been driven from their ancestral lands in eastern Europe in retaliation for the conflict? Was Germany itself not divided and occupied by its enemies, with little prospect of regaining its sovereignty?

German civilians had indeed suffered greatly during the conflict, especially in the final year of the war. And they continued to suffer during the first months of occupation, when much of the country was still in ruins, food was scarce, and the threat of reprisals and violence (and for millions of German women under occupation, rape) was ever present. Germans were in survival mode, and that meant psychological survival as well. This was no moment for introspection and reflection, and certainly not on matters as painful for Germans as their own responsibility for Hitler's rise and the crimes that followed. According to Alexander and Margarete Mitscherlich, whose 1967 book *The Inability to Mourn* attempted to psychoanalyze post-war society,

Germans' emotional response to the Nazi period and the war was marked by denial and repression. The country looked back at the Hitler years—a source of shame and guilt—like the outbreak of "childhood infectious disease," the couple wrote.[22] "It is frightening to see such infantile exoneration techniques," they added, noting that Hitler's crimes would not have been possible without the "enthusiastic support of the collective." The Mitscherlichs concluded: "This attempt to gain control of the past must seem grotesque to the distant observer."[23]

Even before the official creation of the Federal Republic in 1949, the clamor to draw a line under the past—and specifically the crimes of the past—grew louder every year. A crucial target of popular ire was the American-run prison in Landsberg am Lech, Bavaria, where the most notorious Nazi criminals were held (and where 259 of them were hanged between 1945 and 1951). John McCloy, the U.S. high commissioner, came under growing pressure to grant clemency to the remaining prisoners, including from Konrad Adenauer, the first German chancellor after the creation of the Federal Republic, and from Theodor Heuss, the president. Church leaders joined that chorus, as did thousands of ordinary Germans who demonstrated frequently outside the Landsberg prison. In 1951, McCloy finally caved in. Of the remaining eighty-nine prisoners, thirty were released immediately, and forty-nine saw their prison terms reduced. Only ten prisoners had their sentences upheld, including five senior Nazi criminals whose death sentences McCloy confirmed. From a geopolitical perspective, the American change of heart was not without logic. The Cold War was now in full swing, the Soviet Union had turned from ally to foe, and West Germany was needed as a bulwark against Communist advances in Europe. But McCloy's decision was consequential all the same.

It sent the message that a line should indeed be drawn, that the principles established at Nuremberg were obsolete, and that the political needs of today trumped the universal call for justice. That, in any case, was the message Germans wanted to hear, and the one they thought they had received. The country's political leadership did not take long to respond. Less than three months after the Landsberg pardons, the newly established German parliament passed a law that allowed judges, professors and civil servants who had served the Nazi state to return to government employment—even if they had been party members. The legislation was approved unanimously, save for two abstentions. Even the deputies from the Communist Party voted in favor. Three years later, the parliament issued an amnesty law that effectively barred the prosecution of serious crimes, including manslaughter, committed during the final stages of the war. This was the second amnesty law passed by the recently elected Bonn parliament during its brief history. The first, which removed the threat of criminal sanctions from all defendants who faced a prison sentence of less than six months, had been passed as early as 1949. Yet another blow followed in 1955, when Germany regained full sovereignty as a result of the so-called "transfer treaty" with the U.S., France, and Britain. This gave Germany full responsibility for prosecuting Nazi criminals, but also barred trials against all suspects previously put on trial by Allied courts. Crucially, this meant that defendants who had been acquitted due to a lack of evidence—or who had been pardoned—could not be tried again, even if new and damning evidence came to light.

Some of the key beneficiaries of this clause were the prisoners of Landsberg, all of whom would be released by 1958. These included mass murderers like Martin Sandberger, who led Einsatzgruppe 1a, one of the notorious units charged with killing Jews and resistance fighters in the newly conquered territories in occupied eastern Europe and Russia. Sandberger had been sentenced to death in 1948, but received a pardon from McCloy in 1951 and was eventually released seven years later. He shared the same fate as Ernst Biberstein, another *Einsatzgruppen* chief, who was also sentenced to death, pardoned, and released in 1958. Neither man would face trial in West Germany after 1949. Sandberger lived until 2010, Biberstein until 1986. These senior officers had nothing to fear from the wealth of new incriminating material that would be unearthed in the years that followed—while men in far less senior positions were now put on trial. "When Holocaust trials started happening with greater frequency after the 1960s, these offenders often appeared as free men in court to give evidence in support of their former subordinates," Jasch and Kaiser write in their book.[24]

There is no single cause that explains the historical failure of the West German judiciary to prosecute Nazi crimes, and specifically the crimes of the Holocaust. There were practical as well as legal reasons, political reluctance as well as popular resistance. Justice was thwarted by German amnesia and American realpolitik, and by an unspoken agreement between key German leaders to draw a line under the past and move on. At the political and social level, Germany would later adopt a much more enlightened stance. On rare occasions, German courts did bring high-profile perpetrators to justice, notably during the hugely ambitious but ultimately flawed Auschwitz trial in Frankfurt, and a series of lesser-known court cases against SS personnel from other camps. But the number of cases and convictions remained desperately low, and the sentences that were handed down were all too often shockingly light. In 1949, the year the Federal Republic was founded, German prosecutors filed 3,975 formal charges

34

against suspects accused of Nazi crimes, of which 1,474 led to convictions.[25] Only five years later, the number of charges filed against suspected Nazi criminals had fallen to just 49.[26] As the decades went by, case numbers drifted steadily lower. In 1984, less than four decades after the end of the war—with thousands of potential suspects still only in their sixties or seventies—just one Nazi case was brought before a West German court, and there was not a single conviction. In the two decades that followed, prosecutors and courts managed to achieve a grand total of thirty-three trials and eighteen convictions.[27] This meager record was arguably an even greater failing than the reluctance to prosecute Nazi criminals in the early years of the Federal Republic: German democracy had long been made safe; the risk that a more vigorous judicial approach would undermine political stability seemed negligible.

As the twentieth century drew to a close, prospects of a last-gasp campaign against surviving perpetrators of the Holocaust looked faint. The practical and legal obstacles seemed insurmountable, the number of possible culprits was dwindling by the day. It would take a peculiar kind of jurist—stubborn, awkward, maybe even a little insubordinate—to take on such a challenge. Those are rare traits in a profession that is, by definition, beholden to rules, customs, and precedent. But there was one judge in the south of Germany who fit that description perfectly—and it just so happened that in 2006 he was looking for a new challenge.

CHAPTER THREE

Factories of death

The little town of Wangen is about as far from Hamburg as you can travel without leaving Germany altogether. Nestling in the foothills of the Alps near Lake Constance, it is postcard-pretty, filled with colorful, perfectly restored baroque and Renaissance buildings, and ringed by lush meadows and forests. Known as the Allgäu, the surrounding region is famed for producing the best cheeses in the country.

I came to Wangen to meet Thomas Walther, a 76-year-old retired judge with piercing eyes, long gray hair, and dark bushy eyebrows. His shadow loomed large over the Dey trial, even though he never once set foot inside the Hamburg courtroom.[1] Without Walther and the tale of perseverance I came to hear, the man behind the red folder would have likely remained anonymous until his dying days. In the small but borderless world of lawyers and scholars who dealt with Nazi crimes, Walther was something of a celebrity. He was the recipient of awards and prizes, including the Order of Merit of the Federal Republic of Germany. Yet he lived modestly on the ground floor of a terraced house on the outskirts of Wangen, which he shared with one of his daughters and her family. The small garden at the back of the house was filled with brightly colored plastic toys and a playhouse. We sat inside, sipping cappuccinos at his wooden dining table, and Walther started telling me how he ended up hunting Nazis.

His life, he explained, took a dramatic turn in the summer of 2006, just after he retired from his job at the nearby district court. Still only in his mid-sixties, he felt it was too early to stop working. Walther remembered telling one of his superiors that he was at the height of his judicial abilities and wanted to do "something useful and meaningful" after standing down from the court. He wanted a last challenge, and when he saw that the Central Office for the Investigation of National Socialist Crimes was looking for investigators, he decided to sign up.

The Zentrale Stelle ("Central Office"), as it is commonly known, was established in December 1958 to do a job that few in Germany wanted to do: track down Nazi criminals. Based in a former prison in the sleepy Swabian town of Ludwigsburg, Nazi hunting has been its mission ever since. The Central Office was set up in response to perhaps the most famous Holocaust trial in the early years of the Federal Republic: the so-called *Einsatzgruppen* trial that was held in the southern German city of Ulm from April to August 1958. The Einsatzgruppen, or action groups, were death squads made up mostly of SS members and policemen, and were responsible for mass executions of Jews, Communists, partisans, and anyone else the Nazis wanted dead in territories recently occupied by the Wehrmacht. The ten men on trial in Ulm had belonged to the Einsatzkommando Tilsit, and stood accused of murdering more than 5,500 Jewish men, women, and children in the border region between Germany and Lithuania in 1941.[2] The case came to light not because of diligent work by police and prosecutors but because the most senior member of the group, a former Nazi police chief by the name of Bernhard Fischer-Schweder, had been too brazen even by the standards of 1950s Germany. Having successfully evaded identification and prosecution in the immediate post-war period (the denazification process concluded that he was "unencumbered"), Fischer-Schweder eventually threw caution to the wind in 1955. His past caught up with him after he sued the regional government with the aim of winning back his old job as the director of a refugee camp. That brought attention in the local press, where he was soon identified as the former head of police in the Baltic city of Memel, the present-day Klaipėda in Lithuania, and a crucial figure in a series of mass shootings in 1941. Fischer-Schweder had good reason to feel safe: countless other Nazi-era officials—from policemen and judges to bureaucrats and military officers—had indeed been able to resume their careers after the creation of the Federal Republic. In Fischer-Schweder's case, however, the publicity prompted a closer examination of his record during the war and led prosecutors to file murder charges against him and nine others. The trial sparked unusual interest among the German public and was closely covered by the media. The Tilsit killings were remarkably well-documented, as was the cold-blooded eagerness with which some of the accused had taken part in the slaughter: in one instance, the men had even posed for souvenir photos after the shooting was done.[3] Fischer-Schweder had put together an execution squad from forces under his command on his own initiative (he had in fact only been asked to supply men to guard the surrounding area). The verdict made clear that he also played a key role in the actual shootings, checking on victims after the first salvo and providing the *coup de grâce* to those still alive.[4]

Yet even though Fischer-Schweder was a senior SS officer and a committed Nazi, who had volunteered for the mass killings and fired his own gun, the court found him guilty only as an accessory, a minor figure who had merely helped carry out the crime. "All of the accused who took part in the shootings at

Garsden…acted in response to an order, not with the will of the perpetrator but the will of the accessory," the judges found. The men had not wanted to commit the crime "as their own" but had wanted to support someone else's crime. They were, the verdict said, nothing but "tools of the Führer."[5] Fischer-Schweder was sentenced to ten years in prison. The other nine defendants were given prison terms of between three and fifteen years.

Aside from the dubious legal and moral conclusions contained in the verdict, the Ulm case also laid bare a practical weakness of the German approach toward Holocaust prosecutions: the lack of a central authority to investigate such crimes. Germany's criminal justice system, much like its political system, was (and still is) highly decentralized. That meant courts and prosecutors would usually only take on cases that had a clear local connection—if the accused was a local resident, for example, or if the crime itself took place in the district. In Holocaust cases, such a geographical link was fiendishly hard to establish, since the vast majority of victims were murdered in camps and killing fields in Russia and eastern Europe. And without a central register of suspects or a special authority charged with finding them, it was impossible for police and prosecutors to know whether a potential perpetrator was present in their area. The problem was accurately described by Lawrence Douglas, a U.S. legal scholar and expert on Holocaust trials. "Crime tends to be local," he wrote, "and Germany's federated system, like its American counterpart, was well equipped to deal with ordinary criminal acts, but not with a continent-wide campaign of extermination."[6] As the case of Fischer-Schweder showed, Holocaust trials in the 1950s were typically the result of carelessness and coincidence, rather than the fruit of a structured effort by the West German authorities.

The Ulm trial also coincided with a growing awareness among

jurists, politicians, and the wider public that courts were running out of time to prosecute and punish Nazi criminals. The statute of limitations enshrined in Germany's criminal code at the time meant that prosecutors only had a few more years before Nazi crimes—all Nazi crimes—would be barred from going to trial. For manslaughter, that period was fifteen years after the day the crime was committed. For murder, it was twenty years. In practice, this meant charging a former SS man for manslaughter in connection with the Holocaust would be all but impossible after 1960 and for murder after 1965. In just seven years, even the worst mass killers would no longer have to fear prosecution. That prospect caused political unease in Germany, at least in some quarters, and sparked a protracted debate that would lead first to an extension of the statute of limitation for murder, and eventually to its abolition. It also invited critical scrutiny from abroad. Political leaders in Bonn faced especially persistent pressure from the Communist regime in rival East Germany, which delighted in exposing the Nazi links of senior West German officials and attacking the country's hesitant approach toward prosecuting Nazi criminals. In May 1957, the East German regime released a list of "blood judges" who had served the Nazi regime and who were now employed in senior positions in West Germany. It was the start of a campaign that struck at what one scholar has described as the "Achilles heel" of West Germany's efforts to punish Nazi crimes—the fact that so many of the judges presiding over these trials had served loyally under the Hitler regime.[7] The initial list was quickly followed by revelations linking hundreds more West German judges to the Third Reich. The government in Bonn tried to brush off the criticism, but the pressure—both at home and abroad—eventually became too great to ignore.

The first and arguably most important result of that pressure was an agreement between the eleven West German federal states to set up a small authority charged with investigating Nazi crimes. It was up and running in December 1958, just four months after the verdict of Ulm. The man in charge of the new institution was Erwin Schüle, who had served as the lead prosecutor in the Ulm trial. Energetic and resourceful (he was the first German prosecutor to access the vast files of the U.S.-run Berlin Document Center), Schüle had caused a stir with his final plea in the *Einsatzgruppen* trial. His intervention, brief but powerful, urged Germans to reflect on their own moral failure during the Nazi era, and spoke of the "shame that we all feel."[8] He specifically did not exclude himself from that charge and used the pronoun "we" throughout his intervention. At one point he confessed that "all of us were too cowardly at the time."[9] Schüle proved to be an effective leader of the Zentrale Stelle during its early years, but the shame he expressed in the Ulm courthouse in 1958 was more deeply grounded in his own biography than he let on at the time. Schüle, it turned out, had himself been a member of the Sturmabteilung (SA), the Nazi paramilitary wing, and had joined the Nazi Party in 1937. At first, he tried to dismiss the revelations, insisting that he had done nothing wrong. Facing mounting public pressure at home, and new accusations from authorities in the Soviet Union claiming he had been involved in the killing of civilians during fighting on the Eastern Front, Schüle offered his resignation in April 1966.[10] He had become a political embarrassment, but also a symptom of a deeper malaise: in post-war West Germany, it seemed, even the Nazi hunters had a Nazi past.

Then as now, the Zentrale Stelle can be found behind high stone walls, in a squat prison building on the outskirts of Ludwigsburg, near Stuttgart in south-west Germany. The authority's inner sanctum is on the ground floor, past a thick metal door and a corridor dominated by a vast map showing central Europe during the Nazi occupation. At the end of that corridor is a room filled with large metal filing cabinets: an archive—still entirely on paper—containing 720,000 names of criminals, suspects, collaborators, and witnesses from the Nazi period. The names are organized both alphabetically (I easily found Adolf Eichmann's cards, stapled together and marked by a handwritten cross on the front) and by location or the name of the concentration camp. Auschwitz alone occupies several large metal drawers. In its busiest period, between 1967 and 1971, the authority's staff swelled to more than 120, including forty-nine prosecutors and judges.[11] At the time of my visit, however, staffing had fallen to barely twenty, eight of whom served as investigators. Unlike normal prosecutors, the officials at the Zentrale Stelle are barred from filing charges or presenting their case in court. Instead, they act like an early-stage prosecution service: they identify likely culprits, sift evidence, and then pass on their files to ordinary state prosecutors who investigate further and, if justified, file charges.

When Thomas Walther arrived at the Zentrale Stelle in 2006, however, that work had largely ground to a halt. Six decades had passed since the end of the war. It had been five years since a German court had last convicted a Nazi perpetrator. There was, many thought, simply no one left to prosecute. Crucially, that view was shared also by Kurt Schrimm, the director of the Zentrale Stelle at the time, who explained the problem to his latest recruit in weary tones. "He told me: this authority will almost certainly not bring any new cases to trial," Walther recalled. "We have to demonstrate that the accused was directly implicated in the crime, and that won't be possible. The witnesses are either old or sick or dead. They don't know and they don't remember."

Thomas Walther, the retired judge who helped
bring John Demjanjuk to justice.

Over the years, German prosecutors and judges had indeed
convinced themselves that they could only go after suspects
who had killed people themselves, usually with excess brutality,

or whose contribution could be linked to a specific murder or murders. Put simply: they would only charge concentration camp guard A if they could prove that A had helped murder prisoners B, C, and D on a certain date in a certain place. In a normal murder case, establishing this concrete connection was usually simple enough. In the anonymous killing factories of Treblinka, Auschwitz, and Sobibor, it was all but impossible. How could you prove that a guard sitting on a watchtower knew who was being murdered in the gas chamber at any given moment in time?

Walther thought that German prosecutors and judges had got this wrong. And he set out to prove it by going after one of the most high-profile targets still alive: John Demjanjuk. A Ukrainian-born U.S. citizen, Demjanjuk had been sentenced to death by an Israeli court in 1988, after the judges identified him as "Ivan the Terrible," a notorious guard at Treblinka. But there was strong evidence to suggest that Demjanjuk had never been at Treblinka—prompting the Israeli Supreme Court to overturn the conviction. Demjanjuk returned to the U.S. a free man, but soon became the target of sustained efforts by U.S. authorities to strip him of his citizenship and deport him to Europe. Walther became interested in the case in 2008, at a time when Demjanjuk was still fighting his extradition. It turned out that Demjanjuk had indeed served as a so-called "Trawniki man," a camp guard and auxiliary recruited by the SS from the local population—not in Treblinka but at the extermination camp in Sobibor, in southeastern Poland. Crucially, this fact had never been disputed by Demjanjuk's lawyers during the extradition hearings.

Walther knew that it would be impossible to prove that Demjanjuk had contributed to a specific killing. So he tried a different legal route: what if, he asked, the crime that Demjanjuk had aided was not a specific murder inside the camp, but the camp itself? Sobibor, Walther argued, was essentially a "factory of death." Much like a car factory, it depended on a multitude of people who were given separate tasks but who all worked knowingly toward the same goal. The accountant, the cleaner and the security man at a car factory may not know which model is rolling off the plant on any given day, nor will they ever lay a hand on the car itself. But they know the goal that they serve—and that their contribution is required for the success of the overall operation. That same logic, Walther thought, should apply to Sobibor, an extermination camp that—unlike concentration camps like Auschwitz or Dachau—served only one purpose: to murder all the men, women, and children who were delivered to its gates. While concentration camps served at least some other needs of the Nazi state, notably the incarceration of political opponents and the use of Jewish prisoners as slave laborers, the three principal extermination camps at Treblinka, Belzec, and Sobibor left behind almost no survivors: of the 1.5 million Jews who were deported to those three camps, just 120 lived to see the end of the war. The survival rate was less than 0.01 percent. No innocent work was done at Sobibor. Anyone and everyone who helped keep that factory in motion was an accessory to murder.

"The whole thing had to be understood as an industrial enterprise, where everyone works in unison," Walther told me. He would later learn that this line of reasoning had in fact already been accepted by German courts in some cases, albeit many decades ago. But it had been forgotten by the legal community, including by his colleagues at the Zentrale Stelle. Walther decided to pursue it regardless. "I had to prove that the SS man was on duty in a camp from a certain date to a certain date, and that during that time of service a certain number of victims arrived," he told me. "And once I put all that together, I thought that should be enough to show to the prosecution that there was an urgent suspicion, which meant they had to examine: is this enough for formal charges or not?"

Walther teamed up with a colleague at the Zentrale Stelle, Kirsten Goetze, and together they set about building their case. Schrimm, despite initial misgivings, allowed them to pursue their "death factory" theory, and gave them license to track down witnesses and documents in Germany and beyond. Walther, it turned out, had picked an opportune moment to challenge the legal orthodoxy. The Zentrale Stelle was just preparing for its fiftieth anniversary celebrations, in 2008, and Schrimm was keen to show that Ludwigsburg was still relevant. A headline-grabbing new case against a high-profile target like Demjanjuk would be useful to deflect criticism of its meager prosecutorial record in recent years, and might help silence calls for the Zentrale Stelle to be dismantled. Walther warned Schrimm that a change of doctrine would also confirm the wrongheadedness of the previous approach. "I told him, 'If I do this and it works and it turns out to be correct, it will mean that we got things badly wrong here before.' He answered, 'Well, that will be on me.'"

John Demjanjuk was extradited to Germany in May 2009, at the age of eighty-nine. Just six months later, he was wheeled into a Munich courtroom, the eyes of the world trained on him once again. It was the start of one of the most extraordinary criminal trials in recent German history. In stark contrast to the first Demjanjuk trial, in which Israeli prosecutors relied heavily on the powerful but ultimately flawed eyewitness accounts of survivors, the German case was built above all on historical expertise. Following Walther's lead, prosecutors made no attempt to link Demjanjuk to any specific atrocity. Instead, they sought to establish three central facts: first, that the accused was at

Sobibor during the alleged period of time; second, that during that period a certain number of killings took place; and, third, that Demjanjuk had helped those killings because of his functional role in the camp hierarchy. "The prosecution, lacking evidence that the accused had killed with his own hand, developed a rather brilliant theory specifically tailored to the realities of service as a death camp," Douglas notes. "The argument was as simple and irresistible as a syllogism: all Sobibor guards participated in the killing process. Demjanjuk was a Sobibor guard. *Therefore* Demjanjuk participated in the killing process."[12]

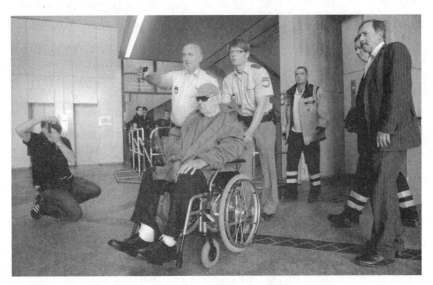

John Demjanjuk, a former guard at Sobibor,
facing justice in a Munich court.

After more than eighteen months and ninety-three hearings, the court essentially endorsed the prosecution's argument—and by extension the arguments developed by Walther and Goetze. It did not matter that Demjanjuk could not be tied to a specific killing. What mattered was that he was there, at Sobibor, helping to keep the factory of death in motion. "The three extermination camps—Treblinka, Belzec, and Sobibor—only served one single purpose: the mass murder of the Jewish population of Europe," the verdict found. "That meant that any action by the accused and all other guards in the camp supported the main purpose of the extermination camp."[13]

Demjanjuk was found guilty of being an accessory to murder in 28,060 cases. He was sentenced to five years in prison but was set free pending an appeal from his lawyers. Demjanjuk died ten months later, in a nursing home outside Munich, before a higher court could rule on the appeal. In strictly legal terms, that meant that his conviction never took full effect. But scholars were quick to hail a "paradigm change" in German jurisprudence.[14] The legal reasoning that led to Demjanjuk's conviction won broad acceptance among academics and jurists almost instantly. Encouraged by Walther's success, the investigators at Ludwigsburg started combing through their archive with renewed energy, initiating a string of new cases and charges and eventually turning their attention to Stutthof, and the handful of its guards and officers who were still alive.

The Demjanjuk case sparked interest also in the state prosecutor's office in Hamburg. Lars Mahnke had taken on the job of prosecuting Nazi crimes in Hamburg in 2010, as part of a wider brief that also included responsibility for crimes relating to the German Army. All of a sudden, the Demjanjuk ruling gave fresh meaning to the role. Mahnke joined colleagues from other federal states and from Ludwigsburg for a series of meetings, initially in Munich, to work out the legal and practical implications. One early priority was the prosecution of any remaining suspects linked to Auschwitz-Birkenau, also known as Auschwitz II, and the Majdanek concentration camp. Mahnke's attention, however, then turned to a different crime: the massacre of 342 civilians by the SS in the Italian village of Sant'Anna di Stazzema in August 1944. Among the dead were more than a hundred children, in one of the worst atrocities committed by German forces in Italy. One of the SS men involved in the killings, it turned out, was still alive in Hamburg. "We were very close to filing charges in what would have been a spectacular trial," Mahnke told me. "We couldn't charge him in the end because at the very last moment he was declared unfit to stand trial. Alzheimer's."

This was, of course, an increasingly common obstacle for prosecutors looking at Holocaust and other Nazi crimes. The suspects that Mahnke and his colleagues were looking at were mostly in their nineties. Whether or not they should stand trial was a medical as much as a legal question—and more often than not it was on medical grounds that cases failed to proceed.

In the late summer of 2016, more than five years after the Demjanjuk verdict, Mahnke was contacted by the officials in Ludwigsburg with another potential case. The investigators had found evidence—a single piece of evidence—linking an elderly resident of Hamburg to the concentration camp at Stutthof. It consisted of a piece of paper confirming receipt of an SS uniform dating from August 8, 1944. The signature on the receipt was that of Bruno Dey. "So he was clothed by the SS—that was the only piece of evidence we had," Mahnke recalled. Sparse as it may have been, the evidence was enough in the prosecutor's eyes to order a search of Dey's house and to tap the suspect's phone. The day of the search turned out to be pivotal: the sudden appearance of four police officers at his doorstep marked the first moment that Dey and his family learned of the investigation against him. He had been questioned by the police before about his time at the camp—but no charges had been brought against him. Now, more than seventy years after he turned his back on Stutthof and fled west, Dey was finally facing the prospect of a trial—and a sentence. Erik Herzberger, the police officer who led the search, found the suspect in a surprisingly talkative mood. Dey decided to waive his right to remain silent and invited his visitor to sit down with him and hear his recollections. Herzberger would later tell the court that he sensed in the suspect a desire to unburden himself. "He said, 'Come with me, I will tell you about it.' I had the feeling that he had a wish to talk about this," Herzberger recalled.

The search itself yielded no fresh evidence. But the policemen returned with a handwritten summary of the conversation between Herzberger and Dey, which included many of the details that would later feature in the trial itself. Mahnke and his colleagues still had months of patient work ahead of them before they were ready to file charges. The suspect's fitness to stand trial remained a constant concern. Not long after the search of his house, Dey's health deteriorated sharply, raising doubts about whether the case would ever come to trial. But at least there was a case.

Without the Demjanjuk trial, and the new doctrine established in Munich, it is likely that none of the subsequent Holocaust prosecutions would have taken place. Without Demjanjuk, no Dey. And without Walther, the stubborn judge from the provinces, there would not have been a Demjanjuk case. Sometimes, it really all comes down to one man and his mission.

There was, Walther told me, always a personal edge to his campaign. Born in Erfurt, eastern Germany, two years before the end of the war, he was too young to remember the horrors of the Third Reich. But he grew up in the knowledge that his own father had behaved with rare courage and compassion, at one point hiding two Jewish families in a shed at the end of their garden and helping them to flee the country. "My father was a very combative, practicing Christian. Today he would be called a do-gooder," he told me. Both Jewish families survived, and kept in touch with his father after the war. One of them settled in Paraguay, from where they sent Walther's father an elegant Parker fountain pen, a prized gift. The young Walther himself made do with the exotic Latin American stamps that graced the transatlantic correspondence. "Even as a small child I knew what my father had done. This was often spoken about," he told me. "This National Socialism insulted my intelligence from early on. I found it hard to understand how something like this could have happened."

Growing up in the 1950s, that kind of openness, which in Walther's home extended more generally to the Nazi period, was certainly not the norm. Traumatized by defeat and stung by shame, most parents chose to envelop their children in a blanket of silence. Walther, in contrast, recalled growing up "on an island of humanist–political free thinkers"—and assuming that the rest of the world was just the same. After his military service and abortive attempts to become a priest, a journalist, and a sailor, Walther decided to study law and eventually signed up to be a judge. Despite being a lifelong member of the center-left Social Democratic Party, he decided to move to the deeply conservative Allgäu in southern Germany, taking up the position of district judge.

His father died many years before Walther joined the Zentrale Stelle, but he served as an inspiration all the same. Walther decided to hand over the Demjanjuk file to the Munich prosecution service on the anniversary of the Nazi pogroms that drove the two Jewish families to seek his father's help. "Every so often I hold council with him, less so now than before—maybe because I am getting closer to him. But on the trip down to Munich, with the file under my arm, I told him, 'You see, Papa? Not so bad, eh?'"

CHAPTER FOUR

"There were rumors"

I returned to Hamburg a few days after the opening of the trial, took my usual seat at the back of the court, and waited for the wooden side door to open once again. After a few minutes, Bruno Dey entered in his wheelchair, his face hidden behind a cardboard file in the now familiar manner. Over the course of the first two hearing days the defendant had remained mostly silent, but that was about to change: today, Dey was going to tell his story, in full and in public, for the first time in his life.

Like most observers, I had been looking ahead to this moment with curiosity as well as unease. I knew Dey had provided substantial—and highly incriminating—testimony during his interrogation by the police and prosecutors before the opening of the trial. That was all on file. But how much could he remember today? How frank would he be in court? Would he succeed in making listeners see his point of view, and start building a case for his defense? What, indeed, was the case for the defense? Dey's lawyer had emphasized in his opening remarks that the accused had arrived at Stutthof against his will, that he had never volunteered to join the SS, and that for decades the German legal system had been content to let ordinary camp guards like Dey live their lives unperturbed. Before the Demjanjuk ruling Dey's chances of ending up in a murder trial would indeed have been negligible. But German justice had moved on. For Dey to escape punishment, he and his lawyer would have to find a flaw in the argument of the prosecution. What that flaw might be was, at least to me and at this point in the trial, far from obvious. They could try to argue that, in the absence of any specific action on his part, Dey's mere presence on the watchtower had made no difference to the killing and dying below; or that he had had no knowledge of the killing and dying below; or that he simply had no conceivable alternative to standing on the watchtower; or that he genuinely thought there was no alternative. That this would be a difficult task was clear, at least to Stefan Waterkamp, Dey's lawyer. He had taken on the case immediately after the raid on the defendant's home. One of Dey's grandsons had called him out of the blue, having found his name and number in the telephone book. Waterkamp had no experience of defending Nazi cases (very few lawyers in Germany did), but he was interested in the period and had studied the Nazi regime's judicial abuses at university, as part of his law course. It was a tough and labor-intensive assignment, made more demanding still by the need to balance the Stutthof case with his everyday work defending suspects in tax fraud trials and other criminal prosecutions. At this point in the Dey hearings, however, there was not much that Waterkamp could do to help his client. It would be up to Anne Meier-Göring, the presiding judge, to question the defendant about his time at Stutthof—and about any other part of his life she deemed important.

I soon realized that there was little that Meier-Göring, a judge possessed of enormous patience as well as forensic curiosity, deemed irrelevant, from Dey's earliest childhood memories to recent conversations with his children and grandchildren. Some questions she returned to again and again, posing them in different ways, on different days, and in different contexts. She was doing her job as a judge, diligently working through all the legal issues that had to be settled. But it felt to me like she was often doing my job as well: more than anything else, she wanted to use this trial to *understand*—to understand what made ordinary men like Bruno Dey take part in the Nazi genocide, why they had climbed up the watchtower, what made them stay there, and how that experience shaped their later lives. So began a difficult, protracted and often painful dialogue between judge and defendant that would carry on, with small interruptions, for nine months, and that delivered some of the most memorable and illuminating moments of the entire trial.

Before Meier-Göring could ask the first question, however, Dey had a prepared statement to read to the court. "I have a great need to let you know how sorry I was for what was done to the people in the concentration camp, and how much pain they had to endure," he said. Dey was also sorry, he added, that he himself had been forced to do his military service in such a "place of horror." His time at Stutthof, he explained, had marked him until today. "The images of suffering and horror have followed me my whole life," Dey said. He had felt pity for the prisoners at Stutthof, but insisted there was nothing he could have done to help them. He had never made use of his weapon, and, on one occasion, had helped prisoners despite knowing that he risked a "big punishment" from his superiors. Dey gave no further details of this incident in his opening statement, which he read haltingly, occasionally stumbling over words, but that reaffirmed the basic line of his defense.

Meier-Göring made no attempt to challenge Dey's protestations of innocence. Instead, she latched on to a seemingly insignificant phrase in his opening statement, one that had little direct bearing on the question of his guilt. In this as in other interrogations, notably with Stutthof survivors who appeared as witnesses, the presiding judge seemed keen to look beyond the deed itself and explore the character as well as the life story of the person she was talking to. "You say that the images have followed you your whole life. How did you deal with that? What did you do with that?" she asked.

"I did not deal with it. I tried after the war to suppress all that. I couldn't speak to anyone," Dey responded. Those harsh years after the war, with no news of his immediate family and no friends and relatives to fall back on, left little time for reflection. "At the time, I had to make sure that I made it through," Dey said, before adding, matter of factly: "I managed to go on living."

Listening to Meier-Göring during these opening exchanges, I was reminded of an interview technique I had myself employed on countless occasions as a journalist. She started off by asking broad, easy-to-answer questions that were not intended to deliver profound or even relevant insights but were aimed at putting Dey at ease—and perhaps lowering his guard. She was throwing him rhetorical "softballs." Her next question, too, landed gently: "What are the pictures you have in your head when you think back to your time in Stutthof? What are the memories you want to share?" she asked.

"I started suppressing all of this immediately after the war, so I could have my peace and quiet. But the pictures would not leave my head. As I said, I saw a lot of dead bodies. And a few other things. [But] I didn't see how they died: whether they were killed or whether they died normally, or not. That I don't know."

Dey was only a few minutes into his testimony, but this assertion of ignorance already seemed dubious. He saw dead bodies, but claimed he did not know their cause of death. *Lots of dead bodies. Inside a concentration camp. And he had no idea how they had died.* Even acknowledging the distance of time, and the peculiar vagaries of memory, this was hard to believe. I was sure Meier-Göring thought the same, but she decided to let it pass. Slowly but surely, however, the pace of questioning picked up. Meier-Göring's tone was calm and friendly, as before, but her questions were now more precise. Were the dead clothed or naked? Where was his watchtower? What part of the camp was this in? Who picked up the dead bodies? What did the cart look like? Where were they taken?

"To the crematorium I presume. I don't know. I didn't follow it."

"You probably followed it a little."

"They must have been taken to the crematorium. Where else would they have been taken?"

Meier-Göring was now steering Dey into increasingly treacherous legal territory, and toward a potentially crucial admission. To find him guilty, she would have to conclude that Dey made some objective contribution to the killings that took place in the camp, even if that contribution was comparatively small. That part of the charge sheet, however, would be hard to refute: his mere presence on the watchtower and around the camp fence clearly served to prevent prisoners from escaping, and to enforce discipline and obedience inside the camp. Without armed guards, ready to shoot and kill from on high, Stutthof could not have functioned, and neither could the gas chamber. That was the objective part. But the court also had to establish a subjective element, or criminal intent. This meant the defendant had to be aware of what he was doing, and of the consequences of his action. And the defendant had to—at least in German criminal law—be shown to have either wanted that outcome, or to have recognized that the outcome was a likely or possible result of his action, and gone ahead all the same. What Meier-Göring was trying to establish, in other words, was one of the most basic conditions for a guilty verdict, namely that Dey knew what was happening at Stutthof. Dey seemed to sense the danger. His answers now came more hesitantly, and when he did respond it was often only to say that he could not remember.

"What did the dead bodies look like?"

"Emaciated."

"So you mean starved?"

"Yes, starved or weakened by the sickness. I cannot say. I don't know."

"Did you ever have thoughts about why these dead people looked so emaciated?"

"Did I have thoughts? How could one have thoughts about this…" Dey fell silent for a moment, perhaps searching his memory for more recollections, or perhaps wondering how to move the conversation back toward safer ground. "I felt terribly sorry for them," he added. "I did not know what kind of food there was in that part of the camp. I did not see it. I never entered these barracks. I did not know what they looked like inside or how they were furnished."

"Did you ever ask anyone?"

"We couldn't enter."

"Did you ever ask anyone who had access to these barracks?"

"I once spoke to the prisoners. Normally we were not allowed to. But I did."

Dey had successfully deflected, at least for a moment, Meier-Göring's line of inquiry. He now began to tell the story he had alluded to in his introductory remarks: how he, at one point during his time at Stutthof, had helped a group of prisoners, despite his fears of punishment. The incident occurred while he was guarding prisoners who had been ordered to build a bunker close to the camp. Two prisoners, he said, had found a fresh horse carcass, and asked Dey whether they could cut off some strips of meat to take back to the camp. "I said, 'Do it.' But I was aware that if I allowed this, and it was found out, that

I could perhaps even have ended up on the other side of the barbed-wire fence. I would have been punished very severely."

Dey clearly attached great importance to this anecdote—the only one from his time in Stutthof that he actively tried to raise during the trial. He probably saw it as compelling evidence, if not proof, that he had tried to maintain his humanity amid the cruelty of life in the camp. Not only was he not a Nazi, but he had in fact helped the prisoners despite the risk this posed to himself. That was not, however, how the anecdote came across to most of us in the courtroom. I was probably not alone in wondering whether this was really the best story he could tell about himself. That he had allowed starving prisoners to cut some strips of flesh from a horse carcass? Even taking into account the extraordinary situation at Stutthof, this seemed like a pitifully small gesture toward a group of starving prisoners. Nor did his perception of the risk he took at the time sound especially convincing. The idea that such a tiny infraction—if it indeed was an infraction at all—would have given rise to punishment, let alone imprisonment in the camp itself, was simply not supported by historical evidence. As the court would hear again and again, camp guards were in fact consistently treated very leniently, even in instances where they refused to do their duty entirely. Meier-Göring, in any case, sounded far from impressed. Why, she asked, would he have been punished?

"I wasn't allowed to give them food."

"Was that written down anywhere?"

"That was clear, we were not supposed to have any contact with them."

Dey's lack of curiosity about the prisoners and their fate would become a recurring theme of the cross-examination by Meier-Göring. She returned to it again and again over the coming months, often making little effort to hide her incredulity (and, occasionally, her exasperation). Did you not ask? Did you not wonder? Did you not see? With one or two notable exceptions, Dey's answers usually fell short. He did not ask. He did not wonder. He did not see. There were times when his denials sounded so improbable that the presiding judge struggled to preserve her calm. One such moment came several weeks later, in mid-November, when Meier-Göring told Dey how many people were deported to Stutthof during his time at the camp. According to historical data, she said, an estimated 40,000 to 50,000 prisoners were brought to Stutthof between the summer of 1944 and January 1945—a vast influx of desperate men, women, and children, many of whom would meet their death under the watchful eye of the camp guards. Dey, however, claimed he saw nothing. The camp, of course, was not intended to provide food, shelter, and medical support for such large numbers, which made the defendant's ignorance not just improbable but also convenient. Had he admitted to knowing of their arrival, he would have had to answer an obvious follow-up question: if thousands of new prisoners arrived every week, where did they go upon arrival?

Dey also claimed that he had never witnessed an execution, or a public whipping or any other form of punishment. He claimed he didn't know where the camp gallows stood. He claimed he never saw the camp's "shoe mountain," the vast pile of shoes left behind by prisoners on arrival. He even claimed that he had never once heard a shot fired during his time at Stutthof.

Dey painted a picture of his younger self as a loner, insecure and fearful, who kept to himself and had no friends among the rest of the SS guards. Other than a single trip to the cinema in a nearby village, he had no recollection of social activities. "We got on but I always set myself apart a little," Dey said when asked about the other guards. "I don't know why but I never had trust in other people."

Nor did he have much contact with his family, despite their relative proximity to Stutthof. Dey never once returned home during his time at the camp, though Dey's father came to visit him on one occasion. The two men went for a walk outside the camp, but when asked what they spoke about Dey said he could not remember. He was similarly evasive when probed, later in the trial, about his conversations with the other SS guards. Dey and his companions usually worked twelve-hour shifts: they spent half the day on the watchtower or guarding the fence, and half the day resting. There was, in other words, plenty of time to talk about what they saw and did. Dey insisted, however, that no such conversation ever took place.

"So you spoke to no one about what was happening in this camp?" Meier-Göring asked, incredulously. "Is that right? None of the other guards told you what was happening in the camp?"

"There were rumors. Occasionally, but you couldn't trust them."

"What kind of rumors?"

Dey hesitated, realizing too late that his reference to rumors had put him on the defensive. "What kind of rumors? None."

"But Herr Dey, you just said there were rumors. What were those rumors?"

The defendant tried another evasive maneuver. "There were some tales that among the prisoners were not just criminals but also political prisoners and also Jews. But what was really said I cannot say. I don't know."

His attention seemed to be slipping away. Lost in his maze of memories and dissimulations, Dey struggled to answer the next few questions. Meier-Göring tried one more time: "Were there also rumors about what was done to them [the Jews] in the camp?"

Long seconds passed before Dey gave a deep sigh and mumbled: "I cannot remember. I no longer know."

There is a reason why the courtroom drama is first and foremost an Anglo-American genre. Over the years, it has become part of the Hollywood canon, with a narrative arc both familiar and satisfying, from the opening skirmishes over jury selection and the high-intensity drama of cross-examination to the emotional closing appeal to the jury. Then the moment of revelation: the jury enters the courtroom, and the verdict is read out. Guilty! Not guilty! The black-robed judge's gavel comes crashing down, the credit starts to roll.

U.S. and British criminal trials are adversarial, meaning they are essentially a contest between the prosecution and the defense. They are exciting and combative by nature. Lawyers face off in front of a jury of laypeople, with the judge largely relegated to the role of referee. The key decision—whether to find guilty or not guilty—is not left to the expert, but to a more or less representative group of amateurs. Unlike the judge, trained to be impartial and experienced enough to see through lawyerly showmanship, they are there to be dazzled, to be seduced and perhaps, on certain occasions, also to be confused. A fine piece of rhetoric and a well-timed question might swing a crucial vote, or destroy the credibility of a perfectly trustworthy witness, or sow doubt over a fact that police and prosecution consider unimpeachable. Whether in real life or on-screen, high-profile criminal trials in the U.S. and England often produce a gripping spectacle.

A German criminal trial, in contrast, is typically a much more staid affair. It is inquisitorial, not adversarial. The court is supposed to establish the truth of the case, not just serve as a stage for a fair fight. Lawyers don't jump up and down and shout "Objection!" They don't seek to sway the jurors with soaring rhetoric while pacing up and down in front of the jury bench. For long stretches, in fact, both the defense and the prosecution in a German court case are remarkably silent. Unlike their counterparts in a U.S. or British criminal trial, they are not the main protagonists. The dominant—indeed, the all-powerful—figure in a German courtroom is the judge. In some criminal cases, the presiding judge is assisted by junior judges and lay judges (Meier-Göring, for example, was flanked by two junior and two lay judges throughout the trial). When it comes to reaching a verdict, their votes count equally. But it is the presiding judges who tower over the proceedings. They sit at the front and center of the courtroom, usually on an elevated podium, and lead the questioning of the accused and of all the witnesses. German judges ask and probe every witness until they are satisfied that there is nothing left to say. They interrogate the accused until they conclude that every fact and argument, be it advantageous or not for the defense, has been exposed. Lawyers for the defense and prosecution plead at the beginning and end of the trial, they can call on the judge to examine additional evidence, and they are entitled to ask questions of witnesses and the defendant once the judge has finished. But if the judge has done their job properly, all they should find themselves left with are crumbs. Nor should German criminal lawyers hope to impress the court with brilliant arguments or rhetorical fireworks. There is no jury of laymen to impress—just a professional judge who has asked all the relevant questions already, and who will make up his or her mind based on evidence, testimony, and years, if not decades, of experience. The German criminal court is not an arena for combat, nor is it a stage for lawyerly stagecraft. It is a laboratory, a place of patient, plodding investigation.

*

In the case of Bruno Dey, there were many moments when Meier-Göring's own version of that plodding investigation seemed to hit a wall. There were sessions when she probed and prodded, but ultimately failed to breach Dey's wall of I-don't-knows and I-can't-remembers. Another such occasion came later on the third day, when the judge turned her attention to an incident, mentioned by Dey in an earlier interrogation with the prosecution, when he did show a flash of curiosity. At one point during his time at Stutthof, he decided to pay a visit to the crematorium, the red-brick building that stood at the camp's eastern perimeter, and whose chimney expelled foul dense smoke day and night. Dey's twelve-hour shift on the watchtower had just ended, but instead of returning to his quarters he decided to make a hasty detour to the crematorium, and to look inside. "I was curious and I wanted to know whether it was true what had been rumored," Dey recalled.

Inside the crematorium, he found several dead bodies waiting to be burned, and a sole prisoner, alive, who apparently formed part of the work crew tasked with keeping the ovens running. The prisoner, Dey recalled, pointed toward one of the dead bodies and asked him whether he was familiar. Dey said he wasn't. "That was the senior Kapo from one of the barracks," the prisoner told him. "He was a good man."

"Was the oven running at the time?" Meier-Göring asked.

"I don't know."

"Did you see how they died?"

"I did not see."

"What were the rumors about what there was to see in there?"

"I don't know any more. I can't say anything about this."

63

"But you just said [there were rumors]?"

"It was said that they burn dead bodies. But how and what none of us guards knew."

Sensing that Dey was not going to budge, the judge shifted her line of questioning onto a different plateau. What, she asked, did Dey think and feel when he saw the scene inside the crematorium?

"How can I explain thoughts and feelings now? I cannot explain. I don't know. It was terrible what one saw there." Dey fell into silence. "I don't know."

"Was this one of the pictures that you could not shake off in later years?"

"That is one of the pictures that…whenever something was awakened…" Dey's response drifted into incoherence. Then, suddenly, there was a flash of anger: "And I was happy until all this here started…"

"This trial here?" Meier-Göring asked.

"Until this trial began. I was happy that I had managed to process this pretty well, that I had a bit of peace and quiet. And now everything is being dredged up. Everything that one no longer knows or no longer remembers. All these cruelties are being dredged up. The sunset years are being destroyed—"

"Herr Dey!"

"This is not how I imagined my old age. Despite everything—"

"Herr Dey!"

Meier-Göring cut short the defendant's outburst of self-pity with unusual sharpness. She had until now shown great patience and forbearance with Dey, allowing his memories to wander freely and some frankly implausible assertions to pass. But she had no intention of letting the man accused of aiding mass murder present himself in court as a victim. There was, however, no stern rebuke. Instead, Meier-Göring made an appeal to Dey to think of the victims and their families—and how they lived their lives after Stutthof. "The people who were in the camp, who were deported there, they too had to carry this with them their whole lives," she reminded him. "And we heard at the beginning of the trial that for the prisoners it is important that the past is not forgotten, but that we deal with it. What do you have to say to that? Do you understand that?"

Dey sounded dejected. His brief moment of anger and self-pity had passed. "But so much has already been said about this," he responded, weakly. His voice trailed off. "The past..." Dey muttered, barely audible.

Waterkamp, his lawyer, intervened at last. "I think a break would be appropriate," he told the judge.

Dey won only a brief reprieve. After the break, Meier-Göring changed subjects, but the pressure on the defendant continued. What, she asked, did he know about the *Judenvernichtung*, the destruction of the Jews?

"Very little or nothing," Dey responded. "I knew that the Jews were taken from their homes and their shops. But where they ended up I didn't know." Once again, Dey's lack of curiosity was striking, though it was also hardly untypical. After the war, similar protestations of ignorance were made by millions of Germans. They saw how their Jewish neighbors were hounded and marginalized, deprived of their rights and their property. Then they saw them deported in their thousands, often in broad daylight, amid ever-shriller antisemitic speeches from Nazi leaders. Not everyone knew of the concentration camps, of course, and as a teenage baker's apprentice the young Dey may well have been among the unaware. But to a contemporary audience, the apparent absence of concern for the fate of the disappearing Jews sounded callous all the same.

Anne Meier-Göring, the Hamburg judge
who presided over the Dey trial.

Meier-Göring pressed on. Had he heard of Auschwitz or
other concentration camps before his arrival at Stutthof? No,
he had not. Had he ever spoken to his parents about any of
this? No, he had not. After leaving his parents' home to start
his apprenticeship as a baker in Danzig, he only returned home
every two weeks. "I went to pick up fresh laundry. My mother
did my laundry for me," Dey explained. "My family had a small
farm; they were busy from morning until night. When I was
home, I wasn't on holiday. I had to work. We spoke about work,
how to do this or that, but not about politics."

"But you must have spoken about Hitler?"

"About Hitler..."

"What people thought of Hitler?"

"Did we speak about this? I cannot remember. Well, Hitler at the beginning got a lot of things done. He got people into jobs, he built roads and things like that, and he re-armed. But why? So that Germany would be strong again. But one didn't know at the time whether there would be war…"

"But Herr Dey, was there also a negative side to Hitler that was discussed in your family?"

"No. As I said, we barely spoke about Hitler at all. Maybe a word here or there but whether this was positive or negative I don't know."

Once again, Dey's memory seemed patchy. But there was little evidence that either he or his family were fervent Nazis. His father had in fact been threatened with imprisonment in Stutthof himself. Dey claimed, however, that his image of the camp was more benign than the murderous reality he later came face to face with. "The concentration camp for me meant that prisoners were kept there, criminals and the like, as well as people from other parties. I thought they were being educated, that they were being told that their thinking was wrong or something like that…"

"So a kind of re-education?"

"Yes, re-education."

"That is what you imagined."

"That is what I imagined."

Dey's personal lack of enthusiasm for the Hitler regime also showed up in his struggle to avoid being drafted into the Hitler Youth. "I didn't want to join any group," he told the court. "I had no liking for marching and things like that. That is why I didn't join, even though my classmates kept on pressing me." His father, too, wanted him to stay clear of the Nazi youth movement. Dey did eventually join, after coming under growing pressure from the authorities. Once he picked up his membership pass, however, he never returned to a meeting or took part in any other Hitler Youth activities. Nor was he in any hurry later on to sign up for the Wehrmacht. More than anything else, he wanted to keep his head below the parapet. When Dey finally received his call-up notice, he told the examining Wehrmacht medic that he suffered from a heart condition that made him unfit for combat. The German compound adjective that Dey used in court, *kriegsverwendungsfähig*, is striking both for its length and cold precision: it literally translates as "able to be used in war." He was sent to hospital where that diagnosis—which Dey claimed was first made when he was at school—would be confirmed. Back at the Wehrmacht office, that meant that his fitness category was changed from *kriegsverwendungsfähig* to *garnisonsverwendungsfähig*, meaning that he could only do military service in the garrison. Thanks to a heart condition that had caused him little trouble until that moment (or indeed later in life), Dey would not be going to the front lines. His chances of surviving the bloodiest war in world history had just risen dramatically.

There was nothing to corroborate or disprove Dey's version of events. But it seemed that the medical examination in Danzig presented a genuine fork in the road. The one he chose—or the one that chose him—led him away from the war and toward Stutthof concentration camp, and ultimately to this courtroom in Hamburg more than seven decades later. Had he not been able to persuade the Wehrmacht medic of his heart condition, Dey would have been sent to the front lines like millions of other young men. He might have killed or been killed, and he might have been caught up in other atrocities on or near the front line. But he would, almost certainly, not have seen a concentration camp from the inside, nor would he have worn the uniform of an SS man.

Dey was sent to the nearby town of Stettin where he received basic military training. He was part of a group of men who, like him, had been declared unfit for combat service. Dey learned to use a rifle, and he learned how to march. After six weeks, his training was over.

Dey looked exhausted at this point. Almost three hours had passed since the start of the hearing, and Stefan Waterkamp, his lawyer, had called for the court to be adjourned some time ago. Meier-Göring finally relented.

"My last question: what did you think was going to happen to you after this training?"

"I thought I would be sent to do guard duty somewhere. I didn't know what I would be guarding, maybe prisoners or maybe a plant of the arms industry. Wherever guarding was needed."

As it turned out, guarding was needed a long train ride further east, just outside his hometown of Danzig, at the Stutthof concentration camp.

CHAPTER FIVE

The wedding photo

It is a late summer night and I am sitting with my parents in the living room of the house I grew up in. Everything here is familiar, from the thick, cream-colored carpet under my feet to the short-backed, slightly uncomfortable armchair I am sitting in. Somewhere beyond the sliding glass door is my parents' beloved garden, with its gnarly old walnut tree, but at this hour everything outside is shrouded in darkness.

Inside, perched on my mother's lap, is a shoebox filled with old family photos. We examine them one by one, passing the pictures between us. The questions we ask are the familiar ones: Who is this? When was this taken? What were they doing at the time? There is one faded photo, perhaps more than a century old, showing my German great-grandfather resplendent in his uniform from the First World War. A later one shows him in uniform once again, this time during the Second World War, wearing the Iron Cross he won in the earlier conflict. Sitting next to him is his oldest son, Helmut, my great uncle, a Luftwaffe officer whose plane was shot down over North Africa in 1941. He is the only German relative I have who was killed in the war, but his presence is keenly felt even today. His sister Dorothea, who mourned him as a favorite brother, chose to honor his memory by naming her first son—my father—after him. The remains of the unknown uncle, the first Helmut, are in a sandy grave in Tunisia to this day.

Most of the images that emerge from the shoebox are innocent fare: a Christmas party in the 1950s, family gatherings in the 1960s, long-deceased uncles and aunts staring back at me in sepia across the years. But we are looking for a specific photo, an image I remember vaguely from my childhood but which I haven't seen in decades. It is my grandparents' wedding picture. I want to see it again to answer a question that has been asked and answered—and quite often not answered—in every German family for at least two generations: *War Opa ein Nazi?* Was Grandpa a Nazi?

I remember the black-and-white photo sitting framed on a bookshelf in my grandparents' living room. (Or was it on the night table next to their bed?). I remember Dorothea, my grandmother, in a simple white dress, standing next to her husband. And I remember Rupert, my grandfather, wearing some kind of uniform, along with an armband bearing the swastika, the symbol of Hitler's Nazi Party. What I don't remember is the photo—or the armband or its meaning—ever being discussed. Even now, I am not entirely sure of its significance. Does the armband prove that he was a member of the Nazi Party, or was it simply part of his uniform? Would he have chosen to wear this outfit on his wedding day or was this dress, in the penultimate year of the war, an official requirement?

To be clear, I am not interested in exoneration. Rupert has been dead for so long, and my personal recollections of him are so distant, that I feel little emotional attachment. But now that I have spent many months following the trial of Bruno Dey I feel an urge to know more about my grandfather, who was born sixteen years before Dey but who would have faced moral quandaries not so different from those that confronted the

accused in Hamburg. To the best of my knowledge, my grandfather never set foot inside a concentration camp; nor do I have
evidence that he was involved in the mass killings of civilians
inflicted by the Nazis on the lands they occupied. But I cannot
be sure. Nor can I help wondering, if things had been slightly
different, if Rupert had been in the shoes of Bruno Dey, would
he have behaved any differently? Watching Dey's grandchildren
sit loyally through the trial hearings, I have to ask, could that
have been my opa in the dock?

After sifting through dozens of pictures of birthday parties
and country excursions, we find the photo. It dates from January
8, 1944, and must have been taken in Rosen, the small town in
Upper Silesia where the couple were married. Rosen, along
with the surrounding region, was part of the German Reich
but became Polish after the war, and today goes by the name of
Rożnóv. The picture shows a timid-looking Dorothea, my grandmother, clutching a bouquet of flowers. She and her new husband are standing in a room that looks terribly gloomy—there
is no natural light to brighten the dark wallpaper and heavy
furniture. I can make out a sofa or daybed on the right, and a
chest of drawers in front of a window. On the wall behind the
couple are three adornments: a hunting trophy, a framed picture
of a deer, and an oval portrait of Paul von Hindenburg, the field
marshal who commanded the German Army in the First World
War and who later, as the last president of the Weimar Republic,
took the fateful decision to appoint Adolf Hitler as chancellor
of Germany. The wedding photo shows Rupert standing on the
right, closer to the camera, a ceremonial sword hanging on his
side and a military cap in his left hand. There is a hint of a smile
playing across his face. And there, just as I remembered, is the
swastika armband. With a magnifying glass in hand, I search
the image for further clues, and find a swastika pin on his chest,

and another emblem showing a broadsword superimposed on a swastika. I later find out that this is the SA-Sportabzeichen, an award for fitness and sporting prowess. The uniform he wears is that of the Reichsarbeitsdienst (RAD), the Reich Labour Service, a Nazi organization tasked with overseeing public works such as draining swamps and building infrastructure. At one point, the Nazis required millions of young Germans to perform work duties under the RAD—in part for ideological reasons but also to reduce unemployment—but its standing and role declined over the years. During the war itself, the RAD supported the construction of military infrastructure. My grandfather, I will later learn, served as a functionary in the organization.

Then we find a second wedding photo, this one a close-up of the couple on which Rupert's arm—and the swastika armband —are cropped out. Still squinting through the magnifying glass, I look down his uniform jacket and find a tiny smudge on his breast pocket. Something has been scratched out, leaving a small but noticeable mark. It is, I realize, in the exact same spot where in the larger photo the swastika pin is visible. Someone—almost certainly my grandfather or grandmother—must have decided later on that it would be best to have at least one photo without Nazi symbolism. Given that they later had no qualms about displaying the larger photo—the one with the swastika armband clearly visible—I am puzzled by this effort to clean the record. Maybe the correction was made immediately after the war, when fears of Allied retribution were at their highest. If so, those fears might soon have been allayed: millions of Germans had similar photos in their drawers after 1945, and compared to some other uniforms captured on camera, my grandfather's would not have raised much of an eyebrow among contemporaries. The scratch mark tells a story all the same: someone wanted to change their history, to remove a stain. I realize this is perhaps the closest I will ever get to hearing my grandfather, a man I knew largely by his silences, make a reckoning with the past: Yes, he was a Nazi. And for one fleeting moment at least, he—or someone close to him—did not want the world around him to know.

Rupert Buck died in 1984, when I was just eight years old. He had been ill for many years, and his mind was clouded by dementia long before I could have a meaningful conversation with him. He had worked as an accountant in a local iron foundry but stopped working a few years before I was born. All I remember is his hard, unsmiling face, his brooding presence at the dinner table, and his habit of joining me in the garden when I was playing football. We would kick the ball back and forth between us without speaking. A talented sportsman in his youth, these kickabouts were perhaps the only way he could communicate with his grandson. Rupert seemed unhappy and confused, but this may be more of a projection than a memory. In any case, he was a marginal figure in a world that was otherwise filled with children's delights. I liked being in my grand-parents' spacious flat on the outskirts of Ehingen, a small town in Swabia, south-western Germany. It boasted a television set much larger than the one we had at home, and fewer restrictions on how much time could be spent in front of it. Above all, there was the kitchen where my grandmother would prepare food so delicious and bountiful that I can still taste it today. There was apple cake topped with buttery *Streusel*, beef roulades filled with pickled gherkins and chunks of ham, homemade raspberry jam, and local specialities such as *Maultaschen*, Swabian ravioli served in rich broth, *Bärentatzen*, or "bear's claws"—dense choc-olate biscuits coated in white sugar—and the strangely named *Seelen*, which translates literally as "souls"—baguette-like, fluffy bread rolls sprinkled with salt and caraway seeds. Waiting for my sister and me on arrival would be extra pocket money and bars of chocolate, elaborate candy eggs for Easter, and piles of homemade cookies at Christmas. The treats mattered. Family history did not—not then, and certainly not to me.

Now it does, but it is too late to ask the questions that matter. I am painfully aware how little I know about Rupert, or why he might have chosen to display the swastika on his wedding day. My grandmother, too, is long dead, as are other contemporaries. Of Rupert's belongings, all I can find in our possession are a few papers and documents: the certificates of his birth, wedding, and death, a school report, some letters and newspaper articles, a hand-drawn family tree. Included among this sketchy collection is a photocopy of the infamous *Ariernachweis*, or Aryan certificate, which was required by the Nazis as official proof that the holder had no Jewish heritage. Rupert's certificate lists the names and occupations of his parents and grandparents, along with confirmation that they were all members of the Roman Catholic Church. The names on the certificate have no meaning to me, nor to my father, but they suggest lives that are hard to imagine today—a late-nineteenth-century world of Catholic farmers marrying Catholic women from the same villages and towns, and dying in the same place they were born. I am struck by how early death came to some. Rupert's maternal grandmother, Katharina, did not live beyond the age of thirty. My grandfather grew up without knowing any of his grandparents, who all died long before he was born in 1910.

It is tempting to fill out the vast blanks in my grandfather's biography with speculation, but what seems clear is that Rupert was an unusually bright and tenacious young man. Despite his humble origins—his father was a signalman on the railways —he managed to complete his high school education with a *Reifezeugnis*, the certificate of maturity that is equivalent to today's A-levels, which would have allowed him to study at a university. In an age before mass education, this was a remarkable achievement: in 1920s Germany, only a fraction of school leavers—less than 5 percent—attained this certificate.[1] Rupert did not attend university, but he did manage to break out of the confines of rural Swabia, at least briefly, and move to Berlin, where he started an apprenticeship at a book publisher. I struggle to find documentary evidence—even a photo or letter—for the period between 1928 and the wedding in 1944. Those crucial years during which Hitler rose to power, and in which my grandfather at some point apparently decided to join the Nazi Party, appear to be a blank canvas.

It seems I am stuck. I ask my parents to trawl through their cupboards and drawers for more documents. I am almost certain that at some point we had other papers. I remember vividly a satirical school magazine from the 1920s, written and edited by Rupert and his fellow high-school graduates. I am also sure I saw, at some point, another letter written by Rupert from his POW camp. My father thinks he kept a denazification paper classifying Rupert as a so-called *Mitläufer*, literally someone who runs along with the crowd. The term became a convenient catchall for the vast majority of Germans who supported or tolerated the Nazis but were not senior enough to warrant punishment after the war. These were the millions of Nazi Party members, Nazi Party voters, and Nazi Party sympathizers on whose support the regime was built. Today, the term is used as a harsh political insult, synonymous with moral cowardice. After the war, however, to be deemed a *Mitläufer* was almost like receiving a clean bill of health. You were one of millions who had simply gone along with the masses.

That document would be fascinating to review now. If nothing else, it would likely provide precise information about my grandfather's association with the party, the year he joined, and possibly even what rank and functions he had. We look everywhere—in the cellar, in the attic, amid stacks of old papers and bills. Nothing emerges.

Then, suddenly, my luck turns. A few months after that evening at my parents' house, I am sitting in front of my computer and tap a few keywords into the search engine. I am directed to the page of Germany's federal archive, the Bundesarchiv. From there I click through to a page with a title that sounds rather too racy for a government archive—and which makes my heart leap: "*War Opa ein Nazi?*" Was Grandpa a Nazi?

The National Socialist German Workers' Party (NSDAP), as the Nazi Party was officially called, kept a meticulous record of its membership, which rose from a few thousand in the early 1920s to 850,000 by the time Hitler was appointed chancellor of the Reich in 1933. It trebled in Hitler's first year in power and kept rising steadily until the end of the war. With defeat imminent and Allied armies closing in, the party sent its membership records to be destroyed—but U.S. forces discovered the archive on the outskirts of Munich before the order was carried out. The list survives to this day, and with it the names of more than ten million members of the Nazi Party. Unless I am mistaken, Rupert Buck should be among them.

Accessing the party list turns out to be surprisingly simple: all I have to do is fill out a form with a few bits of personal information on the Bundesarchiv website. Within days I receive a response from one of the Berlin archivists, asking me to fill out another online form, and to sign a promise that I will pay a fee of €5 for every quarter of an hour of research work done by the archive. A month after my initial inquiry a second email lands in my inbox: my grandfather's records have been found. As I click through the attachments, I find Rupert's youthful face looking back at me, his image fixed more than eight decades earlier. On my screen is a scanned copy of his actual NSDAP membership pass: a two-page document on bright orange paper, which includes a photo of my grandfather in his early twenties, wearing a double-breasted pinstripe suit, a V-neck jumper and patterned tie. The pages contain all the information I was seeking—confirmation that Rupert was indeed a member of the NSDAP, and the date he joined: May 5, 1933. His membership number was 3578524, meaning that more than 3.5 million people joined the party before him—but also that more than 6.5 million held out longer than he did before they signed up. Rupert, it turns out, was not just a Nazi, but an early Nazi. The archivist tells me there will be no fee after all.

I feel neither shock nor surprise, just a strange sense of irritation that it took me so long to find out. Why did I never ask? Why did my parents never ask? I think back to my visit to Auschwitz as a fourteen-year-old, at a time when my grandmother was still alive and well. I sought out and interviewed Holocaust survivors at the time, but it never occurred to me to interview my own relatives, to ask what they knew—and what they did and didn't do at the time. The absence of debate and inquisition, that great, shameful silence about the past, was of course all-pervasive after the war. And in many families, apparently including my own, it lasted much longer than it should have. At the same time, it is important to note that conversations about some aspects of the past did take place. When my London-born English mother met her future husband's family in the late 1960s, she was struck by this contrast: the Germans talked obsessively about the war itself, and specifically about their experience of the war, of the losses and destruction suffered by their side. My father's uncles, who were mostly too young to fight in the war, would tell hair-raising stories of how they would search for unexploded ordnance from the war amid the ruins, and then set off explosions for fun. My grandmother would speak of her desperate flight from Upper Silesia with the Red Army closing in. Warned by my grandfather just in time, she managed to pack up my father, who was only a few days old, and get on one of the last trains out of the embattled region. Temperatures were freezing and—so the story went—those who died on the journey had to be thrown off the moving train, including babies. To what degree these tales were embellished, or indeed sanitized, is hard to say. But one thing struck my mother even then: there was no acknowledgment of the losses and destruction inflicted by Nazi Germany on others—or of the fact that the war had been started, entirely unprovoked, by their country alone. On the rare occasion when the Holocaust did come up in conversations, my mother recalls, it was brushed aside. After all, she was asked, wasn't it the British who invented the concentration camp during the Boer War?

This strange inversion of history was typical of the postwar years, which saw a nation of perpetrators revel in its own victimhood. For many families, not least my own, that warped perspective was grounded in personal experience. They did suffer gravely, both during the war and in the years that followed. To acknowledge that suffering is not to draw a false equivalence, or to justify the lack of empathy with Germany's victims after the war. But I believe it goes some way toward explaining the silence—and the apparent absence of remorse or guilt. Dorothea, my grandmother, lost not only her brother, but also her home in Silesia, which she never saw again. Her husband Rupert, the man with the swastika armband, also paid a heavy price for Germany's crimes. Like millions of German men in uniform, he was taken captive by Allied forces in the final months of the war. He describes his ordeal in one of the rare letters, sent from a Soviet prisoner-of-war camp, we still have: he was part of a last-ditch force sent to halt the American advance in the Sudetenland, in the present-day Czech Republic. After what he calls the "collapse," by which I assume he means Germany's capitulation and Hitler's suicide, Rupert and others surrendered to the Americans, who promptly handed him over to nearby Russian forces. This was a great misfortune: German soldiers who were taken by U.S. or British armed forces had a far better chance of survival—and an early release. The odds were much worse for those taken prisoner by Stalin's Red Army. Of the more than three million prisoners of war held in Soviet Russia, one in three never made it back home. Most spent long years in camps scattered across the USSR, working as forced laborers, on desperately poor rations and with little medical care. Most would have been aware of the murderous conditions under which Soviet POWs had been held in Nazi Germany, not to mention the immense suffering inflicted on the Soviet Union by their side. In four years of brutal war on the Eastern Front, the SS and Wehrmacht reduced vast swathes of central and eastern Europe to rubble, and killed as many as twenty-seven million Soviet soldiers and civilians. The German prisoners had no reason to expect leniency, and none was given. As my grandfather writes in his letter: "For the first time in my life I learned what hunger was. He would be a faithful companion for most of my time here. After four weeks I had the bad luck of falling ill with dysentery. I was hovering between life and death for fourteen days but my strong will not to die like this helped me, over the next two months, to get back on my feet." The letter was sent in April 1948. Three years after the German surrender, and his, Rupert was still a prisoner in Russia.

My grandfather finally came home six months after this letter, so the family story goes, with scars across his back and with just one Russian word he could remember: *Rabota!* Work!

80

*

A year after our trawl through the shoebox of photos, my mother calls me with exciting news. She has looked in yet another long-forgotten drawer and found what I have been looking for all this time: a clear plastic folder, containing dozens of yellowed pages, handwritten and typed letters, official correspondence and court documents relating to Rupert. It seems I will know more about my grandfather after all.

When I finally open the folder at home in London, I find among the brittle papers a handwritten curriculum vitae that my grandfather wrote after the war, when he was looking for work. At last, I can piece together in more detail what he did and when. The document mentions his apprenticeship in Berlin, but also that he had to return home after just three months, because the firm was wound up following the sudden death of the owner. He went on to work in the local post office and then claims to have spent a year "as a soldier in the *Politische Bereitschaft*," which translates as "political standby force," before working in a local bookstore, and eventually joining the aforementioned Reich Labour Service. There he pursued "an administrative career," proudly noting that he received training in all branches of the bureaucracy, from accounting to managing food supplies and payroll. Right at the end of his note, I make a surprising discovery. "I was a party member from 1933–1945, and a member of the SS from 1933–1935."

My grandfather was, by his own account, not just a member of the Nazi Party but a member of the SS. This is news to me—and I wonder what else this collection of papers will turn up.

Perhaps the most important document in the folder dates from August 25, 1949, and was issued by the State Commissioner's Office for Political Cleansing in Württemberg-Hohenzollern, the region in south-western Germany where Rupert and his family lived. It contains the ruling in my grandfather's denazification procedure, part of a hugely ambitious program imposed by the Allies to stamp out any remnants of Nazi ideology and identify those who collaborated with and supported Hitler's regime. Special tribunals grouped Germans into one of several categories—from "main culprit" and "incriminated" to "follower" and "unencumbered"—and imposed fines and punishments accordingly. These were distinct from criminal sanctions, and could result in confiscating a person's assets, barring them from political office or the civil service, taking away their right to vote, or simply a fine. The decision was mostly left to the Germans who staffed these tribunals, whom the Allied authorities trusted not to have had any connection to the Nazi regime.

In Rupert's case, the ruling indeed classified him as a *Mitläufer*, or follower, a common outcome. Only a fraction of the 3.5 million Germans who went through denazification were found to be main culprits or incriminated. My grandfather was barred from holding an elected office until April 1, 1950 (less than eight months after the ruling) and fined 30 Deutschmarks. As far as financial penalties went, this one seemed rather mild: the average monthly income in Germany at the time was about 240 Deutschmarks.[2]

Further down the page, I find confirmation that Rupert was indeed a member of the SS. The ruling neatly lists all the Nazi organizations Rupert belonged to, including his party membership (from 1933 to 1945) and his membership of the Reich Labour Service (from October 1935 to May 1945). In addition to those two affiliations, Rupert was also a member of the SS for more than two years. The document gives further details in brackets: apparently he was a member of the *Polizeibereitschaft*, or auxiliary police, in Ellwangen, southern Germany, between June 1933 and the end of December 1935, the same period he was an SS member. According to the document, he was then expelled from the force due to *Meuterei*, or mutiny—a claim that the tribunal appears to attach great significance to. For the nine men on the denazification tribunal who examined my grandfather's record, the circumstances of his departure from the SS appear to have outweighed the fact that he joined in the first place. As I continue reading the document, I find this passage: "The committee notes that the person in question was excluded from the SS in 1935 for mutiny. He was supposedly not politically exposed, did not exercise political influence on those of a different persuasion, has not damaged or denounced anyone... Since he was excluded from the SS it must be assumed that he did not show any enthusiasm for Nazism. Since there is no other politically damaging information about him, it had to be concluded that his support for the National Socialist reign of violence was only minor."

This strikes me as a remarkably sympathetic reading of the evidence.[3] Rupert may have left the SS long before the genocidal policies of Nazi Germany were formulated and implemented. But the organization's role as the ruthless vanguard of a totalitarian regime was already beyond doubt. The first concentration camps to detain and punish political opponents were in place. The persecution of German Jews was in full swing. Whatever his supposed "mutiny" against the SS entailed, my grandfather's subsequent career—and his continuing membership of the Nazi Party—was hardly indicative of a man distancing himself from the regime.

Leniency and a willingness to let bygones be bygone were, however, typical for the entire denazification program. The general mood is captured with stark precision in another document I find in the folder. It was issued a month after the denazification ruling and comes in response to an appeal for clemency that Rupert sent to the State Commissioner's office. In a few brief sentences on yellowed paper, the commissioner informs him that such appeals should be directed not to him but the French military authorities (which were still occupying that part of Germany after the war). The commissioner—the man formally in charge of "political cleansing" in the region—then adds a revealing note of encouragement: "Don't forget that the responsibility for the gigantic misfortune that has befallen Germany belongs entirely to Hitler and his entourage, not us!" The word "us" is underlined for additional emphasis.

Exoneration was the most typical outcome for denazification hearings, which is why the rulings became known at the time as "Persil tickets." Like the popular detergent brand, they offered the promise of instant cleansing. In my grandfather's case, there may have been an additional reason why the tribunal looked at his biography in a spirit of forgiveness: he had only recently returned from the Soviet Union, where he spent three and a half years as a prisoner of war in the most miserable conditions. At the time of his hearing, Rupert was still classified as unfit for work. Medical reports noted that he suffered from dystrophy, rheumatism, inflammation of the intestines, and poor teeth—all a result of malnutrition. Another report mentioned that he carried scars on both his back and his neck.

Among the papers I find a stack of postcard-sized letters he sent to my grandmother from his imprisonment, via the Red Cross in Moscow. There is also a letter sent to Dorothea on October 10, 1946, by a recent returnee who had been put to work along with Rupert on a *kolkhoz* (a collective farm) near Tblisi in present-day Georgia. The letter states that Rupert spent three months in the camp hospital with jaundice and kidney problems "as a result of malnutrition" but eventually recovered. "He was very depressed that we in the camp were not allowed to write letters and so were unable to hear anything about the fate of our families. Please write to him under the following address: Prisoner of War Buck, Prisoner of War Camp 236 in Tiflis (Caucasus). I hope I have been of service."

The first letter I have that was sent by Rupert himself dates from September 22, 1946, and contains just a few brief sentences, telegram-style: "I am well. Am healthy. Hope the same for you and the relatives. How is little Helmut [my one-year-old father]. Goodbye."

The next few letters are just as brief. Rupert sent his first substantial note only on March 7, 1947, almost two years after the end of the war and the start of his detention by the Soviets. "Dear Thea, In fourteen days it will be the start of spring. I hope that for us prisoners of war spring will come too, and that we will soon return home. I almost can't imagine what that life is like. Three years behind barbed wire, and now within a few months to be free again, without guards, without barbed wire, no longer in a foreign country, home, with beloved people."

The speedy release he hopes for does not come to pass. The wait goes on, and the tiny letters keep arriving, up until the autumn of 1948. Rupert writes of the heat, and his longing for home, but mostly he tries to adopt a reassuring tone. His health is good. He is delighted to receive news and pictures of his son. He hopes it will soon be his turn to come home. On May 16, 1948, more than three years after the surrender of Nazi Germany, he writes to Dorothea for Mother's Day. There must be millions of letters like this one in personal and public archives across the country, but Rupert's note—one of the few documents I have containing his tiny, spidery handwriting—is moving all the same: "Dear Thea! Last Sunday was Mother's Day. My heartfelt congratulations, dear Thea, on the occasion of this feast. You have given life to our boy in pain and under conditions that are hard to describe. For this you shall always have my thanks. Little Helmut, too, will recognize this sacrifice when he is older, and keep you in his heart all the more. It will be our task to educate him in this spirit and to make a useful human being out of him. Thea, please also send my thanks to my own dear old mother, and to your mother. It is only here that you understand what it means to have a wife, a mother, and a family. Today is Whitsun, which is a Sunday here, and a feast that we celebrate in the same way as you back home, and a day when our thoughts, desires, and cares are with you. Please, dear Thea, send my wishes to all acquaintances and friends. Here is to a speedy reunion, Your Rupert."

That reunion finally came five months later. Rupert returned from Russia in October 1948, more than three years after the end of the war and the birth of his son, a child he had never met. Another family story, much repeated down the years, tells how, when Rupert finally showed up at the family home back in Ehingen, my father threw rocks at him. He had no idea who this strange, sickly man was.

This is all I know about my grandfather, the man with the swastika armband, and all I will ever know. His personal story matters to no one except my family, and it is significant only in the sense that it is so entirely unremarkable. The Nazi Party had more than ten million members, and the electoral support of many millions more. Show me a normal German family, and I will show you a grandfather, father, or uncle like Rupert Buck. He was one of countless Germans who carried the regime—and carried out its orders. His story shows in stark and personal terms why it was so hard for German society and German courts to grapple with the legacy of Nazi crimes after the war. For most Germans who had lived through the Nazi period and the

Second World War, a more rigorous approach to prosecuting the guilty would have meant giving up brothers and fathers, aunts and cousins, friends and neighbors. Complicity was everywhere, as were the excuses and justifications that kept both a legal and a wider moral reckoning at a distance. Weren't they all just following orders? Weren't they all somehow unaware of what was really happening? Weren't they all trying to do the best they could in a difficult situation? And had they, after all, not suffered enough as it was?

Rupert was no monster, and neither was he—in strict legal terms—a criminal. No court convicted him, nor would it have occurred to anyone during his lifetime to put a mere *Mitläufer* like him on trial. Membership of the Nazi Party—as abhorrent as it might seem to us today—was never seen as a criminal offense, and in the years after the war it was likely not even an embarrassment. From everything we know, it is highly unlikely that Rupert would have met even the slightest reproach from those around him. As the letter sent by the top official in charge of political cleansing in his region made clear, it was, after all, "not us" who were guilty. There were millions like Rupert. If anything set him apart, it was that he paid a high personal price for the crimes of the Nazis.

No two biographies are the same. It makes little sense to compare the story of my grandfather to that of Bruno Dey. Rupert was thirty when the war broke out, Dey was just twelve. My grandfather was a party member and, initially, also a member of the SS. Dey never joined the party and became a member of the SS only as a result of a military order in 1944. My grandfather spent, by all accounts, the darkest years of Nazi rule working in the administration of the Reich Labour Service. Dey found himself posted to a concentration camp. It was, perhaps, nothing more than coincidence or good fortune that my grandfather served a branch of the Nazi state that was not directly implicated in mass murder. Had I known him better, I might be able to convince myself that his moral fortitude was greater than Dey's, that Rupert—unlike the man on trial in Hamburg—would have said "No." But such fortitude was rare at the time, as it is today.

CHAPTER SIX

"The only route to freedom is through the chimneys"

Marek Dunin-Wąsowicz arrived at Stutthof a few months before Bruno Dey, on May 25, 1944. Other than their age—both were seventeen at the time—the two young men had nothing in common. One was Polish and active in the resistance, the other was German and serving the forces of occupation. One wore the rough striped clothes of the camp prisoner, the other the uniform of the SS. While Dey stood guard in the watchtower with a rifle in his hand, Dunin-Wąsowicz struggled for survival in the filthy, overcrowded prison barracks below. Neither knew of the other man's existence at the time. They never knowingly came face-to-face at Stutthof. That moment would come an entire lifetime later, on October 28, 2019, the fifth day of the Dey trial.

Dunin-Wąsowicz was the first Stutthof survivor to testify at the Hamburg hearing. Dressed meticulously in a dark suit, dark tie, and white shirt, the 93-year-old retired journalist took his seat at the front of the courtroom, accompanied by his lawyer and an official translator. Small in stature, Dunin-Wąsowicz cut an imposing figure all the same. He spoke with confidence and precision, drawing on a prodigious memory and a lifetime of reflection and study. He told the court that he felt a profound sense of duty toward the victims of the Holocaust and a desire, undimmed by age, to fight against racism and demagoguery. He and the accused offered, then as now, a study in contrasts: in court, Dey was hesitant, taciturn, forgetful, and often struggling to provide adequate responses to the questions put to him by the judge and prosecutors. Dunin-Wąsowicz, in contrast, was loquacious, detailed, bursting with facts, memories, and observations that he was determined to share with the court. He took his duties as a witness seriously, but also provided rare moments of levity and charm, complimenting the presiding judge on her looks, and on one occasion addressing Meier-Göring as "*Schönes Gericht*"—"Beautiful Court." In a normal trial this would have undoubtedly earnt him a stern judicial rebuke. As it was, Meier-Göring gave the nonagenarian witness a brief smile and moved on.

Dunin-Wąsowicz described himself as a typical "Warsaw rascal": street smart and quick to spot an opportunity and calculate the odds. He had been good at what camp prisoners called "organizing"—getting hold of extra scraps of food, a decent pair of shoes, or an extra jacket. It was a talent that would prove vital to his chances of survival. But he was also able to be brutal against himself: on one occasion, weakened by long hours of forced labor in the forests around Stutthof, he deliberately crushed his foot under a tree trunk. The painful injury meant he was transferred to the camp hospital, where a friendly doctor was able to nurture him back to strength.

Dunin-Wąsowicz's ordeal, and that of his family, had begun long before his transfer to Stutthof. His mother, father, and older brother had all been active in the Polish resistance against the Nazi occupation. As the youngest, he was tasked mainly with acts of minor sabotage: painting slogans on walls and destroying posters carrying German announcements, but also observing and tracking German troop movements. His brother, Krzysztof, who had previously trained as an officer in the Polish army, took on riskier assignments, while his parents helped organize the funding for illicit activities. Krzysztof was eventually denounced and arrested in April 1944, along with the rest of the family, all of whom were taken to the notorious Pawiak prison in central Warsaw. His brother was tortured and beaten, and sentenced to death. That sentence, however, was never carried out. Instead, the two brothers were sent to Stutthof, where Krzysztof—who not only spoke German but could draw on Polish resistance networks that continued to function inside the camp—was able to look out for his younger brother. "My life was very closely linked with my brother's. He took care of me like a father cares for his child. My brother took part in underground activities in the camp, but I was not involved, and I had no information. After the war my brother told me that he thought the less I know the better for me," Dunin-Wąsowicz told the court.

When Dunin-Wąsowicz was finally released from the camp infirmary after recovering from his self-inflicted injury, his brother managed to have him transferred to his barracks, where they would share a bunk for the rest of their imprisonment. The brothers stayed together, and survived together, until the day the camp was evacuated and the remaining prisoners were driven west, away from the advancing Red Army and toward Germany. This ordeal, too, the brothers survived. "We walked side roads, knee-deep in snow. And there was very cold frost. We had to walk side roads because the main roads were full of fleeing Germans and Wehrmacht troops in retreat," the witness told the court. The evacuation marches from Nazi concentration camps were called death marches for a reason, he added. The prisoners set out with hardly any food and in clothing entirely unfit to withstand the cold. Some locals tried to help them by giving them food, but the SS men had little interest in allowing help to reach the desperate prisoners. "I once saw that people had prepared a large pot of soup, and brought it to us when we made a stop. But one of the SS men kicked it over and all the soup spilled into the snow," Dunin-Wąsowicz said. Prisoners who fell exhausted into the snow and were unable to get up were shot by the SS. "There were many dead bodies. A great many."

Death had been a constant presence, and a daily threat, from the moment Dunin-Wąsowicz set foot inside the camp: "We saw dead bodies every day in the camp, everywhere. At every [morning] roll-call, when the prisoners stood in rows of five, there were dead bodies lying on the ground. They had died of hunger or exhaustion. And every day a special prisoner unit came by with a large cart and large wheels. They picked up the dead bodies and carted them off to the crematorium."

Dunin-Wąsowicz told the court in chilling detail about the public whippings and executions that were carried out on a square close to the main gate. He and other prisoners were made to stand and watch as the sentence was read out and the victims were tied to a special trestle, leaving their backsides exposed. Then one of the Kapos—the prisoners recruited by the SS as supervisors and enforcers, and who were often notorious for their brutality —would carry out the sentence, using a long bullwhip. "As far as I recall no prisoner was able to take more than thirty lashes," he told the court. The gallows stood right next to the whipping trestle, Dunin-Wąsowicz added. Hangings, too, would be carried out in public, with prisoners forced to stand and watch the executions. The witness described two specific executions that he had observed in person, including the stirring last words of a young Russian hanged by the SS: "Don't worry, brothers. Soon our Russian Army will come and take revenge."

Marek Dunin-Wąsowicz (left) was one of six Stutthof
survivors who testified in court.

No less striking was Dunin-Wąsowicz's recollection of the
mood among some of the prisoners watching. "Some comrades
said, 'Damn it, there won't be any lunch again.'" As long as the
executions, roll-calls and announcements took place the prisoners were not allowed to return to their barracks to consume
their measly allocation of food. Desperately hungry and weak,
to some prisoners the prospect of missing out on lunch seemed
more immediately important than the cruel execution of a
fellow prisoner. The camp left little room for pity or mourning.
The obsession with food was all-pervasive. In Stutthof, as in
other concentration camps, prisoners were kept deliberately on
starvation rations, typically only a fraction of the daily calories
required by a normal working adult. Given the terrible living

conditions and brutal workload, those rations were of course even less adequate. According to the official camp history, prisoners consumed on average only 600 to 1,000 calories per day.[1] What that meant in practice, Dunin-Wąsowicz recalled, was a slice of bread and some margarine for breakfast, together with "something to drink that on some occasions was supposed to resemble coffee, and on others, tea." For lunch there was a bowl of soup, made of nettles or turnip or—on rare occasions—potatoes, and for supper again a slice of bread with margarine and a turnip spread. "We were hungry, we were cold, and we were beaten," he told the court. Death came frequently, indiscriminately, by accident and by design, and at the whim of the SS men who ruled the camp with total impunity.

Dunin-Wąsowicz's account was the first given by a Stutthof survivor at the Hamburg hearing, and the most substantial, taking up three entire days. His words lodged themselves deeply in my mind—but then so did those of the other witnesses, even those who were too frail to make the journey to Hamburg and had to speak via video link. These old men and women—many in their nineties, just like the defendant—moved the court in different ways, but all shared the same determination to speak out in public, and perhaps for the last time.

At eighty-nine, Rosa Bloch was among the youngest to take the witness stand. She had traveled to Germany from Holon, a city in Israel just south of Tel Aviv, accompanied by her daughter and her grandson. Bloch told the court that she was just twelve years old when she arrived at Stutthof from the ghetto in Kovno (now known as Kaunas), Lithuania, together with her mother. Hers was a dangerous age to be in a Nazi concentration camp: children under the age of fourteen were generally regarded as too young to be of any use for the hard physical labor demanded by the SS, and most were killed, or sent on to be killed, with their mothers immediately. "My mother was smart and she understood things relatively quickly," Bloch recalled. "Mama knew that children who were too young would be sent somewhere else, maybe to Auschwitz. I was twelve but my mother wrote down that I was fourteen."

A lively and engaging presence in court, the Israeli witness offered a vivid account of her time at Stutthof, including the moment—upon arrival—when she first sensed the terrible danger she and her family were now in. "The first thing I saw [in the camp] was a gigantic pyramid of shoes. When I saw that I thought to myself, there is something different here. Something is not right," she told the court. It was a child's intuition, a basic realization that all those shoes must have once had owners. Where had they all gone? "When I saw that mountain of shoes, I understood: you are not getting back from this place."

Bloch spoke in Hebrew, through a translator sitting by her side, but every so often she would drift into German. When Meier-Göring examined her Stutthof registration card and noted her physical description—"eyes, nose, mouth—normal" —the witness interrupted with a giggle: *Blond! Blond! Ich war eine echte Blondine!*" "I was a real blonde!"

It was the only light-hearted moment in a testimony that brought home in stark fashion the everyday cruelty of Stutthof, as seen through the eyes of a child. Like all arrivals, Bloch said, she and her mother were given a number, and would from then on only be referred to by those digits. "From the moment we arrived at the concentration camp we were no longer human beings, we were a number…the conditions were terrible. I believe that even animals were treated better than we were treated."

For a twelve-year-old girl, still in her growth phase, the lack of food was especially painful. "I wanted to eat. In the mornings we were given a tiny piece of bread with some yellow cheese. In the middle of the day they gave us something they called soup, but it was essentially water. So one day I thought, I have to do something. I was so hungry, terribly hungry, all the time. And one day I got this water-soup and I thought, maybe I can get a second helping, a very small one. I got up and the man who gave out the soup saw me. He picked up a chair and hit me over the head with it, with all his strength…I was full of blood."

Bloch's account echoed much of what Dunin-Wąsowicz had already told the court—about the starvation rations, about the everyday brutality of the guards and Kapos, the terror of the morning roll-call, the public executions, and the industrial killings taking place in one corner of the camp. Was she aware, Meier-Göring asked, of the existence of a gas chamber at Stutthof? Bloch did not hesitate for a moment. "We knew everything about the gas chamber. Because there was a unit of Jewish men who had to drag the dead bodies from the gas chamber…And these men, they could speak to us from time to time, by calling loudly [through the fence], mostly in Yiddish."

There were moments when the testimony of survivors like Bloch and Dunin-Wąsowicz seemed like a history lesson, with little direct relevance to the case against Bruno Dey. But there were moments—such as this one—where the importance of what the witnesses had to say was instantly evident. Bloch's (and, indeed, Dunin-Wąsowicz's) responses to the judge's question about the gas chamber went a long way toward answering one of the most contentious questions hanging over the trial: what did the accused know, and what should he have known, about the mass murder of Jews and other inmates at Stutthof? What did he know about the gas chamber and the crematorium, the executions by gunshot, and the mass deaths caused by the deliberate withholding of food, care, and medical support from sick prisoners? The logic of asking Stutthof survivors those same questions was perfectly simple: if prisoners like Dunin-Wąsowicz and Bloch were aware of the gas chamber, how could a guard like Dey—with his privileged position in the watchtower—claim not to have seen or known? Dey's insistence that he had no knowledge of these matters had always stretched credulity. But it seemed less and less convincing with every survivor who appeared in court. As Dunin-Wąsowicz explained: "Everyone knew about this [the gas chamber]. When the prisoners were fetched by the SS, whether from their place of work or from the barracks, and they didn't return, it was clear they had been murdered. The gas chambers were a 'Polish secret'—meaning no secret at all."

Dunin-Wąsowicz recalled in particular a period in late 1944 when large numbers of Hungarian Jews arrived at Stutthof, only to disappear almost overnight. Pressed by the judge whether he himself saw what had happened to them, a note of indignation crept into the witness's voice: "Please excuse me but I am a thinking person. When I see that thousands of Jews arrive and none of them show up in any of the workplaces later on then I know that they cannot have disappeared into thin air! Something must have happened to them, and that is what prisoners were talking about. Some saw more and the other saw less. But the fact was there was a person, and then there was no longer a person."

Dunin-Wąsowicz did not have to rely wholly on hearsay and deduction to understand what was happening. Following his self-inflicted foot injury he spent several weeks in the infirmary, in a building that directly overlooked the gas chamber and the crematorium. "I saw the gas chamber but I did not see directly [how people were killed there]. When a group of prisoners was taken there you could imagine what was going to happen," he told the court. "When such an event took place and a group of patients in the infirmary went to the window to look, the medic that kept watch over us told us to get away from the windows. He said this could end badly for all of us if the Germans notice."

The crematorium, meanwhile, was impossible to ignore, as was its purpose. "It was a popular topic of conversation [among the prisoners]," Dunin-Wąsowicz recalled. "Every new arrival would ask, 'What is that?' And the response was: 'The only route to freedom is through the chimneys.'"

The accounts of the Stutthof survivors were unlike witness testimony as it is commonly heard in a criminal trial. None of them could identify or remember the accused, nor had they seen him commit any specific crime. There were long periods when their narratives seemed to detach themselves from the trial entirely, not least when they spoke about their anguish after the war, or about how they felt about being in Germany the day of the hearing. These accounts were not relevant to the question at the heart of the trial, namely whether Bruno Dey was guilty of aiding murder. But they were relevant and important in a wider sense. Here was a rare—perhaps a final—opportunity to give a Holocaust survivor the chance to tell their story to a German criminal court. It was an opportunity Dunin-Wąsowicz and others had waited a lifetime for. Cutting them off, curbing their desire to share their story, or limiting them to the brief period under investigation by the court, would have felt like a terrible injustice. I thought Meier-Göring deserved great credit for the way she gave space and time to Dunin-Wąsowicz and the other survivors, allowing them to tell their story at their own pace. She dealt with the elderly witnesses and their often meandering recollections calmly and kindly, occasionally nudging them back toward her path of inquiry but also making clear that she was interested in their whole life story. To understand the crime and its victims, it was important to hear what they had to say—and what they thought they had to say. This was notable when Dunin-Wąsowicz spoke about life after Stutthof, and how his experience there had marked and damaged him for life. Some of that damage came in small and seemingly mundane ways, for example when he realized he was physically unable to change his son's nappies, having lived so long in the filth and stench of Stutthof. "I had to throw up. And that was ten years after I left the camp," he recalled. But Dunin-Wąsowicz also spoke of an emotional numbness that had clouded his later life: "No dead body, no dying person, no one who was tortured or beaten made any impression on me. I became completely indifferent. I know that this is a terrible illness and I was in therapy for a long time to get rid of this," he told the court. "I buried my father and my mother, and I did not shed a tear."

Bloch, too, was asked how she had managed to deal with her memories. "Of course I suffered from this, it impacted me," she replied. But Bloch had also proven herself surprisingly resilient, both in the camp itself and in the years that followed. She had to take care of her mother, who found living and surviving at Stutthof even harder than her daughter (and who died very shortly after liberation). "I am a very strong person, I am always optimistic. That is my character," Bloch said. "After the war I met a man, we married, we started a family, I had children. I always thought you must look ahead, not backward. Life runs forwards not backward. You have to understand that." Her priority, she said, was to take care of her children, not to dwell on her memories. That changed only later. "Later I could recount what I had lived through, but first I had to be strong. That was a lesson for all of us. We had to be strong."

Over the course of the nine-month trial, the court heard the personal testimonies of six Stutthof survivors. Many more provided written accounts of their ordeal, often because they were too weak to appear in person in Hamburg. These statements were read out by Meier-Göring and so became part of the evidence nonetheless. One who did make the arduous journey, in early February 2020, was 92-year-old Henri Zajdenwergier, a French survivor from Paris, who had lost almost his entire family in the Holocaust. Like many of the witnesses in court, he at times struggled for composure. What moved him to tears, however, were not the terrible recollections of Stutthof but the memory of his mother, who had died in childbirth long before the German invasion of France. Hearing the old man sob and sniffle gently at the front of the court, as he spoke of a mother he never knew, was among the saddest moments of the whole trial.

Zajdenwergier was deported to Stutthof in August 1944, having escaped a first round-up of Jews two years earlier that took away his father. He was sixteen years old when he arrived at the camp, and gripped by fear. "I had such fear. I saw what was happening around me, the beatings the deported were getting. I shut out everything, and I tried to make myself as small as possible. Just to become invisible. But I was still beaten a few times when I went to work."

Zajdenwergier was lucky to find a protector, an older prisoner who tried to help the teenager survive as best he could. He would take his food rations from him to stop Zajdenwergier from eating everything in one go, and parcel out the precious calories over the course of the day to keep the boy's strength up. When the prisoners were made to work in the nearby forest, carrying heavy pieces of wood, the older men would place him in the middle of their group, so he had less weight to bear. Other ordeals he was not spared, however—from watching the executions to being forced to stand in wet clothes in the middle of winter. "I lost a bit of my faith in God. I asked myself, 'Where is the Lord?'" Zajdenwergier recalled.

Some of the Stutthof testimonies were almost unbearable in their graphic horror. Halina Strnad, a formidable 93-year-old survivor from Melbourne, Australia, told the court about one particular image that had followed her in her nightmares long after liberation. "One day I found one of the women who had recently arrived [at Stutthof] near the latrines screaming in pain," she recalled. "We got her inside and she gave birth to a five-month-old dead fetus. We had to break a window to cut the umbilical cord. She died of blood loss, and it was my job to [dispose of] the baby in the latrines." The court listened in stunned silence. But Strnad was not finished yet. "A few days later the body of the baby was floating on top of the latrines. I used to see it in my nightmares for many years."

The Australian witness was speaking via video link, but the connection was poor and broke down constantly. This added an excruciating twist to the proceedings, as a court official had to dial into the call again and again. Every time this happened, the video-link software announced cheerfully, "Welcome to the meeting!" followed by, "You are now joining the meeting!" Then Strnad usually had only a few minutes—one more shocking recollection, one more damning indictment of the SS guards at Stutthof—before the line broke down once again.

Meier-Göring became audibly frustrated with this techno-logical farce, but in the end it did little to dim the power of Strnad's testimony. Like Bloch, she had arrived at the camp with her mother. The two were put in a barrack that lacked even the crude, overcrowded bunk beds used elsewhere in the camp. "There was just straw on the floor. At first there were so many of us that we could not stretch our legs. We were like sardines. Soon there was more space because people were dying very fast," Strnad recalled. Both she and her mother fell ill when typhus swept through the camp in late 1944. Deprived of medical support and adequate provisions, and forced to live in unspeakable filth ("Everything was full of excrement"), the prisoners succumbed to the disease in their thousands. Strnad's mother was among them. "I talked to my mother, trying to plead with her to hold on. But she died in my arms," the witness told the court.

Strnad's testimony was brutal in its description of life and death in Stutthof. It was also consequential: as would become clear months later, it was not least her account of the appalling impact of the typhus epidemic that pushed the court toward an important conclusion—namely that the SS personnel that ran the camp had made a deliberate decision to let thousands of prisoners die. This was no neglect, and no mere side effect of the way that Stutthof was set up. It was as clear a case of murder as the decision to fire a bullet in the back of the neck or to close the door of the gas chamber.

Listening to the survivor testimonies in Hamburg, I was reminded of an observation made by Ruth Klüger, the Austrian-born, U.S.-based writer and academic whose memoir of surviving the Holocaust was a surprise bestseller in Germany in the early 1990s. In her book she pointed to a peculiar pitfall when writing or reading a first-hand account of the Holocaust. That same pitfall applied, I now realized, also to hearing first-hand testimony of the Holocaust in court. The problem, Klüger wrote, was that "the author has stayed alive."[2] The first-hand account invited the reader to identify with the statistically improbable character of the survivor; whatever hardship, cruelty, and suffering the narrator experienced inside the camp—and that was now told on the page or in the witness stand—was tempered by the knowledge that he or she ultimately emerged from the hellscape of the camps alive. "One reads and thinks: it all turned out well in the end. Whoever writes is alive. The report, which was begun only with the intention of documenting the great hopelessness, has developed inadvertently into an 'escape story,'" Klüger wrote. "How can I stop you, my reader, from rejoicing with me, now that I am no longer threatened by the gas chamber and heading for a post-war happy ending that I can share with you?...How can I stop you from breathing a sigh of relief?"[3]

Klüger's point was obviously not to criticize or invalidate first-person survivor accounts written after the war. But she wanted readers to be aware of the vast terrible silence that the Holocaust left behind. It was not normal to survive. It was normal to be murdered. Behind every testimony of survival stood six million stories that could never be told.

The sheer improbability of survival was what struck me also in the testimonies of Dunin-Wąsowicz, Bloch, Strnad, and all the others. To escape death in the camps meant beating terrible odds not just once but over and over and over again. There was, moreover, no specific behavior or attitude or work ethic or appearance that made you safe. To be old and frail or young and weak meant certain death. (Bloch, indeed, would have had little chance of survival had her mother not faked her age on arrival.) But even a healthy young man like Dunin-Wąsowicz had to face a hundred "what ifs" to come through alive: what if his brother had not been around to help him? What if there had been no friendly doctor to shield him in hospital? What if his wound had become infected? What if he had not been one of the few Stutthof prisoners to receive a vaccine that protected him against the typhus epidemic that broke out in late 1944? What if he had been told to return to the forest-workers' brigade rather than spending his days in the less grueling leather workshops of

103

Stutthof? What if the irate SS man who found him resting on a pile of rucksacks destined for the Wehrmacht had beaten him even more savagely than he did? Dunin-Wąsowicz might have been flogged to death then and there. He might have frozen or starved on the death march west. He might have been sent to the gas chamber for any reason, or for no reason at all, or been shot in the back of the neck for whatever reason, or for no reason at all. That he survived—and survived long enough to give testimony in Hamburg seven decades later—was indeed a source of joy and comfort, not least to all of his listeners in court. But Dunin-Wąsowicz left the court under no illusion how tenuous his grip on life had been.

Toward the end of the second day of his hearings, Meier-Göring turned toward the witness with a series of questions that were remarkably personal, and far removed from the crimes that were at the heart of the trial. She wanted to know simply how he felt sitting in a German court today, speaking about his memories and coming face-to-face with the accused. Dunin-Wąsowicz responded politely, noting that he had been treated in a very friendly manner by all, and that he had been pleasantly surprised that he had never been asked to show his passport. Germany, he added, was now a friendly country to Poland, and "conscious that we are together in the European Union." Giving testimony, however, had been painful. "Aside from the fact that I am looking at the High Court [Meier-Göring] it is not pleasant to sit here," he said. "I came to this courtroom out of a sense of duty, and because I felt I had to honor my comrades and the 80,000 people who were killed at Stutthof.[4] But I also came to say loudly that I have done everything I can and will continue to do everything I can until the end of my life, to never allow concentration camps again. And I am scared when I look at what is happening, in Germany, in Poland, in France and in many other parts of the world, at a time when nationalism and racism are rising again, and in the final consequence, fascism. That is why I come and speak. And I repeat: I have not come for revenge. I believe in the justice of the High Court. That is all."

Strnad, too, was asked at the end of her testimony whether she had any final words to direct to the court. "In the camp, we said that if we survive we shall have to testify until we die," she responded. "And that is what I am doing now. It is an obligation."

CHAPTER SEVEN

Bullets and birdshit

It is just after midday when Stephan Balliet pulls up in his car
—a spotless gray Volkswagen Golf—outside the small synagogue
in the eastern German city of Halle. Inside are fifty-one worshippers, gathered to mark Yom Kippur, the day of atonement
and the most important holiday in the Jewish calendar. It is a
solemn day, filled with prayer and introspection, the day when
Jews everywhere are called upon to reflect upon their sins and
seek God's forgiveness. Balliet, however, has not come to the
synagogue to pray or reflect, let alone to seek forgiveness. He
has come, armed to the teeth with weapons and explosives, with
one intention only: to commit a terrible massacre.

The Halle synagogue, a nineteenth-century neo-Moorish
building crowned by five little turrets, is set back from the street
and surrounded by a high brick wall. To enter, visitors must
pass through a wooden door and cross a courtyard. Moments
before his attack, Balliet, who is dressed in combat gear and
military-style boots, has switched on a mobile phone camera
that is fixed to his helmet. The assault, live streamed to several
hundred followers on the Internet, begins with an attempt to
break into the compound by throwing explosives and firing shots
at the wooden door. He then tosses a grenade into the courtyard,
apparently hoping that the explosion will force the congregation
to break cover, flee the building, and run into his line of fire. Max

Privorozki, the chairman of the Jewish Community in Halle and one of the worshippers inside, watches the terrifying assault in real time, via the feed of a security camera. "The attacker fired several shots at the door and also threw Molotov cocktails, fireworks, or grenades in an attempt to get inside," he will recall later. "But the door held. God protected us."[1]

Balliet walks along the compound walls, finds another locked entrance, and tries to break down this door, too, with yet more explosives. It is at this point that Jana Lange, a forty-year-old local woman, confronts the attacker, apparently mistaking the loud bangs for fireworks. Balliet kills her with several shots from close range. Abandoning his plan to storm the synagogue, he gets back into his car, drives a few hundred meters, until he sees a Turkish doner kebab restaurant. "Doner. We'll take that," he mutters on his live stream. Balliet tosses a grenade at the front door, and then fires multiple shots inside, killing his second victim, twenty-year-old Kevin Schwarze. After a shoot-out with the police, he escapes—injured and bleeding —to a nearby village, where he steals a taxi and drives on to Zeitz, 60 kilometers south of Halle. It is here that the attacker is finally stopped and arrested by the police. The rampage has lasted just over ninety minutes, but it will remain seared into the country's collective consciousness for years to come. Images of the damaged wooden door spread far and wide, its significance obvious: it was this door alone that prevented the mass killing of Jews inside a German synagogue, by a German attacker, on the holiest day in the Jewish calendar. The attack on the congregation was an outrage, as was the casual slaughter of two bystanders. But it was also a lucky escape: had he broken through the door, Balliet would have committed an atrocity on a scale not seen since the end of the war, a deed so intolerable—unthinkable even—that it would have shaken the country to the core. The date of the Halle assault is October 9, 2019—just eight days before the opening of the Stutthof trial in Hamburg.

The attack hung over the first day of the trial like a cloud, a reminder—if one was needed—that murderous antisemitism had not disappeared from Germany after 1945. It was the first of many moments during the trial in which outside events shattered the calm deliberations inside the Hamburg courtroom. There was, from the outset, something starkly contemporary to the Dey hearings, even if the alleged crimes that were at the heart of the trial happened a lifetime ago. The recent Halle attack, the latest in a series of shocking crimes committed by far-right extremists in Germany, seemed relevant to the trial—as the court itself acknowledged. In her opening remarks, Anne Meier-Göring made a thinly veiled reference to the assault, noting that the Stutthof trial was important "especially at a time when right-wing extremist violence is on the rise." Christoph Rückel, a Munich-based lawyer representing Stutthof victims, referenced Halle explicitly in his opening remarks on the first day of the trial. "The bloody deed in Halle shows that the right-wing-extremist reality must be countered with an unyielding response by the rule of law," he told the court. "It is frightening that on Yom Kippur, the highest Jewish holiday and the day of atonement, there were fifty-one people in a house of worship and they survived only because the wooden entrance door was secure. The prosecution of a criminal case in accordance with the rule of law is the best remedy against far-right messages and messages of hate." Rückel expanded his argument by pointing to the rise of the far-right Alternative for Germany party in recent years. The need to fight back against the resurgence of right-wing extremism, he suggested, extended also to this court.

No trial takes place in a political vacuum, and certainly no criminal trial. The laws themselves may be immutable, but the way judges read them and interpret them is forever shaped by the political and social currents swirling outside the courtroom. If this is true for criminal trials in general, it is especially true for Germany's trials against perpetrators of the Holocaust and other Nazi crimes. These were shaped and molded from the outset by the popular mood and the political atmosphere of the time, and impossible to detach from their moment in history. For much of Germany's post-war history, of course, those pressures acted in one direction only: toward leniency, amnesia, and impunity. Germans wanted to forget about the war, about the Holocaust, and about their own personal responsibility. So the judges, prosecutors, and lawyers inside the courtroom found ways of bending to that pressure. The judiciary was independent, of course, at least in a technical sense: judges were able to rule free from direct political interference. But they were also creatures of their age (and often creatures of the Nazi regime they had served as loyal jurists some years earlier). Their judgments were influenced by the views and values they encountered and absorbed outside the courtroom. The same was true in October 2019 in Hamburg. The Stutthof trial, too, took place in a specific moment in history—and it reflected that moment just as all the previous trials did.

The murders in Halle and the recent spike in far-right violence formed an important part of the social and political backdrop to the trial. For many Germans, however, the autumn of 2019 was unsettling in other ways as well. The era of Angela Merkel, the German chancellor who had governed the country at the head of centrist governments since 2005, was in its twilight years. Merkel had notified the country of her intention to stand down at the next election, depriving the country of a familiar (and still overwhelmingly popular) face at a time when little else in the world looked familiar. The election of Donald Trump in the U.S. in 2016 and Britain's decision to leave the European Union the same year had dealt a heavy blow to Germany and its understanding of the world. Merkel was a symbol of stability that many had grown to cherish. Her careful, cautious, unflashy style of leadership had always had its critics (and increasingly so in the years after her departure in 2021) but it offered a reassuring contrast to the political strongmen who seemed to be on the rise. In one of her final interviews before leaving office in late 2021, Merkel made clear that she too felt a degree of anxiety for the future. "We must be careful that after the great joy over the end of the cold war and the reunification of Europe we don't now enter a phase in which important lessons of history fade away," Merkel told a German newspaper in October 2021.[2] "We must remember that the multilateral world order was created in response to the lessons of the Second World War. There will be fewer and fewer witnesses of this era. In history there is a recurring pattern that people start treating structures with neglect when the generations that created those structures are no longer alive."

The dynamic she described was on display, of course, also in Germany itself. The country, for so long a paragon of centrist stability, had shown itself to be no longer immune to far-right populism. This became shockingly clear a few weeks after my return to Berlin in September 2017, in the federal election that saw the German chancellor win her fourth and final mandate. Her victory, impressive as it was, was overshadowed by the far-right Alternative for Germany party (AfD) winning almost 13 percent of the national vote. It not only entered the Bundestag, the federal parliament in Berlin, but it did so as the third-largest political force in the country and the largest opposition party in the chamber (the two largest parties, Merkel's Christian Democrats and the center-left Social Democrats, formed a "Grand Coalition"). It was the first time since the foundation of modern democratic Germany in 1949 that the far right succeeded in breaking through at the federal level in large numbers: close to six million voters backed the AfD and its nationalist anti-immigration platform—a stunning achievement for a party founded just four years earlier. In parts of the country, most notably in swathes of the former Communist east, the far-right emerged as the largest political force, winning as much as 40 percent in districts around Dresden. Nor did the rise of the AfD as a force in German politics prove a flash in the pan. At the 2021 federal election, the party again won more than 10 percent of the vote.

In its brief but turbulent history, the AfD had already acquired and shed multiple identities. Set up initially as a political vehicle to oppose further EU integration and block a German-funded bailout of the struggling economies in southern Europe, the AfD took a sharp turn to the right in the wake of the 2015–2016 refugee crisis. With the arrival in Germany of more than a million migrants from Syria, Afghanistan, and other majority-Muslim countries, the party seized on a rare opportunity to redraw the political map. In the weeks leading up to the September 2017 election, the AfD carpeted German cities with campaign posters denouncing Merkel's immigration policy: one showed a boat filled with refugees warning of an impending "crime wave"; another showed a pregnant woman and the slogan "New Germans? We prefer to make them ourselves"; a third depicted a piglet and the words "Islam? It does not suit our cooking." There was nothing subtle about the AfD campaign, but it worked. On election night, the biggest cheers in Berlin could be heard coming from the Traffic nightclub on Alexanderplatz, where the party held its celebrations. "We are in the Bundestag and we will change this country," Alexander Gauland, the AfD's figurehead and joint leader, told jubilant supporters. "We will make sure that what the people say on the streets finally plays a role in parliament." His party, he added, would "take back our country."[3]

The AfD's electoral success drew on deep and—until that moment—widely unacknowledged political sentiments. Skepticism toward the European Union continued to play an important role, but in 2017 that anti-Brussels feeling was clearly overshadowed by the party's full-throated opposition to Islam, migration, and Merkel's handling of the refugee crisis. Three years later, at the height of the COVID-19 pandemic, it also led the charge against public health measures imposed by the government, picking up and amplifying hostility to face masks and to the closure of bars and restaurants. In many ways, the AfD tapped into the same political sentiments that had propelled right-wing populists to electoral success around the world: nationalism, law and order, hostility to migrants (and dark-skinned migrants in particular), and opposition to the perceived excesses of "political correctness." But there were also specifically German themes. The party's strong following in former Communist eastern Germany, for example, owed much to a lingering sense of frustration and bitterness over the legacy of reunification. Polls showed that huge numbers of eastern Germans, especially among the older generations, still felt like second-class citizens, mocked and despised by their wealthier western counterparts. The AfD, with its full-on assault on liberal sensitivities, offered those voters a chance to strike back.

Lurking amid that populist *mélange*, however, was an altogether darker and uglier strand: an attempt to challenge Germany's historic consensus around the Nazi period and its commitment to keep both the lessons and the memory of the Holocaust alive in perpetuity. For the AfD, the country's memory culture was a political target as inviting as Merkel's refugee policy. The party's stance was encapsulated in a notorious quote by Gauland, who told a meeting of the AfD youth wing in June 2018 that "Hitler and the Nazis were only a speck of birdshit in more than a thousand years of successful German history."[4]

"The right to reclaim our past." Alexander Gauland, the co-leader of the far-right Alternative for Germany

A few years earlier, such a remark would have been career-ending even for a fringe politician in Germany. Now it was being made by the leader of the third-largest party in parliament—seemingly without consequence. Gauland did go on to voice regret at his comment, though only because he claimed it had been misunderstood. His regret in any case never seemed entirely genuine, not least because both he and other AfD leaders challenged Germany's post-war consensus on Nazism and the Holocaust on a regular basis, and usually in a manner that was designed to provoke and enrage. In another speech, given a year before his "birdshit" remark, Gauland had made a similarly revisionist point about German memory culture. He told a party meeting in the eastern federal state of Thuringia that no other people "had cleaned up their past as clearly as the Germans." He continued: "We should not be reproached for these twelve years [of Nazi rule] any longer. They no longer have an effect on our identity…That is why we have the right to reclaim not just our country, but also our past."[5] As a statement of political intent, Gauland's remarks could not have been clearer. Redefining the past—Germany's past—was now an integral part of the AfD's campaign to win political power in the present. Germans should feel pride, not remorse, when reflecting on the country's history. They should focus on what happened before the Holocaust, and after the Holocaust, but not on the Holocaust itself. Gauland himself, in the same 2017 speech, gave a chilling example of what this meant in practical terms. Germans, he stated, should feel "proud of the achievements of German soldiers in two world wars."[6]

In the AfD's new historiography, even the U.S.-led effort to rebuild Germany on democratic foundations after the war came in for blunt criticism. Jens Maier, a prominent AfD politician in the eastern state of Saxony, told a crowd in the city of Dresden in January 2017 that the Allies' re-education efforts after 1945 had led Germans to become convinced that "we are bastards, criminals, that we are worth nothing."[7] Maier told the cheering crowd, "I hereby declare this cult of guilt to be over! To be over, once and for all!"[8]

It is hard to exaggerate how alien and shocking this rhetoric sounded to Germans reared in the political and cultural mainstream. The centrality of the Holocaust to public life in Germany—and with it the mandate of "Never again"—had been accepted and anchored for decades. It had shaped the country's politics and culture, its approach to education and diplomacy, and provided a moral compass to leaders for many years. For the AfD, however, it was precisely that centrality that was offensive. Its leaders never questioned that the Holocaust took place—they were not deniers in that sense. But they wanted it to play a much smaller role in the German imagination, and—apparently—in the German capital of Berlin, home to the central Holocaust memorial. One of the party's most outspoken hardliners, a former history teacher named Björn Höcke, caused an uproar when he took aim at the Berlin memorial in a speech in 2017. "The Germans are the only people in the world that have planted a monument of shame in the heart of their capital," he declared.[9] The post-war obsession with the Holocaust, he went on, had obscured the suffering of another group of victims: the Germans. "Until today we are not in a position to mourn our own victims," Höcke said. The leader of the AfD branch in the eastern state of Thuringia, Höcke went on to call for a "180-degree shift in memory politics" and a "memory culture that above all, and first of all, brings us closer to the great achievement of our ancestors."[10]

His speech prompted a fresh wave of outrage and condemnation from across the political spectrum, as well as from religious groups and the Jewish community. At the time, Höcke was seen as beyond the pale even by the wider AfD leadership, which sought to ban the so-called *Flügel*, or "Wing," the extreme-right grouping inside the AfD that the Thuringia strongman represented. Not only did the attempt to kick Höcke out of the party fail, he actually went on to strengthen his position in the years that followed. Once the leader of a fringe within a fringe, his particular brand of nationalist, revisionist discourse came to dominate the AfD. This did little to dent the popularity of the party in polls and elections, however. Less than a decade after it was founded, the AfD was represented in all but one of the parliaments of Germany's sixteen federal states, as well as in the federal parliament in Berlin. In the five states that used to form East Germany, the party could count on the support of one in five voters. And while it had yet to break through the cordon sanitaire imposed by Germany's mainstream parties, there was an obvious risk that the country's deepening political fragmentation would mean that the AfD would sooner or later be needed to form coalition governments, if only at the local or regional level.

Pursued with brazen dedication and an evident relish to shock, the attempt by AfD leaders to challenge and subvert Germany's post-war memory culture was met with widespread concern. Yet in some ways, the AfD represented the more acceptable face of Germany's recent far-right surge. Its leaders mostly adhered to the rules of the political game. They denounced political violence and portrayed themselves as defenders of Germany's constitutional order. Their weapon of choice was not the Molotov cocktail or baseball bat but the campaign poster, the political speech, the tweet, and the Facebook post. The same could not be said of the violent thugs and armed neo-Nazis that populated the most extreme fringe of the far-right spectrum—and of whom Stephan Balliet was just one of many examples. Germany long had to contend with a violent far-right fringe, but the Dey trial coincided with a notable spike in deadly extremism.

In June 2019, just as prosecutors in Hamburg were putting the finishing touches to the case against Bruno Dey, a political murder sent shockwaves around the country. Walter Lübcke, a prominent regional politician who had been a vociferous supporter of Chancellor Merkel's tolerant refugee policy, was gunned down in his own garden by a 45-year-old far-right activist. The killer had links to a notorious neo-Nazi group and a previous conviction for setting fire to a refugee center. In a country where few politicians require tight security, Lübcke's death proved deeply unsettling. A chilling message had been sent: mainstream politicians could no longer feel safe in their own home, even if their names were little known outside their region. The simple act of defending government policy—and advocating decency and humanity toward refugees—could be enough to earn a death sentence from far-right terrorists.

In February 2020, four months into the Dey trial, Germans were horrified by news of an even deadlier incident of extremist violence, this time in Hanau, a sleepy mid-sized town near Frankfurt. Driven by burning hatred of foreigners and a desire to "cleanse" the planet of undesirables, a far-right gunman named Tobias Rathjen launched a vicious night-time attack on two bars popular with young Turkish-Germans and others from migrant communities. He shot nine people dead before driving home, where he killed his 72-year-old mother and eventually turned the gun on himself. The morning after the deadly attack I was part of a team of reporters assigned to cover the outrage, and found myself wading through Rathjen's twenty-four-page manifesto, a strange blend of psychobabble, conspiracy theory, and genocidal fantasy. In one passage, he called for the elimination of entire countries and populations, including Morocco, Egypt, Israel, Turkey, Iran, India, Pakistan, Vietnam, and the Philippines. "This would only be the rough cleansing. It would be followed by the fine cleansing," the document stated. "I would eliminate all these people, even if we are speaking about billions of people. It has to be done."

Halle, the Lübcke murder, and the shooting spree in Hanau all received close media scrutiny and broad political attention.

But they were bloody peaks only, that rose amid a high plateau of far-right violence that attracted little to no attention. Official police statistics showed that right-wing extremists committed more than twenty thousand crimes every year, including more than a thousand acts of violence.[11] The danger they pose is, by common consent, significantly greater than that posed by far-left or Islamist extremists.

In a country that prizes political stability, and where the murder rate is comparatively low, these numbers have been a cause for alarm. That some of the deadliest incidents occurred at the same time as the Dey trial was coincidental. But they provided an unsettling backdrop to the hearings, as did the growing presence of the AfD in German political life, and the party's attempt to challenge the country's memory culture from the right-wing fringe.

From the first day of the trial, it was hard to escape a feeling that some important things were going wrong outside the Hamburg courtroom—and that the sense of threat and insecurity outside added both urgency and meaning to the proceedings. The simple act of holding a trial, a fair and open trial, to examine the darkest chapter in German history, seemed to offer an alternative path. It showed that the Holocaust still mattered in Germany, not just as a political and moral imperative, but as a concrete thing that could be prosecuted, and discussed in court, and which a man could ultimately be held accountable for. It showed that for all the braying of the far right, the rule of law still held firm in a country that knew only too well what a descent into totalitarian lawlessness looked like. In that sense, at least, it seemed right that the outside world was allowed to intrude.

Meier-Göring had clearly wrestled with this aspect of the Dey case. When I spoke to her, long after the trial was over, she insisted on the need to strike a balance. Of course the court had to focus above all else on the guilt of the individual, but she insisted that judges could not and should not be blind to the world outside. "I believe a criminal trial should not ignore this. A criminal trial functions only in the framework of a society, and you must be aware of the consequences, and of the impact that a trial and that your verdicts have," she said. "You have to walk a very fine line. On the one hand you need to separate yourself from the voice of the people and from populist tendencies. You have to preserve your judicial independence, of course. But neither must you close your eyes. Because we are part of this society."

Her conviction, as we will see, carried through until the last day of the trial. The verdict Meier-Göring would read out in July 2020 dealt with crimes committed a lifetime ago. But it would have much to say about the present day as well.

CHAPTER EIGHT

The subjective problem

The law faculty of Berlin's Humboldt University is housed in an imposing baroque building known as *die Kommode*, or the "dresser." The pillared facade of gray stone curves elegantly inward, as if trying to embrace the splendor of the square in front. Facing it across a treeless expanse is Berlin's state opera house, erected by Frederick the Great in the mid-eighteenth-century in the style of a Greek temple. To the left stands the main university building, a sober piece of classicist architecture; to the right, a stately nineteenth-century building converted into luxury hotel, and the city's oldest Roman Catholic church. In a capital scarred by war and brutalist rebuilding like few others, the square appears to have survived the ravages of the twentieth century almost untouched. Look more closely, however, and the wounds of history begin to show. Right in the center of the *Platz*, a small glass window has been set into the pavement. It allows a glimpse into a perfectly square white room below, whose 5-meter-high walls are lined with empty bookshelves. A work by the Israeli artist Micha Ullman, *The Empty Library*, commemorates one of the first acts of Nazi barbarity: the public burning of some twenty thousand books by Jewish and left-wing authors on this square in May 1933. A few meters from the glass pane are two bronze plaques bearing a prescient warning by the German poet Heinrich Heine:

That was a prelude only, there
Where you burn books,
You end up burning people, too.

Heine wrote those lines more than a century before the Nazi book burning took place. His own poems and plays would end up in the flames, to raucous cheers from students and professors, along with works by Thomas Mann, Bertolt Brecht, Albert Einstein, Siegmund Freud, and countless others.

The faculty and the square in front are deeply familiar to me. As a student of law in Berlin more than two decades ago, I would cross the traffic light in front of the opera house almost every day, cut across the square, and lock up my heavy Dutch bicycle outside the entrance to the Kommode. Once through the doors, the building changed character abruptly: the baroque facade, it turned out, was just that—a facade. Inside, the library was pure East German functionalism, cheap, glum, and beige. The only touch of artistry was a massive stained-glass window in the center of the library reception hall, depicting a triumphant Lenin pointing the way to the future, with Marx and Engels standing just behind. On hot summer days, when windows were open at both ends of the square, fragments of music would drift across from the opera house rehearsal rooms—shards of beauty to pierce my dull academic duties as a final-year law student.

Those duties consisted largely of writing down thousands of legal definitions, standard problems and theories on filing cards and then committing them to memory. The ability to recall those definitions and theories was crucial to solving the highly artificial and often maddeningly complex cases set by our professors in regular five-hour examinations. These would usually start simply enough, along the lines of "X agrees to sell his used car to Y," or, "Mr. Black wakes up at night and thinks he hears a burglar." The next sentence would add a twist. X might turn out to be a minor, or the car might in fact belong to Z, or the vehicle might contain some costly flaw unknown to buyer and seller. The suspected burglar would turn out to be Ms. Black coming home from a late night. Mr. Black might decide to pull a gun on the shadow appearing at the bedroom door and kill his wife in error. The case description would wind on without mercy, adding layer upon layer of complexity. *Problem erkannt, Gefahr gebannt*, was the mantra drummed into us by our tutors. "Recognize the problem, banish the threat." What they meant was that there was no point trying to skirt around the central complexity of the case. There were no shortcuts. Every layer had to be peeled away, analyzed and resolved, each problem put into the right box, a hundred small steps all leading logically, irreversibly to the correct conclusion. On a good day, this would bring a peculiar kind of satisfaction, comparable perhaps to the sense of accomplishment when you clean up your house after a raucous party—every surface wiped clean, every bit of broken glass swept up and discarded. Solving a legal problem, too, was about restoring order. You took the messiness of life—theft, divorce, a bungled property purchase—and turned it into neat paragraphs of abstraction and reason.

On a bad day (and there were many), the long hours spent rote learning seemed like a pointless waste of time. I had chosen to study law because it seemed like a useful and sensible degree to have, but I had no intention of becoming a judge or lawyer. That frustration was compounded by the sheer dread most of us felt when we thought about our final exams. We knew the statistics: more than a quarter of final year law students failed, forcing them to return to the library and to spend yet another year learning and memorizing the dull intricacies of German law.

I left the law behind as soon as I could, after passing my

first state examination, to pursue a career in journalism. That was more than two decades ago. In the years since, I rarely had cause to think about my legal training, let alone to apply it. But now, in the Hamburg courtroom, I found myself straining to remember those definitions and theories. To my surprise, I also found there was a soothing familiarity to the monotonous cadences of German legal argument, delivered in a language as dry and devoid of life as the surface of the moon.

Lurking behind those courtroom legal exchanges was a question that I found fascinating even as a student: how do we define a murderer?

The answer, it turns out, depends not least on where the killing takes place. In the Anglo-American legal tradition, murder is usually defined as the unlawful killing of another person with malice aforethought, meaning the intention to kill or cause grievous bodily harm.[1] There are differences between English law and U.S. law (which breaks down murder offenses by degree) and even variations between different U.S. states. But the basic idea is rather simple: person A kills person B unlawfully and with intent.

It follows that a killing is not a murder when the killer acted without control, with diminished responsibility or where the death occurred as a result of gross negligence. The killing cannot have been accidental. In such cases, a court in the UK will typically consider a conviction for the lesser offense of manslaughter.

So far, so clear. In Germany, however, the definition of murder is vastly more complicated—with consequences, as we will see, not just for the case of Bruno Dey but for countless Holocaust cases that went to trial before his. The key legal text is section 211 of the *Strafgesetzbuch*, or criminal code, which contains two parts. Part one reads: "Whoever commits murder under the conditions

123

of this provision incurs a penalty of imprisonment for life." The second part says: "A murderer under this provision is someone who kills a person out of lust, to obtain sexual gratification, out of greed or otherwise base motives, perfidiously or cruelly, or by means constituting a public danger or to facilitate the cover-up of another offense."

The concept becomes clearer when you read on to Section 212, which deals with *Totschlag*, or manslaughter. It states: "Whoever kills a person without being a murderer under the conditions of section 211 incurs a penalty of imprisonment for a term of at least five years." That section in turn is followed by further variations of *Totschlag*, such as killing upon request or negligent killing. The overall architecture of German homicide law, then, is this: *Totschlag*, or manslaughter, is the basic offense every time a person kills another person. If there are mitigating circumstances —the victim asked to be killed, for example—the law shifts down to a lesser offense and more lenient sanction. If there are aggravating circumstances—such as greed or cruelty—the law shifts upward to murder.

For a German court to decide on murder, simple intent is never sufficient. Instead, the judges have to weigh carefully whether one of the eight qualifications listed in section 211 applies or not. Some of these so-called *Mordmerkmale*, or "murder criteria," are quite straightforward: the man who kills his wife to inherit her wealth acts out of greed. The woman who murders her husband by poisoning the food at a large dinner party employs "means constituting a public danger." But when is a killing cruel? And what does it mean to have base motives or to act perfidiously? Over the years, those questions have spawned a thousand academic disputes and conflicting definitions, often pitting the jurisprudence of German courts against the views of illustrious law professors. The Federal High Court, for example,

124

has ruled in the past that motives such as racism, revenge, or jealousy constitute base motives. But not everyone agrees that they should: imagine a father killing the abuser of his child. He is clearly acting out of revenge. But is this killing, contemptible as it may be, really an act that society would locate "morally at the lowest level" and marked by "unrestrained selfishness"? Perhaps not. Faced with the vague language of section 211, influential scholars as well as the German high court have tended to argue that "base motives" should be interpreted in a highly restrictive manner.

The murder criterion of perfidiousness is another motive that has sparked fierce academic debates. According to the standard definition, this qualification demands that the killer consciously abuses the victim's unawareness and defenselessness.[2] Killing a victim in his or her sleep is a classic example of this, or poisoning someone's tea, or firing a lethal shot from a hiding place. At first blush, these interpretations seem eminently reasonable. But what about the woman who is beaten and abused by her husband for years, until she eventually decides to suffocate him in his sleep with a pillow? Perfidiousness is generally viewed as reprehensible because it leaves the victim no chance to fight back. But as the example shows, it can also be the only viable weapon of the weak against the strong. The abused wife in the example will spend the rest of her days in prison if she is found to have acted perfidiously. If not, she might well walk free after a few years.

There is another way in which the line between murder and manslaughter—blurred as it may sometimes be—matters profoundly. German political leaders and jurists were finally jolted into action in the late 1950s once they realized that Holocaust crimes, up to and including murder, would soon fall under the statute of limitations. In the case of murder, the statute of limitations was first extended and eventually abolished, which was the reason why the Dey case could be tried in the first place. For manslaughter, however, the laws were left unchanged. With few exceptions, bringing a manslaughter case from the Nazi period to court became simply impossible after 1960. From then on, the only way to bring suspects to justice was by proving that they were murderers—and that in turn meant identifying one of the eight criteria for murder set out in section 211.

German courts generally accepted—how could they not? —that death by asphyxiation in the gas chambers constituted cruelty. This was in part due to the physical pain associated with the inhalation of the Zyklon B gas, and the length of the ordeal. It could take up to thirty minutes before the victims finally succumbed to the lethal fumes. But the courts also highlighted the unspeakable psychological cruelty of those final minutes: it took significant time for the gas to reach all parts of the chamber, which meant victims were forced to witness the panic and horror spread toward them—and often the death of their children, parents, and other relatives along the way. Perfidiousness, too, could often be proved with relative ease, for example when the victims were sent to the gas chamber under the pretext that they were entering a shower room.

In other cases, however, identifying and confirming a murder criterion was hard, notably when it came to bureaucrats and officials who operated far from the actual camps and killing sites. The same problem could arise with SS men, soldiers, and police officers who killed their victims with gunshots (which meant the argument for special cruelty or perfidiousness was harder to make). In those cases, courts had to resort to the more elusive and controversial motivational criteria in section 211, notably "base motives." That led to another complication: those motives had to be present not in the minds of the principal perpetrators, such as Hitler and Himmler, but in the minds of the individuals standing trial, including when they were mere accessories. The Holocaust itself was evidently the result of murderous antisemitism. But was it fair to assume that every member of the camp hierarchy and every official in the SS administration was a murderous antisemite as well? Were they driven by base motives, or were they doing their work because they had been ordered to? Or because they were afraid of the consequences? Or perhaps because they were hoping for career advancement?

The deeper problem, of course, was that courts had to ask such questions in the first place. As critics noted even at the time, the German law's emphasis on subjective, motivational criteria looked horribly misplaced when confronted with the phenomenon of state-organized genocide. As a legal doctrine, it missed one of the central truths of the Holocaust, namely that the precise psychological state of the individual perpetrator rarely made any difference. Their motivation was quite irrelevant to the desperate men, women, and children driven into the gas chamber—or to the Nazi leaders back in Berlin. What mattered was that the killers did what they did, and that they knew what they were doing. What mattered was that the victims did die cruelly, through perfidious means, and for no other reason than murderous racial hatred. In Germany, however, judges in Holocaust trials had to probe the precise psychological motives of every individual defendant, to look into their minds and assess their hatred, their knowledge, their own fears and prejudices, their intelligence, and their excuses. What is more, they had to examine those thoughts and feelings not as they existed in the minds of the defendants today but many years and decades ago, in a situation starkly different from the one they found themselves in at the time of the hearing. For judges keen to find grounds for leniency, this left more than enough space to find them.

This subjective focus is at the heart of another academic controversy that arguably carried even greater significance for the prosecution of Nazi crimes: the distinction between perpetrator and accessory. At a basic level, that distinction is intuitive and often quite obvious: the perpetrator commits the crime while the accessory lends support, by providing information or a weapon, for example, or by helping a thief sell his stolen goods after the act. The perpetrator is the central figure, the accessory remains on the margins. Typically, the latter receives a far more lenient sentence.

In German Holocaust trials, however, that necessary and logical distinction between perpetrator and accessory was stretched to breaking point and beyond. From very early on, courts generally held that only the very top brass of the Nazi state—Hitler, Himmler, Göring, etc.—should be seen as perpetrators. Almost everyone else would be treated as a mere helper, even those who had a direct hand in the killings, and those who wielded enormous power as senior SS or military officers, or top-level government officials. The vast majority of post-war convictions in Holocaust cases were for aiding murder—not for murder itself. This was true even for mass killers like Otto Bradfisch, a doctor of law and veteran Nazi Party member, who commanded a unit of Einsatzgruppe B in present-day Belarus in 1941 and 1942. Under his leadership, the unit was responsible for more than fifteen thousand killings.[3] When he was finally put on trial two decades later, the court found him guilty only of being an accessory to murder—and sentenced him to ten years in jail. Had he been found guilty of a single murder himself, the result would have been a mandatory life sentence. The ruling came despite the court's conclusion that Bradfisch had been part of the firing squads, and that he had "followed orders without any internal opposition and forcefully made sure that his subordinates followed them with precision."[4]

Robert Mohr, also a lawyer by training (who in fact had studied human rights in Geneva before his Nazi career),[5] is another striking example. He, too, served as the commander of an Einsatzgruppen unit, this one stationed in Ukraine. Mohr was ultimately sentenced to eight years in prison for aiding the murder of thousands of Jews, partisans, and mentally disabled in the German-occupied territory. Once again, the court decided that only Hitler, Himmler, and Heydrich should be seen as perpetrators. Mohr, by contrast, was found to only be following orders, and so lacking the "will of the perpetrator."[6]

The court did not even bother to take into consideration the crimes committed by Mohr in his next post—though they are important to me. Having done his time on the Eastern Front, he was posted to Darmstadt, my home town, where he took charge of the deportation of the local Jewish population. According to charges filed by the Darmstadt prosecutor in May 1960, Mohr was accused of causing the death of at least nineteen Jews during his time as the local chief of the secret police.[7] The true number was almost certainly higher, but what the charge sheet lacked in scope it made up for in detail. It went on to identify the nineteen victims by name and by address. Examining the list more closely, I experienced a sudden, unsettling moment of recognition. Among the named victims was Dr. Karl Freund, murdered in Auschwitz, who, I learned, used to live a few houses down from the place where I grew up. There was Dr. Ernst Mayer, whose imposing villa I had cycled past countless times on my way to the local swimming pool. And there was Eduard Wolfskehl, scion of a prominent local Jewish family, whose residence was destroyed in the war and private garden later turned into a public park. As a child, I would often head there in winter with my wooden sledge and spend hours racing down the steep slope. A few years ago, I took my own son sledging there, still entirely oblivious to the tragic backstory.

The charge sheet, unfortunately, never led to a trial. Darmstadt prosecutors finally gave up on their attempt to bring Mohr to justice in 1963, two years before he was sentenced to his eight years in prison in the Einsatzgruppen trial. He lived out the remainder of his life in Solingen, in the Ruhr area, and died in 1989.

Why was he, and why were thousands like him, not convicted as perpetrators? How did German courts manage to classify men who had killed with their own guns, pulling triggers with their own fingers, as mere helpers?

The answer brings me back once again to my days in the Kommode library, and to a particularly dense filing card summarizing the theories and controversies around the distinction between perpetrator and accessory. My once impressive collection of handwritten filing cards went into the recycling bin many years ago, but I still remember the roll-call of peculiar murder cases summarized on this card. Of these, the strangest ruling by far came in the Staschinski case, which was handed down by the Federal Court of Justice in 1962. Bogdan Staschinski was a KGB agent who in 1957 killed two exiled Ukrainian political activists by spraying hydrogen cyanide into their faces (a highly lethal chemical, hydrogen cyanide was in fact the main component of Zyklon B). The murders took place in West Berlin and Munich. A few years later, Staschinski himself defected to West Germany, where he was arrested and put on trial. The court ruled that the agent had acted only as an accessory—despite the fact that he had killed the two victims himself and that the main perpetrators were thousands of kilometers away in Moscow and unable to directly influence or control the situation on the ground. The theory behind this ruling is known as the "animus" or "subjective" theory and is summed up succinctly in a phrase used by the Federal High Court in its ruling: "He did not want these crimes as his own, he had no personal interest in them and did not have a personal will to commit the crime."[8] The court added: "No matter whether it concerns murder or other crimes, the accessory is the one who does not commit the crime *as his own* but who acts as a tool or helper for someone else's crime. The measure of this is the *inner approach* toward the crime."[9]

Unsurprisingly, these phrases and arguments surfaced time and time again in Holocaust trials both before and after the Staschinski ruling. For defendants, they were a godsend. No matter how many victims they had driven into the gas chamber, or shot in cold blood in the forests of Belarus, they could always say that they had not wanted these murders "as their own"—that regardless of what their hands and arms did, or what their voices ordered, what mattered was their "inner approach" toward the deed. The notion that ordinary Germans had been seduced and tricked by the Nazi leadership was deeply entrenched not just in the legal community but in German society as a whole. The rulings against Robert Mohr and thousands like him reflected a specific social consensus, namely that the real perpetrators were not just few and far between, but conveniently dead. The people left to punish were, with few exceptions, deemed to be mere helpers.

In some ways, the emphasis that German criminal law places on the individual and his subjective state of mind is admirable. It is an approach that is rooted in the moral philosophy of Immanuel Kant, and enlightenment ideas about the human ability to exercise free will and choose between right and wrong. If the defendant has no other choice than to break the law—for example, because he was under severe duress or still underage —he will usually be spared criminal sanctions. The freedom and ability to make the right decision, and to choose the wrong path all the same, is a prerequisite for punishment. To establish whether or not that is the case, judges have to look inside the mind of the defendant. In cases of normal criminality—even a "normal" murder—that is of course entirely appropriate. The historic failure of Germany's legal system, however, was to treat the Holocaust as normal criminality—to assume that the best way to prosecute and punish the attempted destruction of European Jewry was to treat it like ordinary murder multiplied by six million, and to ignore the industrial, organized, bureaucratic, and largely anonymous manner of those killings. Look again at the murder criteria in Section 211 of the German criminal code and you realize that they typically assume some form of direct relationship—hatred, lust, greed, sexual desire, jealousy—between perpetrator and victim. That relationship, however, rarely if ever existed between perpetrator and victim in the Nazi genocide. How could it? At Treblinka and other extermination camps, victims were usually herded straight from the train carriages into the gas chambers. Even at Stutthof, as Dey explained repeatedly during the trial, there was next to no direct contact between guards and prisoners. Indeed, the absence of any kind of human bond between the murderer and the murdered was a specific, noteworthy and particularly chilling aspect of the Holocaust. It meant there was no scope for last-minute remorse, or a change of mind. There was no room for pity and no time for reprieve. A "normal" murderer can decide at the last moment to lower his gun, reflect on the terrible act he is about to commit, and turn away. That possibility simply did not exist in the Nazi death camps and killing fields. The Holocaust was a system, it was a factory, it was a chain of command in which responsibility was distributed and shared across ministries, bureaucracies, agencies, and tens of thousands of individuals across an entire continent. Some planned, some ordered, some shot, some shoved, some guarded, some sorted, some experimented, and some incinerated. However hard it was, and still is, to disentangle this web of culpability in the courtroom, the result should not have been that most of those culprits went either unpunished or were sentenced as mere helpers. Yet that was the outcome. That was the result of prosecutors and judges indulging in the fiction that they were dealing with normal criminals and normal crimes.

The one legal term that is invariably absent in German court rulings on the Holocaust is the one that actually fits the crime: genocide. Invented by the Polish-Jewish jurist Raphael Lemkin in 1944, the term was being substantially used as early as 1946 in the indictments at the Nuremberg tribunal, as it tried three specific crimes: crimes against peace, war crimes, and crimes against humanity. It was formally defined by the UN in 1948 as "acts committed with intent to destroy, in whole or in part, a national, ethnic, racial, or religious group," for example by "killing members of the group" or "deliberately inflicting on the group conditions of life calculated to bring about its physical destruction in whole or in part." The UN definition of genocide was incorporated into German criminal law relatively early, in 1954.[10]

Here was a concept, a definition, and a crime that matched the enormity of the Holocaust, which had in fact been developed in direct response to the attempted destruction of European Jewry. In practical terms, moreover, the use of genocide or crimes against humanity to prosecute Nazi crimes in post-war Germany might have allowed courts to avoid at least some of the contortions imposed on them by way of Section 211.

The country's legal establishment, however, never seriously considered it. In the view of German judges and legal scholars, the statute and the three offenses that formed the legal basis for the Nuremberg trials violated one of the most sacred principles of criminal law: the ban on retroactivity. This principle holds that an act can only be punished as a crime if it has been identified as such at the time the act was committed. It is a universal principle—so universal, in fact, that it is commonly expressed in Latin: *Nullum crimen, nulla poena sine lege.* "No crime, no punishment without law." Since genocide was a novel concept—and certainly not a crime recognized in the criminal code of Nazi Germany—German jurists argued that it should not be used to deal with crimes of that period. To this day, there has not been a single Nazi trial in Germany that included charges of genocide.

The question of retroactivity was of course familiar to the jurists who prepared and prosecuted the Nuremberg trials. But they argued that *nullum crimen* was not an absolute principle, and had to be balanced against other interests and demands— notably the demand for material justice. Rigorous adherence to the prohibition on retroactivity would, in the case of Nuremberg and subsequent Nazi trials, only serve to protect criminals who knew perfectly well that their deeds were indefensible and repugnant. There are some crimes, the prosecutors concluded, that are so heinous that they must be punished irrespective of whether or not they were expressly prohibited at the time. Or, as the Nuremberg indictment said: "These methods and crimes constituted violations of international conventions, of internal penal laws and of the general principles of criminal law as derived from the criminal law of all civilized nations."[11]

In practical terms, and despite the seeming weakness of the argument, the debate over retroactivity has long been settled. The trial of Bruno Dey, like all Holocaust trials before, was to be decided on the basis of Section 211 of the *Strafgesetzbuch*. He stood accused as an accessory to murder, not genocide, and the trial itself—notwithstanding the historical interest—was indeed conducted like any other criminal trial.

As a law student, I had studied the intricacies of German legal doctrine with the single aim of making it through the next examination. The murder criteria were entirely abstract concepts, as was the distinction between accessory and perpetrator, and all that arcane mid-twentieth-century jurisprudence by the German Federal Court of Justice. I never realized that it was those doctrinal disputes and academic theories—all of them held in the name of furthering justice—that helped keep thousands of Nazi criminals from being prosecuted.

CHAPTER NINE

"May I embrace you?"

At the end of the seventh day of the Stutthof trial, Bruno Dey received two things not often given in a court of law: forgiveness, and a hug.

Both came from Moshe Peter Loth, a 76-year-old American from Florida who was the second survivor called to testify in the Hamburg trial. Loth, too, had a remarkable story of suffering to tell. His Jewish mother had been sent to Stutthof in 1943, Loth said. She gave birth to him in another camp nearby, but the two of them were soon returned to Stutthof. His grandmother, too, was a prisoner at the camp, where she was murdered in the gas chamber. Though he had no personal recollection of his time at Stutthof, Loth said that he had carried the physical and mental scars from the camp all his life. Nor was his ordeal over when he and his mother were finally released. Separated from her in the chaos of the final war months, he ended up in a Polish orphanage, and suffered severe beatings as well as sexual violence at the hands of Russian soldiers. It was not until 1957 or 1958 (Loth was not sure of the year) that he was finally reunited with his mother, who had meanwhile settled in Germany and married a U.S. soldier stationed in the country. In 1959, the family moved to the U.S., but misfortune followed Loth also to his new home. It took him decades to understand where he had come from and what he had suffered, he told the court. Now he was ready to forgive.

During his testimony, Loth at times struggled for composure. At one point he broke into tears. Toward the end of the hearing, however, his voice was firm and his intention clear. Like the other survivors who testified in court, Loth was asked whether he wanted to address the defendant directly. Unlike most, he was very keen indeed to do so. After probing the defendant on a wide range of themes—including the type of rifle he used and his knowledge of villages and camps close to Stutthof—he asked Dey whether he had any regrets.

"Yes, of course," Dey responded. "I regret everything that happened at the time."

Loth asked the defendant to look at him, and then made a striking plea for forgiveness—from the accuser to the accused: "Would you forgive me for being angry and bitter and hateful to the German people?"

"Yes, of course I would forgive you," Dey replied. "I have no hatred."

Loth now turned to the judge. "Can I approach him?"

The request took Anne Meier-Göring by surprise. Such an approach was unusual, but she had no objections. The judge was in an awkward situation. Loth's drive to get close to the defendant—both physically and emotionally—seemed motivated by a genuine desire for reconciliation. But it also added an unusual melodramatic flourish to a trial that had until now been marked by respectful sobriety. Loth rose from his chair and walked across the courtroom to the table where Dey sat with his lawyer.

"I don't know you," Loth said. "May I embrace you?"

"You may, of course."

Loth now turned to the court: "Pay attention. I will embrace him, and I will forgive him."

He bent down to hug Dey, who simply muttered: "I did not do anything."

"It's all right," Loth said.

The courtroom watched in stunned silence. The quiet was eventually broken by the presiding judge. Meier-Göring called an end to the hearing, and thanked Loth. He responded simply: "Thank you for listening. I am free now."

The embrace made headlines around the world. "Holocaust Survivor HUGS Nazi Death Camp Guard," London's *Daily Mail* announced on its website, claiming that the two men had been brought to tears by the encounter. In the *Times of Israel*, the headline was, "Child Holocaust Survivor Hugs 93-year-old Nazi Guard During Trial in Germany." The Berlin-based daily *Die Welt* asked, "How Can a Holocaust Survivor Hug an SS Guard?" and sought answers from a theologian and psychiatrist about the "power of forgiveness." Loth's gesture, the expert explained, had been a "great human deed" that had brought the victim "inner peace."[1]

A sense of awe at Loth's readiness to forgive lingered also in Hamburg, where the next hearing was called just three days after his memorable appearance. Salvatore Barba, the Munich lawyer representing the American citizen in court, asked to speak, and offered a summary of Loth's testimony. Loth's life, the lawyer noted, had followed a "path of suffering that could not have been harder or crueler." For his client, however, the trial had "closed a causal chain." Both men, Barba added, had turned to "reconciliation and dialogue."

Meier-Göring, too, was keen to return to Loth's gesture of forgiveness, and its impact on the accused. How, she asked, had it felt to be embraced by the survivor? "It was a great relief," Dey answered. "It felt good. I felt sorry and will always feel sorry for what happened to the gentleman. I am happy that he managed to get such a good grip on his life."

Dey seemed keen to explain himself, but he was also—as so often—alive to the danger of self-incrimination. If he admitted to a sense of relief, did that not imply that there was indeed a crime that he should ask forgiveness for? A tone of hesitation crept into his response. Dey stressed once again that he had not been in Stutthof voluntarily, and that he had not witnessed himself any of Loth's ordeals. So what did he mean when he said he felt relief, the judge asked. "Relieved that I could apologize to at least one person. For all the suffering he had to go through... though I did not contribute to it."

The hearing soon moved on to other matters, but to most observers following the trial Loth's gesture was hard to forget. It seemed to transcend the trial itself, a moment of reconciliation that proved beyond doubt the importance and the value of Germany's late search for Holocaust justice. The embrace between the survivor and the camp guard offered moving evidence that these trials were not just about punishing the guilty, but also about helping to liberate the victims and their descendants from lifelong trauma. Loth himself had said so in the starkest possible way after the embrace: *I am free now.*

The uplifting tale of Moshe Peter Loth and his search for redemption broke apart just six weeks after his court appearance. The German news magazine *Der Spiegel* published an article under the damning headline "The Concentration Camp Victim Who Never Was." Based on meticulous research, the story deconstructed Loth's version of events piece by piece. Its conclusion came right in the opening paragraph: "A supposed former prisoner of Stutthof concentration camp attracted attention around the world when he hugged a man accused of being a former guard during his criminal trial and offered his forgiveness. The story seemed too good to be true—and it was."[2]

The *Spiegel* reporters found that Loth was born in a place called Tiegenhof, 20 kilometers from Stutthof. There was no concentration camp there, nor was there any evidence that he was ever held at Stutthof or any other camp. His mother Helene was indeed imprisoned in Stutthof, for a short period of time. But this was long before he was born, and contemporaneous documents showed she was held at the camp not because she was Jewish but for a period of *Erziehungshaft* (instructional imprisonment). According to the *Spiegel* article, this was a disciplinary measure ordered by the Gestapo, the Nazi secret state police, that was usually imposed for minor misconduct such as a perceived "unwillingness to work." According to official documents found by the reporters, Helene Loth was released on April 1, 1943, five months before she gave birth to her son. "There are no documents at all suggesting a second detainment. Indeed, it would seem that there was no second stint in Stutthof at all, and if there was, it must have been for entirely different reasons than those claimed by Loth: his mother couldn't have been kept there as a Jew, because she wasn't one," the article noted.

According to church and municipal registries, both Loth's mother and grandmother were in fact Protestant. Loth's grandmother, Anna, died on August 30, 1943, most likely in a place called Fürstenwerder, near Danzig. There was no evidence that she died in Stutthof, let alone in the gas chamber. That detail in particular made for painful reading: in 2001, Loth had created a page of testimony for Anna at the Yad Vashem Holocaust memorial in Israel. In his submission (which at the time of writing could still be found on the Yad Vashem website) he wrote that Anna was murdered in the gas chambers at Stutthof. Loth also registered his mother on the same database as a survivor.

The magazine stopped short of accusing him of an outright fabrication. "Loth, one has to assume, is apparently mistaken," the article concluded. In his own response to *Der Spiegel*, Loth declared through his lawyers that "not everything can be proved through documents." Many questions were still unanswered, he added, and it had been difficult to verify the information available to him. Loth, the lawyers stated, "had spent his whole life searching for his true identity."

For the court, and for the presiding judge personally, the revelations in *Der Spiegel* came as a blow. All trials rest on the validity of memory, and on the expectation that a witness will speak the truth. That is why perjury—lying under oath in a court of law—is treated as a grave criminal offense and is usually punished with a lengthy prison sentence. In a Holocaust trial, however, trust in the veracity of a witness statement, especially when that witness is a survivor, is of even greater importance. That is in part because of the enormity of the crime, but also because the passage of time makes it so hard to corroborate the observations and recollections shared with the court. Take the example of Bruno Dey's much-repeated claim that he allowed prisoners to cut off strips of horse flesh from a cadaver during a work mission outside the camp. There were no reports or documents to confirm that story, and neither were there surviving witnesses. The same was true of Marek Dunin-Wąsowicz's account of the SS man kicking over a pot of soup in front of starving prisoners during the death march in early 1945—and of countless other testimonies given over the course of the Hamburg trial. Dey's statements were of course subjected to critical scrutiny, and a good deal of judicial skepticism. As a defendant facing a murder charge, he had an obvious interest in presenting his case in a particular light. But the testimony of a Holocaust survivor is treated as almost sacrosanct, whether in court or elsewhere, and more so with every year that passes. Who would lie about such an experience? Who would dream of embellishing such a tale?

The threshold for questioning or doubting survivor testimony is high also because of two other reasons. One is the fear that voicing such doubts might be interpreted as doubting the historical fact of the Holocaust itself. The other is the simple fact that survivor stories are always improbable. For a Jewish prisoner in a Nazi concentration camp, being murdered was normal. Survival was exceptional—and therefore almost by definition the result of a whole series of exceptional circumstances and unlikely events. More than seventy years after the Holocaust, audiences understand this truth implicitly. Whether they are reading a book or listening to a witness statement in court, they are primed to expect the unexpected and believe the unbelievable—and they are right to do so. In the case of Moshe Peter Loth, that trust appeared to have been badly betrayed.

The first trial hearing of the new year took place on January 6, 2020, ten days after *Der Spiegel* published its deconstruction of Loth's life story. Anne Meier-Göring acknowledged the article but said she needed more time to work through a raft of additional documents submitted by Loth's lawyers. Her intervention did little to soothe the anger felt by some of the other lawyers representing Stutthof victims in Hamburg. Chief among them was Cornelius Nestler, the lawyer for Judith Meisel, a Stutthof survivor who had managed to run away from the gas chamber at the last moment but was forced to leave her mother behind, waiting in the line to be murdered. Nestler had been closely involved in a string of late Holocaust trials, including the Demjanjuk case back in 2011. He spent most of his time not in court but in academia, as a professor of criminal law at the University of Cologne. I had met him at an earlier trial and was impressed by his deep understanding of the historical and legal complexities of these cases, and his practical commitment to representing the victims in court.

Nestler spoke calmly but he was plainly furious. Loth's claims, he said, had "simply not been believable." Even after the first few minutes of his testimony it was clear that the court was "being presented with a wild story."

It was hard to disagree. Indeed, what made the revelations in *Der Spiegel* especially troubling was the fact that Loth's testimony sounded—at least in part—highly dubious even at the time. He told the court that both his grandmother and his mother had been sent to Stutthof because they were Jewish. But he also claimed that the person who had arranged their deportation, and the murder of his grandmother, was none other than his grandfather, who had been a "high-ranking Nazi officer." His son—Loth's uncle—was in turn a member of the SS who went on to visit the Stutthof camp on several occasions. If true, this would have made Loth the descendant both of victims and perpetrators of the Nazi genocide—an extraordinary biographical claim, not entirely implausible but, given the lack of documentary evidence, one that should have raised more questions in court than it did. Loth's account was in large parts incoherent and rambling, but every so often he would produce a splinter of graphic detail—usually involving memories of sexual and physical violence. Since he was too young to recall abuses committed by the SS in Stutthof concentration camp, those recollections invariably involved Russian soldiers after the war. In one of the Polish orphanages where he stayed after being separated from his mother, Russian soldiers "came at night and used the children for the benefit of raping," leaving one little girl "bleeding from the front and back." Loth claimed that he was forced to wear a Star of David as a child in post-war Poland, and forced to watch executions when he was just five or six years old. He gave a horrific, and strikingly detailed, description of a mass execution of children supposedly conducted by Russian soldiers one night near a railway station. When it was his turn to be shot, a Polish woman who had become a surrogate mother to him, stepped in, opened her dress and told the soldiers to "take" her instead. "They followed her and they raped her and raped her…I was saved." Later on, as a fifteen-year-old, still in Poland, he was supposedly accused of being a spy and punished harshly: "They knocked my teeth out and broke my hands with an AK-47 [Kalashnikov rifle]."

The violence and abuse—including mass sexual abuse—committed by Red Army soldiers during and after the Second World War is well documented, including some instances when Soviet soldiers raped Holocaust survivors after the liberation of the camps. Indeed, one should never underestimate the human capacity to inflict cruelty on the weakest, no matter when or where. But this apparent orgy of sadism and violence directed by Russian soldiers against children in a Polish orphanage several years after the war stretched credulity all the same. The Red Army may indeed have been omnipresent across eastern Europe during those years, but what were these soldiers doing in a provincial orphanage? The abundance of gore made Loth's testimony appear at times like the script of a schlocky horror movie.

Nestler, meanwhile, took issue with the most obvious flaw in the witness's account, namely his dramatic and convoluted family tale: "The mother was supposedly deported to Stutthof as a 'Half-Jew,' in the Nazi jargon. At the same time her brother served as a Half-Jew as an SS officer. That is in historical terms completely absurd."

Allowing this testimony to be presented alongside that of genuine survivors had been a terrible mistake. "This revelation [in *Der Spiegel*] throws a shadow over this criminal trial," Nestler said. "This publication presents the thesis that Herr Loth, with the help of his lawyers, used this criminal trial for a media-friendly moment of self-aggrandizement, even though he should not have been a co-plaintiff or witness." The damage Loth and his lawyers had done was not restricted to the current trial however, Nestler continued. At a time when Holocaust denial was sharply on the rise around the world, trials like the one in Hamburg were bound to draw suspicion from those who saw a "Holocaust industry" at work. The professor pointed out that accusations of copycat testimony had been leveled already during the Demjanjuk trial almost a decade ago. "We as co-plaintiffs know well that these late Holocaust trials face a particular legitimacy pressure," he warned. The court, Nestler argued, had no choice: it had to establish fully and clearly whether Loth's testimony was wholly or partially compromised.

I was as stunned by the revelations as everyone else. But perhaps I should not have been. There is something powerfully seductive about victimhood: it invites interest, sympathy, and pity. It shields against criticism and blame. And it can provide an explanation, and perhaps even an excuse, for the failures and disappointments we all experience in life. This dynamic applies to all manner of victimhood, from parental neglect and social exclusion to physical abuse. Holocaust victims, however, stand apart. Their torment was singular, their suffering beyond doubt. For those who crave the highest form of victimhood—or maybe just a little bit of attention—assuming the identity of a survivor can be a terrible temptation. As the journalist Helen Lewis observed in an article on identity hoaxers, "a scar on history as big as the Holocaust attracts troubled people who want to affix their own suffering to a grand narrative."[3]

There are thankfully not many documented cases in which self-proclaimed camp survivors have been shown to be fantasists, but they do exist. There is the story of Misha Defonseca, a Belgium-born Canadian author who claimed to have survived the Holocaust after fleeing into the forest as a seven-year-old and joining a pack of wolves. In Australia, a Second World War veteran named Donald Joseph Watt claimed to have been deported to Auschwitz where he was forced to join a *Sonderkommando*, a special prisoner unit, stoking the ovens in which murdered camp victims were cremated.[4] Like Defonseca, he published a book detailing his experience, in his case under the title *Stoker: The Story of an Australian Soldier Who Survived Auschwitz–Birkenau*. Both Defonseca and Watt were forced to recant their claims after they were shown to be false. Perhaps the best-known example is that of Binjamin Wilkomirski, the author of the celebrated Holocaust memoir *Fragments: Memories of a Wartime Childhood*. The book was first published in German in 1995, and soon translated into nine other languages. Wherever it was released, the reviews were rapturous: a critic in the *Guardian* newspaper hailed it as "one of the great works about the Holocaust,"[5] and the book went on to win the U.S. National Jewish Book Award and the Jewish Quarterly–Wingate Literary Prize in the UK. Wilkomirski told a harrowing tale: born in Latvia, he was separated from his parents aged three, sent first to the Majdanek concentration camp and then to a second camp (which is not named in the book itself but that Wilkomirski later identified as Auschwitz-Birkenau). He writes of seeing starving babies so hungry that they chewed their frozen fingers down to the bone, a young boy murdered by the SS for soiling his bunk at night, a bloodied rat emerging from the belly of a woman murdered in the camp. His descriptions of the life and the suffering in the camp were both vivid and detailed—perhaps too detailed: Wilkomirski's book is full of reconstructed dialogue, apparently preserved verbatim in his mind after more than four decades. (Loth, who also wrote a memoir, pulls off a similar feat. There are passages in which he includes long pieces of direct speech, decades after the events took place, and others where he is able to provide the exact hour of the day in which the conversation took place.)

Having survived the camps, and following a spell in an orphanage in the Polish city of Krakow, Wilkomirski is sent to an orphanage in Switzerland, where he is eventually adopted by a Swiss couple. His adoptive parents, the Dössekkers, force him to repress his memories, telling him he must forget all that happened before. But Wilkomirski cannot forget, and nor can he remain silent.

His book, written almost half a century later in simple, elegant prose, made him an overnight celebrity. Wilkomirski traveled the world to speak at universities and book festivals, in synagogues and theater halls. He even went on a fundraising tour for the U.S. Holocaust Memorial Museum in Washington. Then, three years after the publication of *Fragments*, an article written by a Swiss journalist (himself the son of an Auschwitz survivor) made a string of disturbing allegations: Binjamin Wilkomirski was indeed an adopted child, but he was neither Latvian nor Jewish, and nor was he a survivor of Majdanek and Auschwitz. In fact, his Swiss birth certificate showed he was born in 1941 as Bruno Grosjean, the illegitimate son of Yvonne Grosjean, in Biel, a town in the northwest of Switzerland famed for its watchmaking industry. Subsequent reports found a long list of inconsistencies, improbabilities, and inaccuracies in the story of Benjamin Wilkomirski/Bruno Grosjean.[6] Critics such as the historian Raul Hilberg, author of a landmark study of the Holocaust, argued that the story told in the book hovered between the "highly unlikely and the utterly impossible."[7] To give just a couple of examples: children as young as four or five had virtually no chance of surviving one camp, let alone two. With few exceptions, notably involving children selected for medical experiments, infants were usually gassed immediately upon arrival, along with their mothers. There was, moreover, no record of any Jewish children being transported from Majdanek to Auschwitz. *Fragments* was eventually withdrawn by its publisher, as were some, though not all, of the accolades awarded to the book.

Stefan Mächler, a Swiss historian, was hired by the literary agency that represented Wilkomirski to investigate the case in forensic depth. He concluded that there was "not the least doubt" that the celebrated author was in fact "identical with Bruno Grosjean," and that the "story he wrote in *Fragments* and has told elsewhere took place solely within the world of his thoughts and emotions."[8] Mächler argued that the inventions and fabulations were not so much the product of cynical calculation but of childhood trauma relating to his adoption, and "his need to find a story for something incomprehensible." His identity "arose… over the course of four decades, unplanned and improvised, with new experiences and necessities constantly woven into it, and contradictions arising from a lack of any plan smoothed over, though over time with less and less success."[9]

In the case of Moshe Peter Loth, the Hamburg witness, the process of acquiring the identity of a Holocaust survivor happened suddenly and rapidly—but it also came to him late in life. I was struck that both Loth and Wilkomirski—like so many of the other known cases of imaginary Holocaust survivors

—had decided to tell their story in books. Was this a sign that their decades-long struggle to make sense of their lives, to give coherence and shape to a messy and unhappy personal story, had reached a conclusion? Or was it, perhaps, the very act of writing the book that had encouraged them to streamline that narrative, to strike inconvenient facts from the text—and ultimately also the mind? Once they had told their story in written form, moreover, it became impossible to change the narrative. They could not admit to doubts or second thoughts or allow any contradictory evidence to stand. A book, once it has been written and read, becomes permanent and immutable—and so does the life story it claims to tell.

Much like Wilkomirski, Loth had spent much of his life desperately searching for his roots, and scarred by a feeling that dark events in his past had robbed him of the childhood he deserved. Both men had spent a lifetime searching for the ultimate source of their troubles, and in the end convinced themselves—and those around them—that it was the Holocaust where those troubles truly began. Suddenly, it all made sense.

In Loth's case, his personal tale of anguish centered on his abandonment by his mother, and the trauma of spending formative years without her care and protection. "My mother had abandoned me when I was a baby, which in my mind meant that she didn't want me," Loth wrote in his book. "It was a truth I learnt to deal with daily. I suppose one never fully gets over the feeling of abandonment. All the hurt and disappointment from that rejection lingered with me into adulthood as my constant companion. In moments when I least expected it, the hurt would creep in and the pain would overwhelm me."

The book, called *Peace by Piece: A Story of Healing and Forgiveness*, describes how Loth managed to reconnect with one of his sisters in his fifties, and learned from her not only that his mother had been imprisoned in Stutthof, but that he himself was born in the camp. Parts of that story—which as we know are in fact true—were then backed up by an official from the Red Cross. His mother had indeed been a prisoner in Stutthof. The conclusion that Loth drew from that piece of information, however, was wrong—and it set him on a path that ultimately led him to the Hamburg courtroom in the winter of 2019. As he wrote in his memoir: "The reality began to sink in. *I was a Holocaust survivor.*"

Thanks to the report in *Der Spiegel*, that claim had now been convincingly debunked. Loth himself must have realized soon after the January 6 court hearing that he could no longer maintain his role in court. He was damaging the trial and he was damaging himself. One week after Nestler's searing appeal for a full investigation, Loth's lawyer rose in court to announce that his client was formally withdrawing from the trial. The announcement was welcomed by Meier-Göring. Inquiries made by the court after the *Spiegel* article, she said, had shown beyond doubt that Loth's testimony was at least in parts incorrect. One particular claim that stood out for her was the assertion made by Loth in documents submitted to the court that both he and his mother had been tattooed with their prisoner number—a practice that is today widely associated with the Nazi concentration camps but that was in fact used only in Auschwitz. That piece of information alone should have disqualified the witness. But Meier-Göring admitted that she had also been made to feel uncomfortable by the "confused and contradictory" statements given by Loth in court, and concluded right after the fateful hearing that she would not be able to base any of her decisions or conclusions on his testimony. The trial, she added, should now return to the fundamental questions before the court. Loth's testimony had in any case been of only "subordinate significance."

Once again it fell to Cornelius Nestler, the law professor, to offer a counterpoint. He thanked Loth's lawyers for withdrawing their client from the case, but offered harsh criticism of his colleagues all the same. It was "frightening" that legal professionals with experience of dealing with Holocaust cases had failed to spot evident falsehoods, notably the claim of a prisoner tattoo. Nestler's broader concerns, however, concerned the damage done to the credibility of survivor testimonies in general: "Survivors of the Shoah who apply to become co-plaintiffs often have the problem that they have no documents that prove their story and their eligibility. That means courts in many cases simply have to trust their story. And that trust in the fact that co-plaintiffs who claim to be victims of the Shoah don't lie, that trust has been called into question in this case."

The Loth affair indeed cast a shadow over the trial, though perhaps not as starkly as many feared at the time of the revelations. His wild and confused testimony, and the theatrical embrace that briefly made headlines around the world, receded further into the background with every new account given to the court by Stutthof survivors—the real victims of the Holocaust. What lingered, at least in my mind, was a broader question—about memory, and about the reliability of memories that reach back so far in time. The Stutthof trial depended to a large extent on the ability of very old men and women to recall events that took place more than seven decades ago. Dey himself was urged again and again to remember conversations and observations from 1944 that many of us would struggle to remember if they took place a week ago. Who did he speak to and when? What did his comrades and parents tell him? How many people did he see entering the gas chamber? These were deeply consequential moments in his life, which one might expect to have left an indelible impression. But the stories of Loth and Wilkomirski

151

suggest that such memories—or indeed the absence of such memories—can perhaps never be trusted entirely. For the survivors, of course, the occasional gap or imprecision in their recollections was of little consequence. They had been called to testify about their experience and their general memories of life and death in Stutthof, not to provide a detailed description of any particular day or moment or event. The case of Dey himself was different. He was indeed called upon to remember with precision where he was, what he saw, what he thought and did at that time. His struggle with memory was quite different from the one that led Moshe Peter Loth into the realm of fantasy and imagination. But it was no less real—and it would force the court to confront the complex issue of how memory works all over again in the months to come.

CHAPTER TEN

Auschwitz on trial

On the morning of December 20, 1963, presiding judge Hans Hofmeyer opened one of the most consequential criminal trials in the history of post-war Germany. In official documents, the case is referred to by its file number, 4 Ks/263. A handwritten sign outside the courtroom announced it simply as the "trial against Mulka and others."[1] Today the case is known as the Frankfurt Auschwitz trial—the first serious attempt by a German court to punish the crimes committed at the most notorious and deadly of all the Nazi concentration camps. The trial lasted until August 1965, and ended in guilty verdicts for seventeen of the twenty defendants. It marked a turning point for post-war attitudes toward the Holocaust, forcing millions of Germans to confront and acknowledge the savagery of the nation's crimes. To a younger generation, born or raised after the war, many of the revelations about Auschwitz and the camp system were both new and shocking. For older Germans, meanwhile, at least some of the charges presented in the Frankfurt courtroom were only too familiar. But hearing the evidence laid out by German prosecutors against German defendants to German judges in a German court of law came as a clarifying moment all the same. For the estimated twenty thousand members of the public who attended one of the trial's 183 hearings, and for anyone listening to the radio or reading the newspaper during those years, denial was no longer really an option.[2]

The case ought to have been a triumph for German justice, a legal reckoning with the Holocaust that was already long overdue. The legacy of the Frankfurt trial, however, proved to be deeply ambivalent. As would soon become clear, the judgment delivered by Hofmeyer on August 19, 1965, contained flaws that would haunt and hobble the campaign to bring Nazi perpetrators to justice for decades to come. The guilty verdicts in Frankfurt were instrumental in placing Auschwitz at the center of Germany's moral and political consciousness. But they also created a legal precedent that made it increasingly hard, and then almost impossible, to prosecute and sentence other potential defendants implicated in the Holocaust. Conceived as an opening shot, the Frankfurt Auschwitz trial turned out to be more of a closing bell.

The origins of the Frankfurt Auschwitz trial are complex. Like so much else in the story of Germany's early Holocaust prosecutions, coincidence and serendipity played an important role. The first strand in a series of investigations that ultimately led to the trial can be traced back to a letter of denunciation that landed in the post box of the Stuttgart public prosecutors' office in March 1958. It was sent from jail, by a convicted fraudster named Adolf Rögner, who during the war had served as a Kapo at Auschwitz. The letter informed the authorities that a certain Wilhelm Boger, a resident of Stuttgart, had served as a senior SS officer at Auschwitz, where he had been notorious for his brutality.[3] Among other claims he was alleged to have been the inventor of the "Boger swing," a torture device that allowed the SS to hang prisoners from an iron bar in a manner that left their backside and their genitals exposed for beatings.

The letter prompted an investigation by the Stuttgart

prosecutors but also attracted keen interest from the Vienna-based International Auschwitz Committee, an organization of camp survivors that would play a key role in supporting future Auschwitz prosecutions and finding witnesses for the Frankfurt trial. Boger was eventually arrested in October 1958. Later that year, the case was taken up by the newly founded Zentrale Stelle in Ludwigsburg, which decided to expand the probe beyond Boger and investigate the crimes committed at Auschwitz more broadly. Then, in January 1959, prosecutors in Frankfurt obtained documents with the names of victims shot by the SS in Auschwitz and, crucially, the names of the alleged killers. This prompted a separate investigation, both by the Frankfurt prosecutors and by the Zentrale Stelle. After years of judicial neglect, the crimes committed at Auschwitz had sparked formal probes from three different prosecution services in the space of months. But they were moving in different directions, and at a different pace. Someone, clearly, had to be in charge—and that someone turned out to be Fritz Bauer.

Bauer, the chief prosecutor of the federal state of Hesse and the mastermind of the Frankfurt Auschwitz trials, was a towering figure of post-war Germany. Persecuted by the Nazis both as a Jew and a Social Democrat, he made the remarkable decision to return from exile after the war to serve the new democratic Germany as a jurist and civil servant, just as he had before the Nazis rose to power. Bauer stood out from his colleagues in the legal establishment, many of whom had loyally served the Nazi state. Not only had he fiercely resisted the rise of fascism in Germany, he also knew from experience what it meant to be inside a Nazi concentration camp. A prominent leader of the Social Democratic party in Stuttgart in the early 1930s, Bauer was arrested within weeks of Hitler's ascent to power and sent to nearby Heuberg, one of the first concentration camps on

German soil. He spent eight months at Heuberg, which was
run by Nazi police officers and where political prisoners were
subjected to beatings and daily humiliations (though not, yet, to
systematic murder). Later in life, Bauer would rarely talk about
his time at the camp, except to recount how he was forced to
clean out the latrines on a regular basis.[4] Ronen Steinke, his
biographer, argues this was in part due to personal stoicism ("It
was not appropriate to complain of one's own suffering"), but
also out of a sense of shame.[5] When Bauer was finally released
in November 1933, he agreed to sign an open letter published
in a local newspaper that included a declaration of loyalty to
the Nazi regime—"a humiliation that Bauer endures to prevent
worse from happening."[6]

Bauer's desire to downplay his own suffering—and his
Jewishness—after the war also reflected his concerns about
the broader mood in Germany. The lives and careers of prominent Jews in German public life after the war continued to be
blighted by antisemitism and distrust. Bauer himself—a man
who had spent bitter years in exile dreaming of a new democratic Germany—would see his patriotism and loyalty questioned
repeatedly over the course of his career. He in turn had reason
to mistrust his colleagues, especially those who served in senior
police functions or as top civil servants in Bonn, the German
capital at the time. It was that mistrust that led him to share an
extraordinary piece of intelligence—the whereabouts of Adolf
Eichmann, one of the architects of the final solution—not with
the German authorities but with the Mossad, Israel's intelligence
service. Bauer had first received a tip-off suggesting Eichmann
was living in Argentina in 1957. But he feared that involving the
German authorities—whose ranks still included countless former
Nazi bureaucrats—would prompt leaks and allow Eichmann to
flee. Bauer turned to the Mossad instead, deliberately leaving

crucial files open on his desk for an Israeli agent to photograph.[7] In May 1960, Eichmann was captured by Mossad agents, flown to Israel, and put on trial. He was hanged on June 1, 1962.

Bauer had allowed Eichmann to be claimed by Israel, but he was determined to try the crimes of Auschwitz in Germany. His own role in the case, however, was to remain in the background—partly out of concern over public prejudice. Bauer had worked hard to establish Frankfurt as the principal authority in Germany responsible for prosecuting the crimes committed at Auschwitz. The last thing he wanted now was for this landmark trial to be framed as a personal vendetta by a prominent left-wing Jewish opponent of the Hitler regime. Bauer stayed away from the courtroom throughout the trial, instead sending three

Josef Klehr, who murdered thousands of Auschwitz prisoners through lethal injections, on trial in Frankfurt.

157

young prosecutors (all of whom had served in the Wehrmacht) to do the pleading in court. Eighteen years after the end of the war, Germany may have been ready for an Auschwitz trial. In Bauer's view, however, it was not ready for a Jew to be leading the prosecution.

What made the Frankfurt trial so remarkable was not that it sought to punish individual perpetrators at Auschwitz. Such trials had indeed already taken place in Germany after 1945. Bauer's ambition went much further. From the outset, his plan was to prosecute the crimes committed at Auschwitz *systematically*. He wanted to secure individual convictions, but he also wanted to expose the workings of the camp—and the complicity of its vast personnel—in detail to an audience of millions. Bauer's ultimate goal was educational: "If our trial…is to have a purpose, then this trial must serve as a warning and as a lesson to all of us," he told a press conference after the opening.[8]

In the years leading up to the trial, he and his colleagues had amassed a wealth of material and evidence along with a list of 599 suspects. From that list Bauer picked twenty-four men who were formally charged.[9] The selection reflected in part their seniority and the gravity of the alleged crimes. But Bauer also wanted to present a general typology of the perpetrators. He wanted a group of defendants who were representative of the camp system and would allow his prosecutors to show to the court, and the German public at large, how Auschwitz had worked. The first name on that list was Robert Mulka, the adjutant to the commandant of Auschwitz, Rudolf Höss.[10] This made him the camp's second-in-command, and by far the most senior SS officer to stand trial in Frankfurt. Beyond Mulka, the list was striking for the variety of roles and backgrounds of the defendants: it included Victor Capesius, the man in charge of the pharmacy in Auschwitz, and Willy Frank, an SS dentist who, as part of the camp's medical staff, had taken part in the selection of prisoners on arrival. They shared the dock with thugs like Boger and Oswald Kaduk, a trained butcher who served as a *Rapportführer* in Auschwitz. In charge of supervising the daily roll-call, Kaduk was known for acts of staggering brutality, such as trampling a prisoner to death by stomping on his ribcage.[11] Another defendant was the Brazilian-born Pery Broad, who started his career at Auschwitz as a guard but then moved to the so-called Political Department, which was run by the Gestapo secret police and dealt with the registration and interrogation of prisoners. At the lowest rung of the camp hierarchy were men like Stefan Baretzki, a *Blockführer* in charge of supervising a single barracks, and Emil Bednarek, a political prisoner at Auschwitz who was appointed a Kapo. Despite their lowly status, both men were charged as accessories to murder in Frankfurt. They, too, had been necessary to keep Auschwitz and its gas chambers going.

They, too, Bauer decided, should feel the full force of the law.

Hans Hofmeyer, the presiding judge, was in some ways a peculiar choice to steer this sprawling and sensitive trial. Indeed, according to the Frankfurt court's official schedule, the case should have been heard before a different judge, Hans Forester. But the judicial authorities feared that Forester, who was Jewish and had lost his brother in the Holocaust, would be exposed to accusations of bias, and handed the case to Hofmeyer instead.[12] The new judge might have been accused of bias himself, of course, albeit from a different direction. Born in 1905, Hofmeyer had served as a district court judge and a military judge under the Nazis, but—like most of his colleagues—was able to continue his career in the judiciary after the war. In the years leading up to the Auschwitz trial, Hofmeyer had dealt mainly with civil law cases. His past as a judge in the Third Reich was noted by critics, especially from East Germany's Communist regime, but most observers agreed that he presided over the trial fairly and competently.[13] Not a man of sweeping rhetoric, he did at times give voice to his own feelings of horror and sorrow (and made no secret of his contempt for the lies and tricks used by some of the defendants and their lawyers).[14]

The gargantuan nature of the trial was evident from the outset. No court in Frankfurt was big enough to accommodate the proceedings (and the large number of spectators and journalists expected), forcing Hofmeyer to use the plenary hall of the Frankfurt city parliament as a makeshift courtroom. The cast was immense: Hofmeyer aside, there were three other judges and six lay judges, along with two replacement judges and three replacement lay judges. Also present were the three prosecutors sent by Bauer, along with a more senior colleague, three co-plaintiffs, twenty-two defendants and seventeen lawyers for the defense. More than 200 journalists were accredited to cover the trial, including twelve camera teams that crowded into the hall to film the opening day.[15] Every seat in the public gallery was taken, and the queues to enter the courtroom stretched all the way outside the building.[16]

The men at the center of the trial—Mulka and the twenty-one other defendants—showed little sign of remorse. Some of their protestations were stunning in their brazenness. Mulka himself, the second-in-command at Auschwitz, claimed that he had had no idea of the mass killings at the camp. "Personally, I never heard anything about executions in the camp, never reported anything, never ordered anything. I never heard shots," he told the court.[17] Asked about the gas chambers, he responded: "I heard about them, but I never saw them myself."[18] That facade of ignorance was soon shattered, however. Over the course of many months, the court assembled the most detailed and accurate picture yet of the inner workings of Auschwitz. Historians from the Munich Institute for Contemporary History had prepared a whole series of briefings, not just on the functioning of Auschwitz itself but on the history and structure of the SS, on Nazi policy toward the Jews and the nineteenth-century origins of Hitler's antisemitism, on the occupation of Poland, and on the concentration camp system in general. The Munich historians had also been asked to examine the nature of obedience inside the SS—and whether there had been scope for camp personnel to defy orders from their superiors. The answer they gave was the same that emerged in the Dey trial half a century later: whoever wanted to leave Auschwitz could find a way to leave Auschwitz, not least by volunteering to join the troops fighting on the front line.[19]

Experts and historians aside, the court heard the accounts of more than 350 other witnesses, of whom by far the largest group were Auschwitz survivors. It was their testimonies above all that resonated beyond the courtroom. For many Germans, watching the proceedings in person or following the trial through the media, these were some of the first personal accounts of Holocaust victims they had heard—and most were hard to forget. Among the 211 survivors who gave testimony at the trial was Ján Weis, a 47-year-old man from Bratislava who had spent close to three years in Auschwitz. One of his tasks at the camp was to carry away the bodies of prisoners murdered by Josef Klehr, a trained nurse and now a defendant in Frankfurt, who had killed thousands by injecting lethal phenol directly into their hearts with a syringe. Weis was usually made to attend the injection in person—including on one occasion when the victim was his own father. "The defendant Klehr murdered him before my own eyes. That was September 29, 1942," he told the court. "The doors suddenly opened, and my father walked in with another man. The defendant Klehr spoke to both of them, to my father and to the other prisoner who was brought with him. 'Sit down. You will get an injection now, so you don't get typhus.' I started to cry. He was not moved. He gave my father the injection, and I carried him, my father, away."[20]

Weis's account added to a tapestry of horror that was woven in front of the court, one witness testimony at a time. It moved the German public, but it did not move the men sitting in the dock. From the first day of the trial until the last, there was not a word of remorse from Mulka and his co-defendants. Bauer himself noted this in a television interview before the end of the trial: "I must tell you: since December 1963 the prosecutors have been waiting for one of the defendants, meaning one of those directly involved, to find a personal word toward the witnesses, the ones who survived but whose entire families were killed... The whole world would breathe a sigh of relief, not just the prosecutors in Frankfurt. I think all of Germany and the whole world and the relatives of those who died in Auschwitz would breathe a sigh of relief if at last there was one personal word. It has not come and it probably won't come."[21]

Bauer proved to be right. When Hofmeyer called on the defendants to say their final words before the verdict, he met a barrage of evasion and indignation. Capesius, the SS pharmacist who took part in the selection of arriving prisoners at the ramp, told the court that he had not harmed a single human being at Auschwitz: "I was polite, friendly and helpful to everyone, wherever I could be."[22] Klehr, too, pleaded his innocence, describing himself as "a small man [who] was not the master over life and death of these unfortunate people."[23] Bednarek, the prisoner-turned-Kapo, insisted he, too, had done nothing wrong: "I didn't kill anyone, and I didn't beat anyone to death. And if I punished or beat someone, it was because I had to do it to prevent the superiors from taking the gravest measures against the other prisoners. I could not help it. I feel innocent before God and before the people."[24] Mulka, the most senior of the SS men on trial in Frankfurt, spoke only briefly. "With this declaration I place my fate and that of my poor family confidently into the hands of the court, and I do so with the deep conviction that it will take into consideration all the truly fateful circumstances that put me into my unfortunate conflict situation at the time."[25] He expected the court to give a "just decision." Only one of the defendants, Hans Stark, acknowledged a shade of self-doubt when he spoke. "I took part in the killing of many people, which is what I admitted to from the start and without reservation. I asked myself many times after the war whether this made me a criminal. For myself, I have not found a valid answer." Stark, who was nineteen when he took up the role of *Blockführer* at Auschwitz in 1940, concluded his speech by voicing "regret" for what he called his "erroneous path in the past."[26] It was the closest any of the defendants would get to acknowledging their guilt.

In their final pleas, the lawyers for the defense used a broad array of arguments to call for the acquittal of all twenty remaining defendants. Some called into question the veracity of incriminating survivor testimonies, often based on small and unrelated moments of confusion made during their—frequently traumatic—periods in the witness stand. Others dismissed the legitimacy of the Frankfurt case itself, denouncing it as a political or show trial. Beyond such sweeping accusations, a popular line of defense was that the SS men charged in Frankfurt—including Mulka—had had no choice other than to follow their orders. Hans Laternser, a veteran trial lawyer who had previously acted for the defense at the Nuremberg war crimes tribunal, offered a particularly striking version of that argument. In Frankfurt, he had taken on the defense of Capesius, and other SS men, whose tasks included selecting which prisoners would be sent straight to the gas chambers on arrival. Hitler, the lawyer declared in his closing speech, had ordered the killing of all Jews living under German control, which meant their fate was sealed long before the trains reached the gates of Auschwitz. The SS men responsible for the selection at the ramp could therefore not be accused of murdering those they sent to be gassed immediately. They had not killed those who were sent to be gassed but had in fact saved those who were spared the gas chambers. As Devin Pendas rightly notes in his book on the Auschwitz trial, Laternser's "terrifying sophistry" ignored the crucial fact that, for most prisoners who survived the selection, death had not been averted but merely postponed.[27] Living on hunger rations in filthy, overcrowded barracks, exposed to the everyday cruelty of the guards, and forced into hard physical labor for up to twelve hours a day, most prisoners at Auschwitz would meet their death sooner rather than later, and often in the very gas chambers they had escaped on arrival. The selection was no act of salvation—it was an integral part of the Auschwitz killing machine.

Hofmeyer delivered his verdict over the course of two days in mid-August 1965. It had been, he said, a trial whose "terrible content had given it the character of the extraordinary." Auschwitz would forever be linked to the "inferno" that had been revealed over the course of the past twenty months. But Hofmeyer was also at pains to stress that the trial had remained, at least in his eyes, an ordinary criminal trial, and that his verdict was guided by the same laws and principles that guided an ordinary criminal judgment. "It is the task of every criminal trial to test the validity of the charges raised by the prosecution, and to examine only those facts that have to be understood to decide those charges.

The court does not have the right to pursue other goals," he said. "Even if this trial drew attention far beyond the borders of this country and has been named the 'Auschwitz trial,' it remained for this court a criminal trial against Mulka and others. What mattered for the decision of this court was only the guilt of the defendants."[28]

The court handed down guilty verdicts for seventeen of the remaining twenty defendants. Three were acquitted. Mulka, the adjutant of the camp commander, was sentenced to fourteen years in prison; Capesius, the pharmacist, to nine years; Broad to four years. They and eight other defendants were deemed to be mere accessories to murder. Much harsher sentences were imposed on the lower-ranked but more brutish of the defendants, who were mostly convicted as murderers. Kaduk and Boger received life sentences, as did Klehr, the man who injected lethal phenol into the hearts of thousands (although the court found him guilty of only 256 such killings). In that sense, and despite Bauer's grand ambitions, the Frankfurt trial followed the long-established lines of argument developed by the German judiciary since the end of the war: perpetrators who acted with brutality and killed with excess cruelty met the full force of the law; those who were one or two steps removed from the direct killing found leniency, despite their seniority and their power of command over the thugs. The case of Boger—the suspect whose arrest in 1958 had started the Auschwitz proceedings in the first place—exemplified that contrast: the court found that he had participated in at least one selection at the arrival ramp, which led to the gassing of at least a thousand deported Jews. Since Boger had apparently not acted with particular eagerness or brutality or ruthlessness during the selection, the court found him guilty for his role in the selection only as an accessory to murder, not as a murderer himself. His sentence for this particular crime was just four years in prison. But the court also found him guilty of torturing to death five Auschwitz prisoners in person. For these killings he was found to be a murderer, and given a lifelong prison sentence. Four years in prison for a thousand deaths, a life in prison for five deaths: there was a certain judicial logic to this outcome but it seemed puzzling nonetheless. As Pendas writes, "the disproportion between the number of victims and the severity of the sentences in the two instances is striking and clearly indicates that the weight attached by the court to torture as an indicator of subjective motivation far exceeded that which it gave to genocide."[29]

In Boger's case, at least, the ultimate outcome was undoubtedly correct. He spent the rest of his life in jail, dying behind bars in 1977. The court's reasoning with regard to Mulka, meanwhile, was arguably even more problematic. Despite his seniority and his role as adjutant to the commandant of Auschwitz, despite the fact that he once ordered a prisoner beaten to death in front of his eyes, despite the fact that he personally signed orders for more Zyklon B to be delivered to Auschwitz—despite all these facts—he was sentenced only as an accessory to murder. Hofmeyer had evidently struggled with this particular decision, devoting four whole pages of the judgment to the question of whether Mulka should be treated as an accessory or a perpetrator. The verdict carefully weighed his role and responsibilities, his background and his likely motivation. It was possible, the judge argued, that Mulka had indeed acted with the "will of the perpetrator," echoing the then-dominant legal theory that made the distinction between accessory and perpetrator dependent on the subjective motivation of the defendant. But it was also possible, Hofmeyer continued, that he fulfilled his role in Auschwitz above all out of obedience and a "misguided sense of duty."[30] The specific nature of Mulka's crime was that it took place within a "gigantic organization built for the killing of millions of people."[31] He had been "ordered into this apparatus" and served as "a cog in the killing machine," the verdict argued.[32] In the end, Hofmeyer gave the benefit of the doubt to the defendant. Mulka spent the next three years in prison but was released due to ill health in 1968 and died one year later.

There was at least one other serious problem with Mulka's sentence. The presiding judge had been keen—almost certainly too keen—to draw an impeccably clear connection between specific acts committed by the defendant and a specific killing. Hofmeyer managed this by highlighting a radio message from October 2, 1943, faithfully reproduced in the final verdict, in which Mulka ordered a truck to drive to Dessau and pick up "materials for the resettlement of Jews."[33] That material, the verdict noted, was known by SS personnel to be Zyklon B, the poison gas used in the gas chambers. Another piece of evidence that was given extraordinary prominence was Mulka's effort to secure four airtight doors for the construction of additional gas chambers at Auschwitz. These orders were deemed a specific contribution to the killing of at least 3,000 victims in the chambers (four train arrivals with 750 victims each), satisfying the court's need for a concrete deed. As a piece of detective work, the reference to the radio message was undoubtedly impressive. From a legal perspective, however, it was disastrous. By attaching so much importance to a concrete but minuscule piece of evidence, Hofmeyer had set an impossibly high standard for future courts and future cases. What if there had been no such radio message? What if there had been no evidence trail linking Mulka to the gas-chamber doors? Would that have meant that the Auschwitz second-in-command should have left the Frankfurt court a free man?

The fundamental flaw in Hofmeyer's verdict was that he

decided to break the great crime of Auschwitz—where the Nazis murdered more than a million innocent people—into tiny shards and splinters. The presiding judge went to extraordinary lengths to isolate from the mass of victims a series of individual cases: a prisoner beaten to death by Boger, a few hundred prisoners injected with phenol by Klehr, four transports of victims gassed to death with the help (but not at the orders!) of Mulka. The harshest penalties were reserved—as so often in post-war German courts—for the lower-ranking and lesser-educated brutes, in part because it was often easier to connect them to individual acts of murder and cruelty. The doctors and pharmacists, the jurists and bureaucrats, whose responsibility was greater but also more diffuse, met with comparative leniency.

Hofmeyer's approach helped secure important convictions, which were ultimately also upheld by the Federal Court of Justice. But his verdict missed a crucial truth about Auschwitz and the Nazi genocide. The Holocaust was not primarily the work of brutes and sadists intent on battering individual victims to death. It was the industrial killing of millions by a criminal state, employing all the resources of state power and all the industrial and technological facilities at its disposal. The individual motivation and the subjective state of mind of the defendants, to which the court dedicated immense attention, were largely irrelevant to the crime. Hofmeyer's insistence that the trial had to follow the exact same principles as an ordinary criminal trial was wrong, because the crime itself was anything but ordinary. The court in effect treated every killing and every group of new arrivals who were sent to be gassed as a separate and largely unrelated crime. Bauer himself lamented in an essay some years after the verdict that the Frankfurt court had "atomized" the mass killings at Auschwitz.[34] Cornelius Nestler, the Cologne professor of criminal law who appeared in Hamburg as a lawyer for a Stutthof survivor, described the approach as both "grotesque" and "absurd."[35] The German historian Werner Renz, meanwhile, argued that the Frankfurt court's "erroneous description of the historical events led to an incorrect legal assessment."[36] To illustrate his point, he cited a period in the summer of 1944 when three trains carrying three thousand deportees each arrived in Auschwitz every day over many weeks. To be present at the ramp meant "participation in constant mass murder" that followed a specific division of labor.[37] To disassemble this process, as the Frankfurt court had done, was "incomprehensible."[38]

The damage, in any case, was done—especially after the Federal Court of Justice upheld the verdict in February 1969. The Auschwitz ruling left German prosecutors with guidance —or at least with the impression—that they had to prove a suspect's participation in a concrete and specific crime, and that the mere presence in a concentration camp, irrespective of the role and responsibility, would not be enough to secure a conviction. Whether this requirement could indeed be read clearly from Hofmeyer's 700-page verdict remains a matter of dispute. Yet lodged within the Auschwitz ruling was at least one other formidable disincentive for prosecutors: the decision to impose relatively lenient prison sentences on Mulka and other key defendants. This proved problematic above all for any attempt to launch proceedings against SS personnel further down the hierarchy. If even the high-profile criminals in the dock in Frankfurt got away with a few years in prison, what point was there in prosecuting guards and other lowly SS personnel, whose contributions to the Nazi genocide were much less significant? Capesius, the man who sent thousands to their death during his ramp duty, was sentenced to nine years. Even the crimes of Mulka, the second-in-command at Auschwitz, were deemed to be worthy of just fourteen years in prison. Other high-profile defendants got away with five years or less. With those convictions in mind, the mere thought of prosecuting men like Bruno Dey seemed absurd.

One striking example of this was the failure to see through the prosecution of SS truck drivers at Auschwitz whose task it was to transport weak and elderly arrivals straight to the gas chamber. This was, even by the restrictive standards of German jurisprudence, a clear and causal contribution to the passengers' eventual murder. Yet the case against them was abandoned in 1970, after state prosecutors ruled that their guilt was in any case likely to be minor. The decision referred explicitly to the Frankfurt Auschwitz trial, noting that some senior SS officers who had taken part in the selection of arrivals had received prison terms of only five years or less. "The guilt of the members of the *Fahrbereitschaft* [drivers' pool] should be measured by comparison with these sentences. On this basis their guilt appears to be minor."[39]

As Nestler writes in his analysis of German jurisprudence at the time, "in this way, a practice was established that effectively put an end to the persecution of Nazi crimes."[40] It would take almost three decades for that to change—by which time all but a handful of perpetrators were already dead.

The legacy of the Frankfurt Auschwitz trial has been a matter of fierce debate among historians and jurists for decades. It succeeded in placing the Holocaust, and Auschwitz in particular, at the center of the nation's collective consciousness. It helped silence those who sought to deny or belittle the crimes of Nazi Germany. As Gerhard Werle and Thomas Wandres conclude in their study of the Auschwitz trial, "the outstanding achievement of this trial was the incontrovertible establishment of what happened."[41] The trial also stripped away many of the excuses—legal and moral—that had shielded the perpetrators in the decades after the war: as the Frankfurt verdict made clear, SS men had indeed been able to remove themselves from Auschwitz. Hitler and Himmler were not the only men guilty of genocidal crimes. German courts were in fact able to pronounce men like Klehr and Mulka guilty, despite the immense complexities of the case.

Yet in other ways the message that emanated from the trial was problematic. Much of the public and media attention was focused not on Germans' broader responsibility for the Holocaust or on the culpability of the SS and Nazi hierarchy, but on the bestiality of men like Kaduk and Boger, and their bloody record of killings and torture. As Pendas notes in his book, press articles at the time were filled with references to "monsters," "demons," "beasts" and "devils."[42] That focus was unfortunately amplified by the sentence itself, which, as we saw, placed far greater emphasis on individual acts of cruelty than the systematic nature of the Nazi genocide. In that sense, at least, the Frankfurt trial provided a convenient psychological outlet for the majority of Germans. They were left to believe that "the Holocaust was caused by the deviant motives of a few sadistic individuals, and that torture, not genocide, was the most important characteristic of Auschwitz."[43]

Bauer, the architect of the Auschwitz trial, died of heart failure barely three years after the Frankfurt verdict. He had argued vehemently against the doctrine established by Hofmeyer's court until the end, insisting that anyone serving in a Nazi concentration camp was criminally responsible for all the killings that took place from the day they arrived until the day they left.[44] That view had been rejected by the Frankfurt court, and ultimately also by the Federal Court of Justice, in a ruling Bauer did not live to see himself. But the power of his argument lived on, and ultimately triumphed in the remarkable series of verdicts that

171

started with John Demjanjuk in 2011. The groundwork for these late Holocaust trials was laid by Bauer, in part through his legal arguments but also because he bequeathed to German judges and prosecutors a moral clarity and sense of purpose undimmed by the passage of years. That legacy shone through in the trial of Bruno Dey, just as it did in the other late Holocaust cases: "When you are ordered to do something that is unjust, when it breaks an iron norm like the norms laid down in the Ten Commandments, which everyone must know, then you must say no," Bauer once told an interviewer. "That is the fundamental message that has to emerge from these trials: you should have said no."[45]

CHAPTER ELEVEN

The dancer and the bookkeeper

A few weeks before the opening of the Stutthof trial, on a bright and sunny autumn day, I walked down a street in central Budapest, carefully scanning the imposing belle-époque buildings for a particular address. I was in the Hungarian capital for a short family holiday, but also because I wanted to meet an extraordinary woman and hear her story.

Éva Pusztai-Fahidi was a 94-year-old survivor of Auschwitz, the author of several books, and a passionate dancer who had recently starred—despite her advanced age—in an award-winning autobiographical dance film. She was also, by a strange twist of fate, the mother-in-law of Thomas Walther, the German judge who helped bring John Demjanjuk to justice back in 2011. Walther had met Pusztai-Fahidi's daughter after agreeing to represent the elderly survivor in a case against a former Auschwitz camp guard. In a story that was otherwise marked by relentless sadness and loss, their encounter offered a rare chapter with a happy ending.

Pusztai-Fahidi lived in a light-filled apartment between Budapest's main shopping street and the Danube. She led me past a corridor lined with shelves full of cacti to her spotless kitchen, where we sat down at a small table. I unpacked my notebook and recorder, while she made tea for her visitor. As soon as she started speaking, I was transfixed, both by her story and by her voice. Her German was precise, and marked by the peculiar intonation of old central Europe, an accent that was once widely heard but that has now all but vanished. It reminded me of the way my great-grandmother—who grew up in Silesia, in present-day Poland—spoke.

I was interested to hear about Pusztai-Fahidi's early life in Debrecen, the provincial capital of Hungary's north-eastern plains with a Jewish community numbering ten thousand before the Nazi invasion. I wanted to know about her time in Auschwitz, where most of her family perished. But I had also come to ask her about an event that happened many decades after the end of the war. Walther had told me that his mother-in-law had served as a co-plaintiff and witness in another landmark late Holocaust trial—the case against Oskar Gröning, the so-called "Bookkeeper of Auschwitz." Gröning was brought to trial aged ninety-three before a court in the north German city of Lüneburg in 2015, and convicted of being an accessory to murder in at least 300,000 cases. He was sentenced to four years in prison, a verdict that was ultimately upheld by the Federal Court of Justice—the first and only judgment so far in the history of the late Holocaust trials that was confirmed by the highest criminal court in the land. Gröning died in 2018, before he could start his sentence, but his case acted as a further spur to prosecutors up and down the country to pursue the last surviving perpetrators.

Pusztai-Fahidi's family was Jewish but secular. She told me she had no recollection of celebrating Jewish holidays or keeping kosher; only her grandmother used to light a Sabbath candle on Friday evenings, and say a prayer. But even as a teenage girl she was aware of antisemitism—a sense that she wouldn't be welcome in or invited to certain houses, and that some children wouldn't come to her home either. The situation of Hungary's Jews grew steadily worse over the course of the 1920s and 1930s, starting with a law that limited their access to higher education, and deteriorated sharply with the outbreak of the Second World War, which ushered in a succession of increasingly repressive

"It is terrible to have such fear, every second of the day."
Éva Pusztai-Fahidi, the Auschwitz survivor who gave
testimony in the 2015 trial against Oskar Gröning.

regimes in Budapest allied with Nazi Germany. The country's Jewish community was marginalized and expropriated, shut out from most professions, and subject to constant harassment. But it remained shielded from the Nazis' genocidal plans until March 1944, when Hitler ordered the invasion of Hungary. In an attempt to protect himself and his family, Pusztai-Fahidi's father had formally converted to the Roman Catholic Church in 1936. "He thought he could save us like that," she told me. "But he was not so smart to realize that he should have taken us away rather than converted. He did not have that horizon." In the end, his professed Christian faith did nothing to save him, or most of his family.

Pusztai-Fahidi herself had no idea what was coming. A passionate dancer and accomplished pianist, her dream was to become a professional musician. "I was kept in an ivory tower. I reproached [my parents] so many times. If only they had told me what was happening, I could have steeled myself. Had I known what was coming I would have been prepared," she said. "But no. Until the last minute I sat at my piano."

The Wehrmacht rolled into Debrecen on March 19, 1944, a Sunday. Pusztai-Fahidi's childhood home, a two-story villa with a large garden, was requisitioned for a German officer and his *Putzer*, or manservant. Her family was allowed to stay in the house, but both parents and their two daughters were confined to a single room. "Every day he [the officer] would come into our single room and boast how cultured he was. But he didn't know Heinrich Heine. And we never spoke about Thomas Mann," Pusztai-Fahidi recalled, seemingly still perplexed at the man's lack of education a lifetime later. For a few precious weeks longer, she was allowed to continue her piano practice. The reprieve, however, was brief. In late April 1944 the German occupiers ordered all of Debrecen's Jews to move into a ghetto in the western part of the town. Every Jew was allocated no more than four square meters of living space; Pusztai-Fahidi and nine members of her extended family shared a single room. On June 26, 1944, she was put on a train to Auschwitz.

Oskar Gröning had at that point been in Auschwitz for close to two years, serving as an *SS-Unterscharführer*, a junior squad leader. Born in a small town near Hanover in 1921, he had been an eager recruit to the Nazi movement, joining the Hitler Youth early on and signing up for membership of the party as soon as he turned eighteen. One year later, he joined the SS, keen to be a part of what was regarded by many Germans at the time as an elite formation, more glamorous and selective than the ordinary armed forces. "The SS was a caste, and we wanted to be part of it," Gröning told the court in Lüneburg.[1]

He was sent to Auschwitz in September 1942 to serve in the foreign currency department, which in turn was part of the administrative section responsible for processing the vast amounts of cash and valuables that were taken from Jews de-ported to the camp. Most of his work was done sitting at a desk, but at times he had to join the SS officers and guards at the ramp when a new train of deportees arrived. If Gröning harbored any illusions about the shocking reality of Auschwitz until then, they were dispelled on the very first occasion he stood at the ramp. Among the new arrivals, it turned out, was a Jewish mother who had tried and failed to hide her baby in a suitcase. "She had calculated that she could avoid the selection like this. An *SS-Rottenführer* [squad leader] took the baby, bashed it against a truck, and the screaming stopped. My heart skipped a beat. I went to the man and told him: You can't do that."[2]

But, of course, he could. Murdering innocent people, includ-ing babies, was no moral outrage at Auschwitz—it was what the camp had been built for. And, as it turned out, Gröning's objections had to do more with the blunt method of murder employed by his fellow SS man, and less with the murder itself. Even seventy years after the event, speaking on the opening day of his trial, the distinction still seemed to matter to him. "It would have been different had he taken his pistol and shot it," Gröning said.[3]

It would not be the last shocking and perplexing thing the defendant said in court.[4] But there was another side to Gröning. The defendant was no irredentist old Nazi; nor was he trying to push aside all responsibility for his actions in the past. Unlike most of the old men who stood trial in this last wave of Holocaust prosecutions, Gröning had clearly started wrestling with his conscience as he grew older. Indeed, one of the reasons why he was in the dock in the first place was because he had been willing to speak out both in the German and the international media, and talk about his time in Auschwitz. He spent nine hours talking to the BBC for a documentary in 2005, and the same year he gave a long interview to *Der Spiegel* that caused waves in his home country. "Talking helps," he told the journalist.[5] What animated Gröning at this point in his life was—at least in part—his anger at the rising tide of Holocaust denial. A fellow stamp collector had some years earlier given him a copy of *The Auschwitz Lie*, a book by Thies Christophersen, a neo-Nazi activist and former SS member. Gröning returned the book with a letter telling his friend that he himself had witnessed the murders in the gas chamber. The exchange prompted a first attempt to set down in writing his recollections of the camp, followed by more detailed versions that he had bound and sent to friends and relatives. Asked by the *Spiegel* interviewer in 2005 whether he felt any guilt, Gröning gave a response that foreshadowed a line of defense also used by Bruno Dey in Hamburg. "Guilt really has to do with actions, and because I believe that I was not an active perpetrator, I don't believe that I am guilty."[6] He had been only "a small cog in the gears." Legally speaking, Gröning insisted, "I am innocent."

Given the pervasive lack of interest in lower-ranking SS officers and guards from German prosecutors and judges at the time, it was easy to see how he came to that conclusion. But times changed—and nine years later the Bookkeeper of Auschwitz found himself facing trial after all. His tone, too, had shifted slightly. Concluding his opening testimony on the first day of the trial, Gröning stated that in moral terms he was unquestionably guilty. Addressing the judge directly, he added: "Whether I am also guilty in a criminal sense, you have to decide."[7]

Pusztai-Fahidi and her family arrived in Auschwitz on July 1, 1944, after a journey that would haunt her for the rest of her life. Around eighty men, women, and children had been crammed into a barren cattle carriage, with no windows, no space to sit or lie down, and equipped with just two buckets: one for drinking water, which ran out almost instantly, and one to be used as a toilet. The stench and the heat, she recalled, were "terrible." I asked Pusztai-Fahidi whether she and the other passengers had been aware—even dimly—of the fate that awaited them at the end of their journey. "No, no. We thought we were going somewhere where we had to work," she told me.

When their train finally reached its destination, it seemed to her as if she had "landed on the moon." The first thing she noticed were the prisoners in their "ridiculous" striped clothes that looked like pajamas. "They immediately started talking to us," Pusztai-Fahidi recalled. "They asked us, 'How old are you?' I was already eighteen at the time, but there were also younger children there. They were told [by other prisoners] to lie about their age and say they were sixteen. Because if you said you were fourteen you were automatically sent to the left side, the bad side."

Only she and one of her aunts ended up on the right side. (The aunt survived Auschwitz but took her own life soon after the end of the war. "She could not live with her memories," Pusztai-Fahidi told me.) The rest of her extended family—including her mother, father, and younger sister, and her cousin, who was traveling with a baby—were sent to the left, and from there to the gas chambers. "Suddenly I was alone. There was no one from my family," she recalled. It took some time for the truth to sink in. Still confused about where her parents and sister had gone, she eventually asked the Kapo, the prisoner functionary, in her barrack about their fate. The Kapo, herself a young woman, pointed to the smoke rising above the camp. "'There they are.' And then she laughed. We asked her why she was being so cruel to us. And she said: 'I truly hate you very much because I have been here since 1942. And from 1942 until now you were living at home, and you had parents, and you went to school. And I was already here.'"

Pusztai-Fahidi survived Auschwitz because she was young, and strong enough to be selected for factory work not long after her arrival at the camp. She ended up being sent to a vast munitions plant in Allendorf, near Frankfurt, where she was put to work along with thousands of other slave laborers. The work was hard, the factory was "terrible"—but compared to the death camp Allendorf seemed like a "paradise," she told the court in Lüneburg. Still, Pusztai-Fahidi was in Auschwitz long enough to experience the daily fear, and the constant punishments and humiliations inflicted on the prisoners—as well as the pervasive threat of death. In her court testimony, she recalled the physical transformation inflicted on her and a group of schoolgirls from Debrecen shortly after her arrival and the initial selection: "We had our heads shaved and were stark naked," she said. "We were spoilt girls, and there we stood." She also remembered the stench of burnt flesh that hung in the air day and night, and the terrible screams emanating from the so-called "gypsy camp" in early August, when thousands of Roma and Sinti were taken away to be gassed over the course of two days. And she remembered the SS guards and officers, the men who kept the Auschwitz death machine running day and night, without mercy—and without the slightest fear of retribution.

For the vast majority of them, retribution would indeed never come. Out of six thousand SS men who served in Auschwitz and survived the war, only a fraction were sentenced for their crimes.[8] Oskar Gröning, however, lived long enough to be caught up in the slipstream of the Demjanjuk decision. His blunt interview with *Der Spiegel* in 2005—in which he essentially confessed his direct participation in the Holocaust—drew immediate interest from the officials at the Central Office in Ludwigsburg (at a time when very few cases did draw the office's interest). They sent a note to the state prosecution service in Frankfurt, which had traditionally taken charge of most Auschwitz crimes, but after a cursory examination the chief prosecutor there concluded there was no case to answer. It took another nine years—and, crucially, the judgment in the Demjanjuk trial—for that view to change. It also helped that the Frankfurt prosecutors handed the Gröning case to a more energetic colleague in the defendant's hometown of Lüneburg. Jens Lehmann, the chief prosecutor for the district, moved with speed and pragmatism: one key decision he took early on was to restrict the charges against Gröning to the 300,000 Hungarian Jews who were gassed in Auschwitz as part of a distinct and time-limited *Aktion*. This meant ignoring the countless victims who were murdered in the camp between 1942 and the summer of 1944 (when the defendant was already posted to Auschwitz). But it also meant a speedier trial, a better chance of securing a conviction before Gröning's health deteriorated further, and a way to address any lingering judicial concerns about the previously entrenched legal doctrine demanding that Holocaust perpetrators had to be tied to a "concrete" principal deed. The Demjanjuk case had broken with that doctrine only very recently, and it had yet to be confirmed by the country's top court.

The Gröning trial opened on April 21, 2015, to huge public interest both in Germany and abroad. More than half a century after the landmark Auschwitz trial in Frankfurt, a German court would once more—and perhaps for the final time—examine the crimes committed at the most notorious concentration camp of them all. The case was remarkable for many reasons, but not least because in Gröning it had a defendant who had spent long years reflecting on his own role and responsibility, and who was able and willing to articulate his thoughts—however shocking and misguided they seemed at times—with clarity and urgency. He also offered a frank and vivid description of what life at Auschwitz was like for an SS man like himself—and the outsized role that alcohol played in that life. "They gave us vodka and tinned sardines. Vodka, vodka, vodka was the essential drink. I still remember today how the seal [on the bottle] was opened."[9] The alcohol may have helped dull the senses, but so did the simple fact that after some weeks and months most SS men simply became used to the horrors. Gröning had spoken about this process in his *Spiegel* interview ten years earlier. "I settled in over time. Or perhaps, to put it better, I became part of internal emigration," he told the magazine.[10] His use of the term "internal emigration" was, of course, farcical: it had begun to be used after the war to describe the situation of critics of the Nazi regime, including artists and writers, who remained in the country after 1933 and engaged neither in overt support nor opposition to Hitler. Though accurate in some ways, it was also a convenient defense for Germans who didn't dare to resist, and were too comfortable to go into exile. For an SS man in Auschwitz to describe his position as such was, in any case, absurd. What Gröning said next was revealing, however, in its portrayal of life on the other side of the concentration camp fence: "Part of living in Auschwitz was perfectly normal. There was a vegetable shop where you could buy soup bones. It was like a small city. I had my unit, and gas chambers were irrelevant to that unit. There was one side of life in Auschwitz, and there was another, and the two were more or less separate."[11]

"I can only ask for forgiveness from God." Oskar Gröning, the so-called Bookkeeper of Auschwitz

To be clear, this was no plea of ignorance. Gröning told the court that he had learned about the camp's murderous purpose immediately upon arrival, when he was told by his SS bunk-neighbors that Jews who were no longer able to work were being "disposed of" at Auschwitz. At the time, he saw no need to question that purpose: "We had been drilled to follow orders, no matter what happened next. We were told, 'You have to do this because otherwise the German people are doomed,'" he told the court. His superiors, in any case, seemed to regard him as a model officer. On his personnel file they noted: "He performed all duties that were entrusted to him with diligence and care. Gröning's character is without flaw. His soldierly manner is firm and correct at all times. In ideological terms he is steadfast."[12]

The defendant said that he requested a transfer from Auschwitz on three separate occasions, the first coming immediately after he witnessed the brutal murder of the baby by a fellow SS man at the ramp. On that occasion, however, he was talked out of his request by a superior officer. Gröning supposedly made another attempt to be sent away toward the end of 1942, this time after he observed a gassing of Auschwitz prisoners at close quarters. His third and final transfer request—and the only one that is recorded in his personnel file—came in October 1944. This time it was granted.

Sitting in court a lifetime later, Gröning was confronted with the consequences of his actions, and inaction, in the starkest manner. Day after day, he would watch and listen as Auschwitz survivors and their descendants gave testimony, spoke about their suffering and—at times—turned to him with rage and incomprehension. One such moment came on the eighth day of the trial, when Kathleen Zahavi, an 86-year-old survivor from Toronto, Canada, told the court about her experience at Auschwitz. Toward the end of her testimony, she addressed the defendant directly: "Herr Gröning, you have said you are morally culpable. That is not enough. You volunteered for this. You knew what was happening in Auschwitz," she told him. "I hope the images follow you for the rest of your life. You were allowed to grow old in freedom. My parents were not. They were not at my wedding. My children never met their grandparents. Even if I survived, I was never as free as you were." Zahavi was now shaking with rage, but she carried on: "I want to show you the Nazis did not get rid of all of us. I came all the way from Canada for this trial. It is the last thing I can do."[13]

The defendant did not look at Zahavi once during her speech.

Yet as the trial went on, there were signs that Gröning had indeed absorbed some of the painful truths revealed by the witnesses. On the thirteenth day of the hearings, he broke his silence with a personal statement that was read out by his lawyer. It included some of his well-worn defenses, along with the assertion—deemed highly unlikely by experts consulted during the trial—that he had only been present at the arrival and selection of a prisoner transport on three occasions. But he also offered perhaps the most nuanced examination of his own guilt of all the defendants who were brought to justice over the previous decade. "Even if I was not immediately involved in these murders, my role contributed to the functioning of the camp at Auschwitz. That is something I am conscious of today," he told the court.[14] His efforts to suppress this realization at the time were "inexplicable" to him now. It was at this point that the defendant used a phrase so perceptive that it was picked up years later by Meier-Göring in her interrogation of Bruno Dey in Hamburg. Perhaps, Gröning said, he had simply succumbed to the *Bequemlichkeit des Gehorsams*: the "comfort of obedience."[15]

His words described with painful accuracy the attitude of millions of Germans during the Nazi period, but there was a ring of universal truth to them. Of course there is comfort in following orders and directions, in not having to think for yourself, in passing responsibility up the ranks. That is true today, even for

185

those of us lucky enough to live in liberal democracies governed by the rule of law. And it was undoubtedly true for Germans living in Nazi Germany—and those who served in Auschwitz, Treblinka, and Bergen-Belsen. I didn't take Gröning's reference to the comfort of obedience as an attempt to excuse his deeds (in legal terms it was wholly irrelevant). It was valuable all the same. His remark offered one of the most succinct explanations for German behavior under the Nazis I had heard to that date. That it came from a former SS man at Auschwitz was remarkable.

There was at least one other remark made by Gröning that was destined to live on, and ultimately find its way into the Stutthof verdict five years later: Auschwitz, Gröning declared toward the end of his trial, "was a place where you should not have taken part."[16] It was a realization that came too late—far too late—but that resonated all the same. It summed up with childlike simplicity the moral and legal demand made on men like Bruno Dey and Oskar Gröning, then and now, and which both of them ultimately failed to follow.

His statement in Lüneburg ended with an explanation why he had not and would not ask for forgiveness in court. He felt guilty for his role in the Holocaust, he said. "I stand before the survivors and the relatives of the victims with humility and regret. Yet I have deliberately not asked for forgiveness. In light of the scale of the crimes committed in Auschwitz and elsewhere such a plea is not for me to make. I can only ask for forgiveness from God."

Pusztai-Fahidi appeared in court on the fourth day of the trial, as one of the first survivors to testify. She told the court about her life in Debrecen, the shock of the German invasion, the brutality of the Hungarian police who helped the Nazis round up the Jewish population, the horrors of the train journey to Auschwitz, and the existential judgment delivered by anonymous

SS men during the *Selektion*. "It was just a tiny gesture, to say go to the right or go to the left. At the time one had no idea what it meant. A trauma for the rest of your life."[17] Pusztai-Fahidi recounted the same story she would tell me years later in her apartment in Budapest—how her desperate question about the fate of her family was finally answered when the *Kapo* pointed toward the smoke coming from the crematorium, and how she was transferred to munitions work in central Germany. Her ability to craft beautiful and profound phrases to describe the most unspeakable of crimes impressed me greatly during our meeting. I later realized that it had been the same in Lüneburg, where she provided one of the most eloquent of all the survivor testimonies. Asked by the judge whether she and her family had taken any belongings on the journey to Auschwitz, she responded: "Everything that you once owned in life you can get back. There is only one thing you can never get back and that is your life. We learned to live without a toothbrush, without anything and without anyone."[18] Toward the end of her testimony, Pusztai-Fahidi spoke about the present—and why her appearance at the trial was so important to her: "I must say that it gives me a kind of satisfaction to be able to speak in front of a German court," she said. "What was a crime then is still a crime today, and for all eternity. For me, this is not about punishment, it is about judgment and about society taking a position."[19]

She told me years later in Budapest that her appearance as a witness and co-plaintiff had in fact been, "the most important thing I did in my life." Given her remarkable biography, this was a surprising statement. I asked her to explain. I had to remember, Pusztai-Fahidi said, that the SS men in Auschwitz were untouchable and all-powerful. "They were gods in the world," she explained. "One of them actually said this, I later read. He said: 'Above me is only God.' And it really was like that. You cannot imagine the power these people had. They could do whatever they wanted. There were no limits." That memory of utter helplessness was perhaps the most important reason why survivors like her cherished the opportunity to see men like Gröning in the dock —and to do their own part to secure a conviction. "I knew that he had behaved and felt like God. I had to be so afraid of people like him. And it is terrible to have such fear, every second of the day. That I could now speak against him in a court of law—that was simply miraculous," Pusztai-Fahidi told me.

For many survivors, the simple act of telling their own story and that of their murdered relatives was hugely significant, despite—or perhaps because of—the passage of time. I was struck, both in Hamburg and when I read testimonies from other trials, how often these witnesses spoke of the sense of duty they felt toward the dead. Thomas Walther, who acted as Pusztai-Fahidi's lawyer in the Gröning trial, wrote after the verdict that appearing in court had allowed the survivors to build "a bridge to the victims."[20]

It was always tempting to use terms like catharsis and closure when describing the impact of these late Holocaust cases on the survivors and their families. But Walther's more modest claim—that speaking in court had allowed them to connect and reconnect in a new way with their loved ones—was probably more accurate. And it was, as Pusztai-Fahidi had made clear, immensely important all the same. There was no closure after Auschwitz. There was no way a guilty verdict in a German court seventy years later could be cast as a happy ending. But justice mattered all the same.

Had it not come too late, I asked Pusztai-Fahidi toward the end of my visit.

She shook her head. "It's not too late," she said. "It is never too late."

CHAPTER TWELVE

"Where is my guilt?"

At times it was the silences that spoke most loudly.

They lasted only a few seconds, but to Dey's listeners in the courtroom, who were hanging on every one of his words, they could feel like minutes. They were brief moments of capitulation, tacit acknowledgment that the defendant had nothing left to say in his defense. Silence meant that Dey's ability to explain and evade had reached a limit. That not even a whispered I-don't-remember would do. Such was the weight of the question, or the weight of the evidence, hanging in the air.

One of the most poignant silences came on the fourth day of the trial. Dey seemed more exhausted than usual. He struggled to follow the meandering flow of Meier-Göring's questions during the first half of the hearing, which drifted from the color of his uniform and the layout of the camp to his duties as a guard and—once again—his relationships with the other SS men at Stutthof. His responses came more slowly and in more stilted fashion than in previous days, occasionally drifting into outright incoherence. After an hour of fruitless probing, Meier-Göring ordered a break. Lawyers and journalists mingled in the hall outside the courtroom, wondering what would come next. Dey had been wheeled away to a separate room for a moment of rest. For him, the worst was yet to come.

Back in the courtroom, Meier-Göring asked Dey to turn his

memory back to the occasions when he did his guard duty on one particular watchtower—the one that stood closest to the gas chamber and crematorium.

"When you stood on that watchtower, you knew that over there were the crematorium and the gas chamber. Is that right?"

"Yes, I think that was said. I cannot say that so clearly."

"But that is what interests me," Meier-Göring replied. "When did you hear for the first time that there was a gas chamber there?"

"I don't know when that was, the first time. At the start one assumed..." Dey searched for the right words, or maybe the right memories. The building, he said, had initially been used for purposes of disinfection. He had not known, at least not at the beginning, that it was a gas chamber. Meier-Göring repeated her question: when had he learned that it ultimately served a different use? Dey hesitated, again. He could not remember. Maybe, Dey suggested, he had picked up talk from the other guards. He now spoke in fragments, leaving sentences unfinished and words drifting in the air. Amid the haziness and the hesitation, however, I sensed a bit of steel. Dey was aware that he was in dangerous territory, and his flight into vagueness seemed like a deliberate strategy. Meier-Göring, however, persevered.

"But you knew [about the gas chamber], at least that is what I understood, before you stood up there on the tower?"

"Not in the beginning, what happened there."

"But later?"

"Later one did hear, and then one knew," Dey responded. Tellingly, he had started using the impersonal pronoun when referring to his former self, as if talking about another man. "When one stood there, or when one had to stand up there on the tower, one thought, 'Hopefully nothing will happen today.' Those were the kind of thoughts one had."

Hopefully nothing will happen today. Meier-Göring had, gently and patiently, steered Dey and his memory back up on that watchtower. She was determined to keep him there a little while longer, and gave him a small nod of encouragement: "Of course."

Dey carried on. He was still struggling to finish his sentences but the meaning of what he said—and what he saw—was clear all the same. "One could do nothing to stop it, if…what I said previously, that people were brought into…that I saw that people were brought into the gas chamber…One could do nothing to stop it. And I also didn't know why they were brought in there."

Some people in the courtroom—those who were familiar with the protocols of earlier interrogations—knew that lurking behind his halting response, and behind that amorphous "it," was a specific incident, something Dey had witnessed, that he remembered well, and that he had spoken about already. In fact, the incident had been on file since 1982, when Dey had been questioned as a witness by police investigating a separate case. What he had told them was, even by the generous standards of the German judiciary at the time, almost certainly enough to land him in court. He was lucky that police and prosecutors at the time had shown no interest. Meier-Göring, however, was very interested indeed.

"Tell us about this. You already spoke about this when you were questioned in 1982. What did you see there?"

"That people were taken in there."

"Into the gas chamber?"

"Into the gas chamber, and that the door was closed. That is what I said. And that a little later, I don't know how long, one heard screams and rumbling. I didn't know why. Or what was done to the people there. I didn't know."

"What did you think?"

"What did I think? I thought, 'What could that be? What are they doing with those people in there?' That is what I thought. But I had no concept of what they could be doing."

His response was feeble, and indeed directly contradicted what he had told the court a few minutes earlier. Meier-Göring was quick to remind him: "But Herr Dey, you just told us that there had been talk earlier about what was happening inside the gas chamber."

"Yes but what was happening in that moment, as I said, that I didn't know. When there were screams…What was happening to them in there today? I didn't know that they were being gassed."

Meier-Göring, sounding slightly annoyed, pushed back. "But Herr Dey, you can't tell us things like that. This is not what you said in 1982. In 1982 you said clearly that you saw people being led into the gas chamber."

"Yes, but I didn't see how they were taken out."

"But you heard screams. And you said during your questioning in 1982 that you heard screaming, not for ten minutes, but for some minutes, and then there was silence. And then there was silence. And then there was silence, Herr Dey."

Meier-Göring repeated the phrase three times, to a defendant struck mute and a courtroom holding its collective breath. This incident, the moment when Dey looked down from his watchtower and saw a group of human beings herded into the gas chamber, suddenly felt of almost unbearable significance. We would never know the identity of the people who were being led to their death, nor the precise time and date of their murder, and not even their exact number. But Dey's observation, hazy as it was more than seven decades later, suddenly made the unimaginable crime of the Holocaust imaginable. It had become concrete, specific, and graspable. What Dey saw was a fragment

192

of a fragment—one comparatively small set of killings in one comparatively small concentration camp—but it was indisputably part of the Holocaust nonetheless. Over a period of years, that very same terrible scene could have been observed hundreds of times a day, in concentration camps in Germany, Austria, and much of occupied eastern Europe—in Treblinka, in Auschwitz, in Sobibor, in Majdanek, in Belzec, in Mauthausen, in Chelmno, in Sachsenhausen. But who was left today, two generations later, who had seen those scenes? And who was left to put on trial?

Dey was. And every word he had to say, every desperate splinter of recollection, seemed precious and relevant—to the judge, to the prosecution, to the survivors represented in court, and, in a small way, to me too.

Dey, however, still offered resistance. And then there was silence, Meier-Göring had declared three times. "Yes but why?" the defendant responded.

"Why was there silence?" the judge asked back. "You know the answer. We all know the answer."

"Today, yes. But at the time, when I was standing there, I didn't know the answer yet. I don't believe that I knew it."

"What is the answer you would give today?"

"Today I know. That is…well…"

Silence. Meier-Göring waited, but then gave the answer herself. "The people fell silent because they had been gassed, because they had died, because they were killed, because they were murdered. And, Herr Dey, that is surely what was rumored among your comrades."

"Yes but not at that precise moment we are talking about," Dey responded. He now shifted into the conditional, still resisting the judge's assertion that he knew what the scene in front of him signified. "It didn't necessarily happen this way. It could have been different. But what it was I cannot say. I already said

I didn't know what happened. I was thinking, 'What could that be?'"

"What were your thoughts about this?"

"As I just said: what is happening there? But I did not have any images in my head."

"To be honest, that is not at all what I mean, what pictures you had in your head."

Dey, once again, sought refuge in uncertainty. "I could not have said with 100 percent certainty that they were being gassed. I could not say that because I didn't see it."

"But you had heard it before?"

Dey, perhaps confused by the judge's reference to hearing, asked back, "Does one hear gas escape?"

His question sounded crass as well as evasive, and Meier-Göring seemed duly annoyed. "You heard from other people that people were being gassed there. That is what you heard."

"Yes."

"And now you are seeing with your own eyes that people are being led in there, and you are hearing screams and you are hearing rumbling."

"Yes."

"Yes."

Dey sighed deeply. He said nothing. Meier-Göring had, it seemed, finally worn down his defenses. Into the silence, she brought Dey back to a small but revealing remark he had made earlier. "You told us earlier that when one stood on this watch-tower, one thought, 'Hopefully nothing will happen today.' What did you mean by that? Hopefully nothing will happen today."

"Yes, I thought, hopefully...no gas will be brought in or..."

"Hopefully people won't be led into the gas chamber again. That is what you meant."

"Yes."

*

Time to exhale.

Whatever else was going to happen in the trial, that final "Yes" had brought Dey a step closer to a conviction. Meier-Göring's patient, insistent questioning delivered the reward she—along with the prosecution and the multitude of lawyers representing Stutthof victims—had been looking for. Dey had just admitted that he saw people being led into the gas chamber. He has also admitted, crucially, that he knew the fate they were being led to. His objective contribution to their killing, the guarding of the camp, the manning of the watchtower, was never in doubt. But he had now also confirmed the subjective element, his criminal intent: he knew what was going on. He had not willed or desired the death of the prisoners in the gas chamber. But he knew that death was waiting for them. Through the fog of obfuscation and amnesia, a moment of clarity at last.

Meier-Göring was keen to press on but she paused to acknowledge Dey's readiness to remember and reveal, hard won though it was. It had, she said, been "insanely hard for all of us and painful to talk about this." But it could not be helped. "It doesn't help you either [not to talk about it]," she told Dey.

"I want to continue saying what I know," he responded.

"Exactly."

"And not gloss over things."

"Exactly."

"Or remain silent about things. Because it wasn't me who did it."

"Exactly."

"And I wasn't in favor of the things that were done there, or in agreement, with the fact that people were being imprisoned who had done nothing wrong."

Dey's statement was, in a narrow sense, correct: it was not he who was leading the prisoners into the gas chamber, it was not he who sealed the door and fed the deadly gas into the chamber. Nor did he actively desire those killings, let alone cheer them on from his watchtower. That this should be known mattered to him, as it would matter to anyone. In legal terms, however, these protestations were largely irrelevant. He was not on trial for committing murder, but for aiding murder. All that mattered was that he had provided objective assistance to the killings—which he did in the form of his guard duty—and that he knew both about the murders and about his contribution to them.

More was still to come, on a day that saw the defendant face his most painful—and most incriminating—memories yet. Dey went on to recall a second time he saw prisoners being led into the gas chamber, only that this time he also observed a man doing something on the roof of the chamber. What that man did exactly Dey was no longer able to recall, but even without further details the implication was clear: the defendant very likely witnessed an SS man dropping the deadly gas pellets into the chamber. Then another memory spilled out, of a time Dey saw prisoners being led one by one into the building that housed the crematorium. Here again, the relevance was immediately obvious to those familiar with the charges. Lars Mahnke, the lead prosecutor, had made clear in his opening plea that he was seeking a conviction in relation to three distinct cases of murder: first, the gassing of prisoners; second, the shooting of prisoners in the back of the neck; and, third, the mass deaths through illness and starvation at the height of the typhus epidemic that swept the camp in late 1944, during which the SS denied any kind of treatment to the prisoners. Of those three categories, it was the second that Dey had likely observed when he saw prisoners being led to the crematorium building. "It was said that they had to go to a medical examination because they would somehow be sent to a work assignment outside the camp. So they had to have a medical before that to see whether they were healthy," Dey explained. "That's what I heard and that's what I assumed. That was what was said to the people before they were led in. And they went of their own free accord with the doctor or medic or whoever that was. In any case, someone in a white coat."

This indeed sounded ominously similar to the description of the perfidious SS method of shooting unsuspecting prisoners that was provided by Mahnke at the start of the trial: prisoners would be asked to attend a medical examination in a separate room of the red-brick crematorium building. There they would be received by SS men wearing white coats and carrying clipboards, who after asking a few opening questions would demand a height measurement. The prisoner would be made to stand next to a measuring stick attached to a wall. A simple mechanism would then open a slit to the neighboring room, where another SS man stood waiting with a pistol at the ready. As soon as the slit opened he would fire a shot into the back of the prisoner's neck, killing his victim. Once the body was removed and the blood washed from the floor, the next prisoner would be asked to step in.

"How many did you see going in?" Meier-Göring asked.

"I don't know. Maybe ten or fifteen or twenty. I don't know."

"Were those men or women?"

"I think they were men. They were wearing suits."

"And did they come out again?"

"No."

Realizing the implication of what he just said, Dey quickly offered an alternative explanation. Perhaps there was a second entrance to the room that he was unaware of, and through which the prisoners had left—alive—after their examination?

197

Meier-Göring pushed back, but the defendant's concentration had now started to seriously wane. After a protracted but fruitless back-and-forth over the gassing of prisoners in train wagons at Stutthof, which Dey appeared to have no personal recollection of, the defendant's patience snapped. "I don't want to say anything more," he told the judge. Meier-Göring relented, calling an end to the hearing.

It had, she remarked, been an exhausting day.

There would be many more such days in the weeks and months that followed. Another that stayed in my memory was Friday, November 15, 2019, the eighth day of the hearings. It was the first time that Bruno Dey was confronted not just with what he saw and heard at Stutthof, but with his own personal responsibility for the crimes committed at the camp. For the defendant, perhaps understandably, this was not an easy idea to grasp. Throughout his trial, Dey argued with vehemence and conviction that the murders at Stutthof had nothing to do with him, that they had taken place without any contribution from him personally. *Ich habe ja nichts getan.* I didn't do anything. *Ich wollte das nicht.* I didn't want that. Dey would repeat these phrases over and over again, as if intoning a spell to ward off evil.

That Friday, Meier-Göring decided to challenge this spell at last. As so often, she did so not by confronting the defendant and his world view head-on. Instead, she sought to guide him to a different viewpoint, one careful question at a time.

"This is a point I would like to speak to you about," she opened. "You say again and again that you didn't do anything. But at the same time, we know, and you have admitted that, you were there."

"Yes."

"So when you say, 'I didn't do anything'..."

"I stood guard."

"What do you mean when you say you didn't do anything?"

"I didn't make anyone suffer."

"You mean: not with your own hands?"

"Yes."

Dey reminded the court that he had not been at Stutthof voluntarily. He was following orders, he said, and those orders were to stand on the watchtower and look out to make sure that "all was quiet." He had never done anything to the prisoners, not even annoyed or insulted them.

"So what you mean when you say, 'I didn't do anything,' is: 'I didn't treat anyone badly. I didn't shoot anyone. I didn't, with my own hands, help others to kill.'"

"Yes, that is correct."

"Should I therefore understand that you therefore have no guilt?"

"That is my understanding. Why should I be guilty? Where is my guilt? Where is my guilt for what happened there? That is what I ask myself over and over again. What could I have done? What more could I have done?"

Dey's sudden barrage of questions was intended as a protestation of innocence—but it also laid bare one of the trial's central moral and intellectual conundrums. To find the defendant guilty of being an accessory to murder, the court would have to conclude not only that his presence and actions there objectively helped the killings and that he had criminal intent. It also needed to establish that there were no grounds for justification or excuse. One of the best-known examples of a legal justification—both in German and English law—is self-defense: a court will typically not convict a defendant who deliberately injures or even kills a person if that person has attacked him first. Another example is what German lawyers call *Notstand*, or necessity, which allows defendants to avoid punishment for committing a crime if they faced a "present danger to life, limb, liberty, honor, property, or another legal interest" that cannot be otherwise avoided. Dey's experience at the camp did not fit easily into any of the established categories of justifications and excuses. Following orders—that most archetypal of Nazi defenses—had not been accepted as a valid excuse in German courts for decades. In strictly legal terms, Dey and his lawyer would struggle to convince the court that his actions should be justified or excused. From a moral perspective, however, the question seemed important all the same. What kind of behavior, what degree of fortitude, must we expect from a young man like Dey, standing on the watchtower of a concentration camp in the autumn of 1944? Meier-Göring, too, seemed interested in hearing Dey's answer. Though, as usual, she took a slight detour. If he was not guilty, she asked, who was?

"The government at the time, the regime that was in power," Dey responded.

"Who do you mean?"

"Yes, who? The party and those who instigated everything."

"You mean Hitler?"

"Yes, he was the most responsible."

Dey's answer in the Hamburg courtroom echoed the convenient myth that Germans told one another in the immediate post-war years, and that was shared by German prosecutors and judges at the time. The Holocaust, in their eyes, was the responsibility of Hitler and the Nazi leadership. All those below —including senior officers, bureaucrats, and executives—were helpers at worst, and innocent at best. Dey went on to argue that even the commandant of Stutthof, Paul Werner Hoppe, did not necessarily bear guilt. Asked who in the camp was responsible, he responded: "I don't want to blame anyone, nor do I want to

200

excuse anyone. Herr Hoppe was the head of the camp and he had the main responsibility for what happened there. He also had his orders and had to pass those on. But who is responsible for the abuses and all the injustices that happened there and who is guilty I cannot say."

Meier-Göring asked again: "My question is—and I am sure you have thought about this over the course of the trial—who bears the guilt for the fact that people were murdered in Stutthof?"

"I don't know."

Sensing a dead end, Meier-Göring opted for a new angle of inquiry. Could guilt, she asked, not also derive from the mere fact that someone remains in his place when a crime is committed? Should Dey, in other words, not have found a way to somehow remove himself from Stutthof?

The question was met with incredulity from the defendant. "There was no way to sign yourself out," Dey responded. Any move to leave Stutthof would have landed him in "more trouble." A transfer to the front lines, perhaps the most obvious exit route, was not on the cards, he claimed, because of his heart condition. He had, after all, been officially certified as unfit to fight on the front.

Could he not have simply climbed down from his watchtower?

"You were not allowed to leave your station."

"What would have happened if you had climbed down?"

"I don't know. I cannot give you an answer. I don't know what to tell you." What, he asked, did the judge want to hear from him?

"The truth!" someone in the courtroom shouted. I could not make out who had intervened, but Meier-Göring was happy to endorse the sentiment. "Yes, exactly," she said. "The truth."

Dey seemed to be growing more and more irritated. The judge's questions, her insistence on probing possible alternatives to his youthful obedience, clearly made no sense to him. He insisted, over and over again, that there was nothing he could have done at the time. As an individual, he was powerless to help the desperate prisoners, even though he felt pity for them. "I could not just say, 'I'll go down and open a gate.' How should that have happened?"

On this occasion, Meier-Göring decided to let the matter rest. But she returned to the question of Dey's guilt, and the question of what he might have done differently, four weeks later, on the tenth day of the trial. Her questions sounded harsher than in previous hearings; on one occasion, when the discussion turned once again to the arrival of tens of thousands of Jews deported from Hungary and from camps further east at Stutthof, and his claims that he never saw them, she came close to accusing him of lying. After the break, Meier-Göring made an attempt to summarize Dey's own version of events—what he saw and didn't see, and how he viewed his role at the time.

"Well, Herr Dey. You told us today once again—and we have heard this many times—that you were aware that the Jewish prisoners in any case had not done anything wrong. That they were only in the concentration camp because they were Jews, and you also told us that you felt sorry for them. You also told us that you observed that people were being gassed. You told us about this incident. You told us, Herr Dey, that you saw hundreds, if not thousands, of dead bodies that were carried out of the barracks in the morning, that the dead were emaciated and were thrown onto a cart and driven to the crematorium. You told us all that. So I want to ask you again: when did you understand—or did you even understand—that what was happening in front of your eyes was a crime against humanity?

That what was being done to these people was a crime? Did you understand that?"

By Meier-Göring's standards, this was an unusually long speech. And it had the desired effect. By using his own words and his own admissions, she confronted Dey with a seemingly inescapable conclusion. She had connected all the dots for him —and now left him little chance other than to see the line.

"Yes, of course," Dey responded. "I regarded this as a crime, what was being done to these people. Because punishing the innocent is in any case a crime, in my view."

"In my view as well," the judge responded. "Did you think this also at the time?"

"Yes."

"Or did you think: 'This is okay?'"

"No, I didn't."

In legal terms, Meier-Göring was now making progress. Dey had just acknowledged that he understood the fundamental criminality of Stutthof. What he had yet to accept, however, was his own part in those killings. Piercing that defense was the judge's next task. "Did you at some point start thinking that you should not take part in this crime?" she asked. "Did that thought ever enter your head: 'I must not take part in this?'"

"I could not run away. I had to follow the order I was given to go to the watchtower and stand guard. Running away, walking away—that was not possible."

"My question is about the step before that," the judge responded. "You see that a crime against humanity is taking place, that innocent people are being killed. And you stand on the watchtower and you ensure that they cannot escape. My question is, before you even thought about running away, did you think: 'I must not take part. It is wrong that I am standing here on the watchtower?'"

"I did have those thoughts, but I still say, what should I have done against this? Should I have ignored an order?"

Meier-Göring's question was simple enough to grasp but Dey was struggling to answer it in a meaningful way. He seemed genuinely baffled by the idea that he should have questioned, let alone ignored, an order from his superiors. His view, then as now, was, "I am not the one giving the orders or making the decisions, so what kind of responsibility could possibly be attached to me?" This was the position characterized with remarkable self-perception by Oskar Gröning, in his trial a few years earlier, as "the comfort of obedience." The phrase captured something important about the culpability of the guards and clerks, the junior bureaucrats and ordinary soldiers involved in the Nazi genocide. Many of them would, had they served another nation in war, never have dreamed of aiding and committing the kind of crimes that took place under the Nazis. For many of them, however, taking part, going along, not objecting, seemed like an easier, more comfortable, and less risky choice to make. More comfortable, even, than simply walking away.

"Herr Dey, do you understand that this is a different question?" Meier-Göring insisted. "To stand there and to say, 'I must not do that, I must not take part in killing innocent people. What can I do against this? How can I distance myself from this?' Did you have these thoughts?"

"I had the thoughts, but I could not act upon those thoughts," he responded. "I could not distance myself from the orders that were given without putting my own life in danger."

Dey's repeated insistence that he was only following orders, and that it was not his place to question those orders, failed to impress Meier-Göring. Was he not aware of the concept of criminal orders, she asked. Even the Nazis' own military criminal code had made clear, in Article 47, that soldiers were not required to follow an order from a superior officer if that order was criminal in nature. Had that thought not occurred to him? No, it hadn't.

Dey, I realized, had still not understood the point of the judge's question. He kept on insisting that he had been powerless to stop the killing, and incapable of helping the prisoners. That was not, however, what Meier-Göring wanted to know from him. She wanted to know, simply, whether Dey had understood that he was contributing to a terrible crime, and that he should have removed himself—or at least tried to remove himself—from the machinery of death in Stutthof. Dey was, of course, under no obligation to incriminate himself by providing the answers that the judge was looking for. But her pleas for frankness from the 93-year-old defendant became steadily more insistent, and her interventions more impassioned. Even if this moment of moral reckoning came seventy-five years too late, Meier-Göring was determined to confront Dey with that choice all the same.

"Now you are on the watchtower. You have become an SS man. And you see that innocent people are being murdered. Now you are standing there and you are participating. That would be the opportunity to say: 'I must not do this. I cannot reconcile this with my conscience that I am standing here. I cannot stand this. I have to remove myself.' That is the question that I am asking myself—whether you asked yourself these questions at the time?"

"I asked myself those questions but who should I have told? How should I have removed myself? I could not tell this to any of my superiors, that I don't want to take part and stand guard here."

"Why not?"

Dey was, finally, lost for words. Meier-Göring broke into the hushed silence that had descended across the courtroom. "That is a serious question, Herr Dey," she declared. "Why not?

Why couldn't you go to a superior and say, 'You know what is happening here is a crime! Innocent people are being killed here. I—won't—take—part—in—this!'"

Those final six words were shouted more than spoken, every word sounding as if it was followed by an exclamation mark. The presiding judge seemed, for the first and only time during the trial, on the verge of losing her composure. I was glad of the outburst. The question she was raising was, to me, the most important of the whole trial. It was directed at Dey, but she might as well have shouted it at an entire generation of Germans—at my grandparents and all my friends' grandparents, at everyone who was there at the time, keeping quiet, following orders, fleeing into the comfort of obedience. Why had they not walked away? Why had they not said no?

Dey's insistence that there was no way for a guard like him to refuse an order sounded—superficially at least—like a compelling argument. It conformed to the general perception of a Nazi concentration camp as a system both murderous and absolutely hierarchical and ruthless. But while the camps were indeed murderous for the inmates, there was at least some leniency and tolerance for SS personnel who showed moral qualms about the industrialized killings taking place. As Meier-Göring pointed out, there were numerous examples of guards and other personnel who asked for a transfer—and whose wish was granted. There was, strikingly, not one documented case of an SS guard executed for refusing to serve in a concentration camp.

There was, however, another flaw in Dey's argument: if he could not refuse an order to stand guard on the watchtower, he surely could not have refused any order—including an order to herd prisoners into the gas chamber, or shoot at Stutthof prisoners with his own gun? How far did obedience—and the defense of obedience—go? Standing on the watchtower was evidently not the same thing as murdering prisoners with your own hand, both from a legal and a moral perspective. But this was a difficult discussion from the point of view of the defense nonetheless. It was Dey himself who brought it up, however, in response to a question about what he regarded as a criminal order.

"A criminal order would have been if they had told me you have to shoot someone. That I wouldn't have done, of course."

"That you wouldn't have done?"

"That I wouldn't have done."

"What would you have done, Herr Dey?"

"I would have refused, of course."

"And then what?"

"I don't know what would have happened to me. I didn't know at the time either. What could have been done to me..."

"Yes, exactly."

"But I would have refused that."

"But standing on the watchtower and preventing people who are being killed from running away, that was okay?"

Dey sighed deeply. Silence. The judge's question had landed like a punch to the gut.

"Well...I can't answer that. But it certainly wasn't okay."

Meier-Göring pressed on. How did he even know that there would have been harsh consequences if he had refused an order? Dey had just admitted that he didn't know what would have happened to him had he refused to shoot a prisoner. So how could he be sure that he would have faced severe punishment had he refused to stand on the watchtower and do guard duty? Was it really fear of punishment that kept Dey on that watchtower, or had it perhaps simply been easier to follow orders? "Did you too escape into the comfort of obedience?" Meier-Göring asked. "Was it not simply more comfortable to be obedient?"

"I did not do anything to anyone," Dey responded, with stubborn insistence. "I had to follow the order I was given to stand guard, and I followed that. I didn't think that I was going to endanger anyone or save anyone if I refused. I never had that thought. If I had refused to stand guard there, well, maybe I would have gotten away but someone else would have come [and taken my place]. That's what I thought. This would have served no one. I would have harmed only myself. No one would have been saved."

This was a new line of defense. Dey appeared to be conceding that he could indeed have secured a move away from Stutthof, but that it would have made no difference to the killing. It was not an argument he had used before, but Dey seemed keen to drive home the point. "If I had left no one would have been protected in any way. The post would have been filled by someone else immediately," he added.

"Exactly," Meier-Göring responded. "Because there were others who thought the same as you did. I must follow this order. But if everyone had refused to follow this criminal order it would indeed have helped everybody. Because then all of this would not have been possible."

"Yes. If everybody had done that." There was a hint of sarcasm in Dey's voice.

"Yes, then maybe you should have been the one who started."

Silence, again. Meier-Göring carried on: "Yes! Have you ever thought about that? That someone should have started with this?"

"That person would have disappeared instantly."

"Herr Dey, this may come as a surprise to you but there is not a single person who was killed for refusing an order in this manner. No one has found historical proof of this. But there were many who said exactly that: we would have been killed. I could not get away from this. I had to follow the order or I

208

would have been killed. But those who did it, who asked to be transferred, who refused the orders, were actually not killed. Does that surprise you, Herr Dey?"

"During my time no one was transferred from there."

"But you didn't speak to anyone. You don't know that."

"Somehow one would have found out."

"Yes, because they all stood there like you and thought: there's nothing I can do now. I am standing here now and doing my duty. I won't help anyone and will only harm myself if I remove myself from here."

Dey fell silent again. The judge's words were more than a mere observation, more than a rhetorical device to make him think and question himself. They sounded—to me, and perhaps to Dey, too—like condemnation already.

"Good. I will say it again," Meier-Göring added. "The Nazis killed millions of innocent people, but not a single SS man who refused an order was killed. That in any case is what the historical evidence shows."

The judge was not done yet. And neither was Dey. He reminded the court that he had tried to persuade a senior officer to send him to a Wehrmacht canteen or bakery. So he had tried to get away from the SS. Meier-Göring, however, was quick to counter. That incident, she reminded the defendant, had taken place long before his arrival at Stutthof. Once at the camp, had he asked for a transfer? He hadn't.

The hearing was almost over but the judge made two last attempts to help Dey see that he was no innocent bystander, and that he, too, had to take responsibility for the murders at Stutthof. The defendant had said earlier that he would not have helped a single prisoner if he had abandoned the camp, or if a transfer request had been requested. Whatever the truth of that assumption, there was one person who he would certainly have helped—himself. "Because then you would not have taken part in this crime," Meier-Göring explained. "Would that not have been at least something?"

"I cannot say anything more about this," Dey responded.

"Herr Dey, you say you did nothing. You say you are not guilty."

"I don't see any guilt on my part. Because I caused no one to suffer."

"Not directly, you mean."

"Not directly."

"Would it have been possible to keep the concentration camp running if there had been no guards like yourself, Herr Dey?"

"If there had been none…I don't know."

The conclusion was already inescapable, but Meier-Göring had one last idea up her sleeve. Imagine, she told the defendant, that someone here in the courtroom suddenly got up, pulled a gun and threatened to kill everyone present. Imagine also that I, the judge, then ordered the police officers present to leave the courtroom and barricade the doors. The gunman kills everyone. Who, Meier-Göring asked, was to blame for the massacre? She answered the question herself: "Of course the person who had brought in the gun and killed everyone. Probably also myself, who gave the order to close the doors so that no one could escape. And what about the police officers, who locked the doors and prevented all the people here inside from escaping. Are they guilty?"

Of course Dey saw the comparison the judge was trying to draw. Of course he saw there was only one correct answer to the question. Yet he still resisted the pull of that answer. Instead, Dey simply questioned the logic of her hypothetical scenario. He doubted that the police officers would have followed the order. And why, he asked, would Meier-Göring have given that order, since she would have placed her own life in danger as well by locking the doors?

The hearing carried on for a little while longer but Dey said little of substance. He seemed exhausted, as did Meier-Göring. She ended the session with the usual formula, but this time it sounded like she meant it.

"I have no more questions."

CHAPTER THIRTEEN
A legacy of stones

A short walk from Munich's onion-domed cathedral stands a house of worship that is, in its own way, every bit as remarkable as the famous Frauenkirche. The imposing Ohel Jakob Synagogue has a base of rough, cream-colored stone that evokes the Western Wall in Jerusalem, topped by a steel and glass cube that floods the wood-paneled interior with sunlight. Opened in 2006, it forms part of a cluster of buildings that house a Jewish museum, a bookshop and café, a Jewish school and kindergarten, the offices of the Jewish community of Munich, and a kosher restaurant. It was a bold piece of architecture, and an even bolder statement of intent: seven decades after the Holocaust extinguished Jewish life in Munich, the community had returned to the heart of the Bavarian capital.

The improbable post-war story of Munich's Jews can be told in simple numbers: in May 1945, there were no more than sixty Jews left in the city. At the time of my visit, a year before the opening of the Stutthof trial in Hamburg, there were almost ten thousand. What those numbers failed to capture, however, were the extraordinary tales of perseverance that made the revival of Jewish life in Germany possible. I had come to Munich to hear perhaps the most remarkable of them all: it belonged to Charlotte Knobloch, an 86-year-old survivor of the Holocaust, who had led Munich's Jewish community for more than thirty

years. We had arranged to meet at Einstein, Munich's only certified kosher restaurant, a few floors down from Knobloch's office.
To access the building, I had to pass through a metal detector
and a booth manned by Israeli security guards—a reminder that
Jewish establishments from Pittsburgh to Paris had every reason
to feel threatened. Knobloch arrived in a blaze of color and
fabric that hinted at her training more than half a century ago
as a seamstress. She wore a bright pink jacket and matching scarf
in black, pink and turquoise. Her earrings, too, were strikingly
colorful: two large, translucent purple stones, set in gold. We
passed a minute or so in silence, as Knobloch looked over several
pages of notes prepared by her assistant, summarizing the themes
I wanted to tackle. She raised a skeptical eye: "You want to go
over all that? We'll be talking for hours!"

Knobloch was right to worry about time. Even a cursory
examination of her life would have required far more hours
than our lunch allowed. But I had come to Munich not just
to listen to Knobloch's personal story, but also to understand
what felt like an increasingly urgent challenge for Germany and
the country's culture of Holocaust remembrance: the gradual
disappearance of the generation of survivors. For as long as I
could remember, there had been people like Knobloch around
to tell their story and to bear witness. Their role in German
public life was special: their views and warnings were treated
with a degree of reverence that transcended all political and
social divisions. There was also, perhaps, a sense of reassurance
that came with their pronouncements: as long as Knobloch and
other survivors were there to speak—whether in schools, lecture
halls, or television studios—there seemed little reason to fear that
the Holocaust would fade from the nation's memory. Yet that
time was drawing to a close. What would happen when their

voices fell silent? What would happen when the story Knobloch was about to tell me was confined to books alone?

Born in 1932, her life was turned upside down by the rise of Nazism when she was just four years old. Her mother, a gentile who had converted to Judaism, was unable to withstand the social and political pressure placed on her, and decided to abandon the family. As Knobloch wrote in her autobiography, "Her fear was greater than her love for me." Knobloch's first brush with Nazi ideology, she told me, came as a little girl: one day, she tried to enter the local playground to meet up with neighborhood friends. She found the janitor's wife barring her way. "Our children will no longer play with Jews. Go home," she was told. Knobloch was hurt, angry—and stunned: "I had never even heard the term Jew before," she recalled. Her home was an observant one, but it had never occurred to her to see herself as different from her playmates. Worse was to follow, notably the terrors of the Kristallnacht (the "Night of Broken Glass") on November 9–10, 1938, when hundreds of synagogues and thousands of Jewish shops were sacked and destroyed. Her father, a prominent Munich lawyer, had been warned of the organized riots in advance, and decided that he and his infant daughter would be safer on the street, walking all night amid the thugs and bystanders. "We came up to the synagogue and I saw the smoke and asked my father, 'Why isn't the fire brigade coming?'" she recalled. "It was then that I realized that we were not only being pushed to the margins, but that they were after our lives. Even as a child, I understood this perfectly."

Part of the tragedy of Knobloch's family was its deep emotional bond with Germany. Her father, Fritz Neuland, had fought for the Kaiser in the First World War, and had the medals to prove it. He also felt a profound attachment to German culture

Charlotte Knobloch, the Holocaust survivor from Munich who
helped rebuild Jewish life in Germany after the war.

and ideas: Knobloch remembered the portrait hanging next to
her father's desk, showing the stern face of Immanuel Kant,
Germany's great philosopher of reason. Unlike his brother,
who emigrated to the U.S. in 1936, Neuland stayed put. He, too,
survived the Holocaust, but his mother—Knobloch's grandmother—perished in the camps. "I never spoke to my father
about this later on. I didn't want to sound like I was making a
reproach," she told me. "But I know that he reproached himself.
Everyone did. This was such an issue for many people after 1945.
Why did God spare me but not the others?"

She herself survived thanks to a young woman named
Kreszentia Hummel, a former maid in her uncle's house, who
agreed to hide her in her family's farm in rural Franconia. For
almost three years, this daughter of Munich's Jewish bour-
geoisie became Lotte Hummel, the illegitimate child of her

new protector. Shunned by other villagers, her only friends, she remembered, were the farm animals she took care of. "I spoke with them so much…They knew everything about me."

The moral courage displayed by Hummel was exceptional. Not only did she take the risk of hiding a Jew, she also endured the taunts from villagers mocking the bastard child. Knobloch would later learn that Hummel—a devout Catholic—had made her own private pact with God: she would save the little Jewish girl from Munich in the hope that God would protect her two brothers serving on the Russian front. Both men indeed returned safely.

In May 1945, Knobloch was reunited with her father, who had managed to survive the last years of the war in forced labor. For Knobloch, who was just twelve when the war ended, it was clear there could be no future for Jews in Germany. "Nobody wanted to stay in the country of the murderers," she recalled. "I no longer had a home, I no longer had a homeland. I just wanted to go, and never see these people again." Her father had other ideas. He had considered himself a patriot before the Nazis rose to power; he was not turning his back on the country now. Too young to leave by herself, Knobloch had no choice other than to stay as well. She hated it. "I never had the sense that people were ashamed. People would say: 'Oh, we missed you. How are you doing?'" she said. "The boy who used to spit at me suddenly seemed delighted to see me again. He just said, 'How much you have changed!' As if I had been away on holiday." She married Samuel Knobloch, another survivor, and gave birth to the first of three children. Somehow, the right moment to leave Germany never came: "There was no decision to stay—it just happened."

At first, Knobloch said, "Jewish life took place only among us… We lived in the country, but not with the country." That started to change only in the early 1980s, in part because of the landmark television series *Holocaust,* which rekindled reflection among Germans about the Nazi crimes. Knobloch told me she never spoke about her experiences during that period with her children. "That conversation never took place. We didn't want it because we were ashamed. We knew the question that would have come. And then I faced that question some years ago from my granddaughter [who was born and raised in Israel]. She went to Auschwitz and then wrote me this long letter with the headline, 'How can you live in this country?'" Knobloch argued that, in political terms at least, the Jewish community in Germany remained a significant asset for Israel: "I am convinced the Jewish state needs friends, and that the Jewish state needs a strong Jewish diaspora. I think [Israel] should be quite pleased that we exist."

Knobloch herself was as determined as ever to keep going. Her views and her presence were in demand as rarely before. But with every year that passed there were fewer Shoah survivors left who could speak of their experiences, and none—at least in Germany—could match the force of Knobloch. What would happen, I finally asked, when her generation was gone?

"It will be different," she answered. "The stones will have to speak."

The stones, indeed, are speaking everywhere, and new ones are being sunk into the ground every year. Germany's physical landscape of remembrance is unique—and uniquely dense. An official survey of memorial sites dedicated to the victims of Nazi rule that was completed in 2000 filled two volumes and ran to 1,864 pages.[1] Many more have been built since. The list runs from small plaques and humble crosses to ambitious contemporary sculptures and sprawling historical sites. It includes former concentration camps like Buchenwald and Dachau, which serve as memorials and museums alike, and the vast architectural ensemble that was once the staging ground for the annual Nazi Party rallies in Nuremberg. There is the razed former seat of the Gestapo and SS in Berlin, which was converted into an exhibition space aptly called the Topography of Terror. The house of the Wannsee conference on the outskirts of Berlin is now a museum, as are countless historical buildings and sites from the Nazi period across the country. The vast majority of memorials are dedicated to victims, or to specific groups of victims. But there is also a growing number of sites that serve as physical reminders of the perpetrators, like the Wannsee villa where the final solution was discussed and planned in January 1941. A separate category concerns landmark public buildings and sites that date from the Nazi period—like the former Ministry of Aviation (now the Federal Ministry of Finance) in Berlin or the Haus der Kunst gallery in Munich—that are still in official use today. Over the years, German cities have become increasingly adept at tackling the difficult historic and aesthetic legacy of these spaces: more often than not, the best solution is to keep the buildings and their dark history visible, while providing sufficient context to avoid any sense of glorification. In some cases, that approach was applied even to monuments that predate the Nazi period, but that offer a similarly problematic nationalist and militaristic message. One striking example is the Victory Gate in Munich, a nineteenth-century triumphal arch dedicated to the Bavarian army. Heavily bombed in the Second World War, it was rebuilt with its original dedication on one side and a new, decidedly non-triumphal inscription on the other: *Dem Sieg geweiht, vom Krieg zerstört, zum Frieden mahnend.* "Dedicated to victory, destroyed by war, urging peace."

The broader history of Germany's post-war memorial building is fascinating and complex, and closely traces the broader shifts in public attitude toward the Holocaust and German guilt.

From the immediate post-war years right up until the 1960s, the prevailing mood in society was one of self-victimization: Germans wanted to remember their own suffering, and forget the suffering they had inflicted on others. This led to a flurry of monuments, typically bearing Christian iconography, that were dedicated not to the victims of the Holocaust but generically to the "victims of war," or the "victims of war and terror."

There was one right outside my school in Darmstadt, where the bombed-out remains of a neo-gothic chapel had been left standing as they were, with the 1954 addition of a seven-meter-tall granite cross, and the inscription: "In memory of the dead, they rest in peace. As a reminder to the living, hold fast to peace." The site was treated, by us teenagers at least, with little piety: on summer nights it was a popular place to meet friends, listen to music, smoke, and drink countless bottles of beer from the brewery around the corner. Whether consciously or not, the memorial chapel did not feel to us like a particularly sacred or meaningful place.

The deeper problem, of course, was that behind the bland admonishments for peace lurked a glaring omission. By focusing on the victims of war in general, monuments like the one outside my school erased any distinction between those who started the war and those who suffered its consequences, while ignoring the victims of the Holocaust altogether. The ruined chapel, like so many memorials built during that period, was a physical representation of a prevailing post-war narrative that emphasized German victimhood—and de-emphasized German guilt. Memorials were typically placed in and around cemeteries—providing a distinctly Christian context—or alongside existing monuments to the dead of the First World War. At the same time, former camps and prisons as well as prominent Nazi buildings were either destroyed or revamped to serve new uses, their original purpose now hidden from sight.[2]

The post-war desire to blur the dividing line not just between different groups of victims but even between victims and perpetrators proved surprisingly enduring. After German unification in 1990, the conservative government of Chancellor Helmut Kohl faced the challenge of how to deal with the central war memorial of East Germany's Communist regime. The site, located in the neoclassical Neue Wache building on Berlin's Unter den Linden boulevard, had been dedicated to the "victims of fascism and militarism." It housed the remains of two of those victims—an unknown soldier and a resistance fighter murdered in a Nazi concentration camp—and featured a large depiction of the state symbol of the Communist regime, a hammer and compass surrounded by a ring of rye. There was an obvious need for a new design after 1990, but Kohl—a historian by training—pushed for a solution that caused bitter controversies. He called for an enlarged version of a famous sculpture by the pacifist artist Käthe Kollwitz, depicting a grieving mother with her dead son, to be placed in the center of the Neue Wache. Kollwitz, whose own son was killed in the First World War, had sculpted the work on a smaller, more intimate scale in the late 1930s. She referred to the piece at the time as a *pietà*, the traditional depiction of Mary holding the dead Jesus in her lap. Inside the Neue Wache, the inscription on the floor below the sculpture read: "To the victims of war and terror."

Critics—including the Central Council of Jews in Germany —were quick to speak out and took aim in particular at its nebulous dedication. Here was another landmark memorial, in the heart of the German capital, that failed to make a distinction between victim and aggressor, and that appeared to include the murdered Jews of Europe only as part of a diffuse mass of victims. *Der Spiegel* described the new memorial on the eve of the opening ceremony as a "lazy, anachronistic compromise," arguing that a "warrior memorial in the Christian tradition is not suitable for a place that should above all be dedicated to the murdered Jews."[3] The controversy was not just limited to the culture pages of German newspapers: a week before the opening, protesters chained themselves to the Neue Wache and loudly denounced what they called the "mockery" of Germany's victims.

Kohl's misjudgment was striking not least because the country's broader approach to memory culture—and memorial building—had mostly moved on a long time ago. From the 1960s onward, spurred by the Eichmann trial in Jerusalem and the Auschwitz trial in Frankfurt, Germans had begun looking at the Nazi period in a different—and more self-critical—light. This shift included a new focus on the Holocaust and its victims, and a more clear-eyed view of German guilt for the horrors inflicted by the Nazi regime. One consequence was a renewed interest in former concentration camp sites such as Dachau and Bergen-Belsen, which now finally received the attention they deserved. After decades of neglect, Dachau was turned into a memorial site and documentation center in May 1965. Bergen-Belsen had been declared a memorial site a decade earlier, but it, too, had been largely ignored until 1968, when the regional government added a documentation and exhibition center and paid for a restoration of the site. Over the decades that followed, public attention started to turn to lesser-known concentration camps and to emblematic sites that were linked to other Nazi atrocities, like the clinics where SS medical personnel murdered disabled patients as part of the regime's "euthanasia" program, or the vast factories where Jews and Soviet prisoners of war were forced into slave labor. In 1989, Berlin unveiled its first modest memorial to the fifty thousand homosexuals murdered by the Nazis—a victim group that until then had been almost entirely ignored. The small plaque was controversial at the time (the city's public transport authority, on whose property it was placed, resisted at first) but it was representative of a much broader shift: in towns and cities across Germany, there was a growing clamor to recognize all victims of the Nazi regime, in ever more sites, in ever more creative ways, and—often—in increasingly large and ambitious structures. The German capital was at the forefront of that movement. In the words of the historian Mary Fulbrook, the city emerged as the "commemoration capital of the world, certainly as far as displays of shame, remorse, and responsibility are concerned."[4] Like many foreign observers, she was struck by the peculiar—and perhaps unique—nature of Germany's new landscape of remembrance: "Most nations commemorate their heroes and martyrs; contemporary Germany, by contrast, displays the enormity of its crimes."[5]

It was also in the late 1980s that the idea for the most ambitious memorial project yet was first floated: a national memorial site dedicated to the murdered Jews of Europe. The driving forces behind the project were Lea Rosh, a prominent television journalist, and the historian Eberhard Jäckel. Their initial proposal, published in February 1989, called for the memorial to be built on the plot of land in West Berlin that once housed the headquarters of the Gestapo, Hitler's secret police (and later became the home of the Topography of Terror exhibition center). The site bordered the Berlin Wall, which duly collapsed just seven months later. German reunification brought immense joy, but it also rekindled fears in parts of Europe, and indeed among some German intellectuals, about German hegemony. A surge in neo-Nazi violence in the early 1990s, notably in eastern Germany, and a series of deadly attacks on the homes of migrant families and asylum seekers, provided another source of anxiety. Against this backdrop, and perhaps stung by the criticism of his clumsy intervention in the Neue Wache, Chancellor Helmut Kohl and his government eventually threw their weight behind Rosh and Jäckel's project. The fall of the Berlin Wall had freed up huge tracts of land in the former heart of the city, notably around the Brandenburg Gate—prompting the backers of the memorial to call for a new location on a sprawling site just south of the gate, and only a few meters from where Hitler's Reich Chancellery had once stood. Kohl approved, paving the way for the Berlin regional government in 1994 to launch an international competition inviting artists and architects to submit their designs for the memorial. The contest was always likely to be controversial, but among the 528 entries were some that baffled even the most open-minded observer: one artist proposed to build a giant ferris wheel on the site, but instead of passenger cabins the structure would use cattle carriages like the ones used to deport Jews to the concentration camps. Another entry called for the construction of a crematorium tower belching out real smoke day and night. There was also a suggestion to blow up the Brandenburg Gate—and leave the rubble as the memorial.

The jury eventually selected a proposal by four German artists to build a huge sloping concrete plate that was to be inscribed with the names of all known Jewish victims of the Holocaust. The winning design—much like the competition itself—attracted close scrutiny as well as sharp criticism. One concern, raised not least by the Jewish community, was that the concrete slab was suggestive of a Christian tomb, and therefore inappropriate for a memorial to the murdered Jews of Europe. The German chancellor, too, took exception, and vetoed the design—plunging the project into crisis and forcing a second competition. It took another four years and countless further controversies until a new design—by the American architect Peter Eisenman—was approved in a formal vote by the Bundestag. Work started on the site in April 2003, and the memorial was finally unveiled in May 2005 in the presence of the German president, the German chancellor, the presidents of the German parliament and constitutional court, the head of the German Jewish community, Lea Rosh and Eberhard Jäckel, and much of the country's political, cultural, and business elite. The first speaker, President Wolfgang Thierse, noted the "great emotional power" of the site, describing it as a "symbol in concrete for the utter incomprehensibility of the crime."[6]

The need for a memorial, he argued, had arisen not least from the fact that Germany's memory culture was at a transition point: "What today can still be narrated vividly by contemporary witnesses must in future be transmitted by museums, by works of art. We are, at the moment, within a change in generations, a shift in the tides, as some may phrase it. National Socialism, war and organized genocide will become less and less the living experience of contemporaries to the events. They will become ever more events of history. There is a shift under way from personal memory, individually certified, to a collective memory transmitted by knowledge. The memorial is the expression of that transition."[7]

The presence of the entire German establishment at the unveiling ceremony suggested a degree of social and political consensus that was in truth hard to find. Controversies—and, indeed, confusions—surrounded the monument from the very beginning. Who, exactly, was it for? For the victims? For the perpetrators? For the perpetrators to remember the victims? And which victims precisely? In its official dedication, the Berlin memorial was unequivocal: it was a memorial for the murdered Jews of Europe. That had been its intended purpose all along, and given the scale of Jewish suffering and the centrality of antisemitism to the Nazi worldview it was a legitimate choice. But it meant that millions of other victims—Communists, Social Democrats, and other political opponents of Nazism, Poles and Soviets, Sinti and Roma, prisoners of war and partisans, homosexuals and the disabled—were excluded from the site. Some felt unease at their exclusion, arguing that it was not up to the descendants of the perpetrators to draw distinctions, and by implication a hierarchy, between different groups of victims. Others worried that the sheer scale and prominence of the project—the memorial covered 19,000 square meters, or close to five acres of ground—could be misread as an attempt to finally draw a line under the country's culture of Holocaust remembrance. Others pointed out that the memorial was conspicuously silent, both in its dedication and its design, on the question of who actually committed the murders. As one critic remarked: "The title doesn't say 'Holocaust' or 'Shoah'; in other words, it doesn't say anything about who did the murdering or why—there's nothing along the lines of 'by Germany under Hitler's regime,' and the vagueness is disturbing."[8]

There was also the polarizing figure of Rosh herself, whose drive and personal dedication to the memorial project was not always matched by depth and subtlety of thought. This became clear in stunning fashion during the unveiling ceremony, when Rosh announced in her speech that she intended to bury a tooth she had found and taken from the Belzec extermination camp seventeen years earlier at the new Berlin memorial. "I picked this one up and took it. I held it tight in my hand. And at that moment I promised myself, I swore that we would build a memorial for those murdered. And that this tooth would find its place in that memorial. Today, almost exactly seventeen years later, I can keep that promise," Rosh declared in her speech.[9]

The backlash was immediate. Not only had Rosh misused this most solemn of occasions for a gesture of theatrical self-indulgence, but she had also defied Jewish burial rites—angering both Jewish community leaders in Germany and the director of the Belzec camp memorial. Rosh eventually returned the tooth to be buried where it was found.

The story of Berlin's Holocaust memorial is so complex, its ambition so great and so obviously impossible to meet, that it is not easy to approach the site with an open mind. The fact that it has emerged in the years since its opening in 2005 as an important Berlin tourist attraction—the backdrop to a million selfies—adds another layer of complexity. There is an underground information center and museum, but it is the memorial itself that forever fascinates visitors. It seems inviting and forbidding at the same time, darkly beautiful, and prompts visual associations almost instantly: a sea of stone, a concrete labyrinth, a forest, a canyon, a graveyard.

I passed the Holocaust memorial countless times when I lived in Berlin. On occasions, I would stop and walk among the smooth, dark concrete steles, and experience the strange sense of dislocation and unease that follows you as you move further along the sloping ground. I returned to the memorial on a recent visit to the German capital, and that same sensation was produced almost instantly: the noise of the busy metropolis fell away, as did the view of the surrounding Berlin skyline. The sky was visible only when I looked up, and even then it appeared only as a narrow cross-slit, framed by the sharp edges of the steles above. It took just a few steps to feel utterly lost amid the dense, towering slabs. The effect on the senses was undeniable, and strangely impressive. By shutting out the world, the memorial forces you to turn your thoughts to the event it had been built to commemorate. That, in any case, was the intention. But there was, I felt, also a faint echo of the fairground attraction—the haunted house, the carousel, even the ferris wheel: a sense of momentary physical dislocation, a brief shudder, followed by the relief (or disappointment) of a return to safer and firmer ground. The architect, Peter Eisenman, had done a formidable job, I thought. But could a Holocaust memorial really be well designed? Could it be effective? Should it?

There is only one other Holocaust memorial that competes with the Berlin field of stone in scale and ambition. It is grand yet tiny, ubiquitous yet often invisible. And it will remain, deliberately and forever, unfinished. For the past thirty years, German artist Gunter Demnig has been placing his *Stolpersteine* —stumbling stones—into the urban landscape of cities across Germany and Europe. Each one is shaped like a small paving stone, capped in brass, and inscribed with the name of a Holocaust victim, their date of birth and the location and year of their death. Demnig and his team of supporters then place it into the pavement outside the entrance of the home they lived in, or occasionally their place of study or work. Many of the stones are placed at the request of descendants but in some cases it is the new inhabitants of the buildings from which the victims were deported who initiate the procedure. The upkeep and cleaning of the stones is left to the neighborhood. The proliferation of these stones—there were more than 90,000 at the time of writing—has created an entire new set of rituals and traditions, most notably the placing of candles and flowers next to the Stolpersteine on January 27, Holocaust memorial day. Walking through Berlin, where thousands of stumbling stones have been laid over the years, on the evening of January 27, always made for a haunting sight: freshly polished brass glinting in the candlelight in street after street, passersby stooping down to read the inscriptions and take in the names.

227

Stolpersteine, or stumbling stones, marking the names of Holocaust victims on the pavement outside their former homes.

Once you start to pay attention, the Stolpersteine are impossible to ignore: I doubt there was a single excursion or journey I made in Germany—from my Berlin flat to the office, from my parent's house to the local shops—that did not involve passing by one of Demnig's stones. There was one on my street, two on the way to the bakery around the corner, two more between my flat and the nearest supermarket. On the five-minute walk to my son's school, we would pass no fewer than six.

As Demnig himself has argued, the project resonates above all because it does not seek to capture or memorialize the vast, amorphous crime of the Holocaust itself, but the individual. "It goes beyond our comprehension to understand the killing of six million Jews," he once told a U.S. interviewer. "But if you read the name of one person, calculate his age, look at his old home and wonder behind which window he used to live, then the horror has a face to it."[10]

The Stolpersteine, too, have their detractors. Among the most prominent is Charlotte Knobloch, who argued that Demnig's stones were not an appropriate way to commemorate the victims of the Holocaust. In her view, the very idea that people could literally step on the names of the dead, and that the stones were exposed to everyday dirt and filth, was intolerable and akin to desecration. Under pressure from Knobloch and the Munich Jewish community, the city government in 2015 issued a formal ban on placing Stolpersteine on public land. Holocaust victims should instead be honored by plaques and steles at eye level, the city decided. That decision, too, was hotly contested.

For Knobloch, the survivor of the Holocaust and veteran of a thousand struggles over Holocaust memory and Holocaust commemoration in Germany, the stones that may ultimately matter the most were the ones that surrounded us as we finished our lunch. The synagogue and cluster of buildings that grace Munich's Jakobsplatz today were to a large extent the fruit of her vision and dedication. "Sometimes I catch myself thinking this cannot be true. Every day, when I arrive here, I draw such happiness from seeing the synagogue and the museum and the community center," she told me. "What is amazing is not just that we have this, but that it has become so accepted. When the tourist busses stop here, I often hear the Munich guide say: 'And here you can see *our* synagogue.' I cannot imagine anything more beautiful."

For Knobloch and many others, the decision to build a new temple in the city where Hitler plotted his rise to power was deeply significant. It was, she told me, the moment she decided to "unpack her suitcase"—to finally admit to herself she had made Munich her home, despite the past. That suitcase, she added, would remain unpacked. Unlike some of the former leaders of the Jewish community in Germany, she did not want to be buried in Israel, but in her hometown of Munich. And, despite the recent worries about rising antisemitism, she seemed keen to leave our conversation on an upbeat note: "Of course I am worried. But I have great faith in young people, and I mean both Jewish and non-Jewish. I think they will take on the responsibility, and that is ultimately all that matters."

Knobloch's optimism was both moving and encouraging. She had fought all her life to rebuild her community from the ashes of the Holocaust, and to remind her fellow Germans of the lessons from that disaster. And she had left behind her own legacy of stones. We finished our meal, said our goodbyes, and I headed back to the railway station. But before I turned the corner I looked back one more time at this striking complex of buildings in the heart of Munich, a new bastion of Jewish life in Germany, and a monument to survival—both her own, and that of her people.

CHAPTER FOURTEEN

A trial on the edge

The court hearing on February 26, 2020, started on a surprisingly hostile note: Stefan Waterkamp, the lawyer for the defense, called for the presiding judge to be removed from her post on grounds of bias.

It was a bold move, and one that seemed at odds with Waterkamp's courtroom stance until then. He had intervened on behalf of his client on numerous occasions, but his tone had never previously been this confrontational, and there was never a sign that the defense was intent on torpedoing the entire trial. Now, four months into the proceedings, Waterkamp was arguing that Anne Meier-Göring was unfit to lead the trial. He accused her of showing blatant disregard for Dey's health by extending the previous hearing beyond the maximum two hours recommended by medical staff, despite what Waterkamp claimed were clear signs that the defendant had no longer been able to follow the proceedings. Her failure to end the hearing on time had put Dey at risk, and suggested that Meier-Göring was more interested in the speedy conclusion of the trial than in his health. This had left Dey with the impression that the judge was "degrading him to a mere object."

Meier-Göring was evidently taken aback by the application. If successful, Waterkamp's move would not just remove her from her role as presiding judge, it would almost certainly also force a retrial. Given Dey's age and health, it was far from certain that prosecutors would get a second chance to put the defendant in the dock. The decision on whether or not there were grounds to assume bias would be taken later on by her fellow judges, without Meier-Göring's presence or involvement. But she was in no mood to let the accusations from the defense stand unanswered. "I deny that I in any way tried to continue the hearing despite his inability to follow the proceedings," the judge told Waterkamp. She had kept an eye on Dey throughout the hearing, she said, and had brought it to a close as soon as she noticed that the defendant's attention was flagging. Meier-Göring's tone remained friendly, but now a sense of indignation crept into her response: "I am actually the first to pay attention to how your client is doing. I really find this a little…well…it's the way it is."

Lars Mahnke, the chief prosecutor also weighed in, describing Waterkamp's move as "shrill." He, too, had observed Dey throughout the last hearing day and never noticed any sign of deterioration. Besides, it was the defense lawyer's job to defend his client's interests and notify the court of any sign of health risk. "You obviously didn't do this part of your job at all the day before yesterday," Mahnke told Waterkamp.

In truth, Waterkamp knew that his application had little chance of success. The bar for removing a judge on grounds of bias was high. Even if Meier-Göring had allowed the occasional hearing to run on for longer than previously scheduled, it seemed a stretch to argue that this was reason enough to break off the trial. Waterkamp was genuinely concerned about his client's health, however, and his application was an attempt —arguably a heavy-handed one—to remind the court of its duty of care.

The hearing was the last before the court took a three-week break, allowing tempers to cool off and for the court to come up with a formal response to Waterkamp's application. Within days, however, the case against Bruno Dey would face a far more serious challenge—and from an entirely different source.

The first case of COVID-19 in the city of Hamburg was detected within twenty-four hours of that contentious hearing. A pediatrician from the university hospital in Hamburg–Eppendorf, a short drive from the Hamburg criminal court, was found to have contracted the virus on February 27, 2020. Like many Germans during the first wave, he had become infected while skiing in Italy, which was among the European countries hit hardest at the start of the pandemic. The first German to die from COVID was also a man from Hamburg (though he had contracted the virus and died while on holiday in Egypt). Within weeks, authorities across the country started shutting down public life. In Hamburg, the city government issued an emergency decree on March 15, 2020, ordering the closure of all theaters, cinemas, libraries, museums, galleries, and swimming pools, as well as the zoo and the planetarium.[1] Public gatherings and sporting events were banned. The government also shut down all brothels and strip clubs, plunging Hamburg's famous Reeperbahn red light district into darkness. Even the city's historic fish market was shut down for the first time in more than 300 years. One day after the decree was issued, Hamburg closed its schools.

One of the few public institutions that was kept open at the start of the pandemic was the court system. But the risk posed by the virus to the Stutthof trial was evident. Even in the early weeks of the pandemic, it was clear that COVID-19 posed a particular danger to the elderly. At ninety-three, Bruno Dey was among those who had every reason to expect that an infection with the coronavirus would be lethal. There was no vaccine at the time, protective equipment was in short supply, and hospitals had yet to find effective ways of treating the infected. Beyond such medical considerations, the onset of the pandemic prompted a wholesale reordering of priorities. The need to contain the virus and protect the population was at the front and center of everyone's mind. Even a criminal trial as historically significant as the one against Bruno Dey seemed trivial when set against the public health crisis unfolding around the globe. As important as it was to bring the last perpetrators of the Holocaust to justice, was this trial worth the risk, not only to Dey but to other participants as well? The answer to that question was—at least in the eyes of the defendant and his family—a matter of life and death.

The strictures of Germany's *Strafprozessordnung*, the law governing how criminal trials are conducted, offered little help to Meier-Göring and her fellow judges. On the contrary: some of the core tenets underpinning the code stood in direct opposition to the sudden public health requirements prompted by COVID-19.[2] One was the demand that criminal trials must be concluded as swiftly as possible, which meant hearings could be interrupted for no more than one month. Another rule demanded that all participants, and notably the defendant, had to be present in court in person. There was nothing in the procedural law that allowed trials to be held, even for a brief period, online or virtually. Finally, there was the requirement for criminal trials to take place in public, which meant more people—and more potential carriers of the virus—inside the courtroom. Given the one-month rule, Meier-Göring's most immediate problem was time. The last hearing had been held on Wednesday, February 26. The next was scheduled for Friday, March 20. Delaying the hearing by even a week would risk scuppering the whole trial. Mindful of the problem, the German Ministry of Justice was at that very moment racing to come up with a fix: a new procedural rule that allowed trials to be interrupted for longer than a month to prevent the spread of COVID-19. But that provision would be published in the official register only on March 27, and take effect the day after—too late for the Stutthof trial in Hamburg. The court had a decision to take, and it had to take it fast.

Two days before the scheduled hearing day, on March 18, 2020, an email landed in my inbox. It was from Kai Wantzen, the judge who served as the court's chief press officer, confirming that the hearing was going to go ahead after all. "The appointment is indispensable for the continuation of the trial," his message noted. The hearing itself would last only ten minutes, and would involve only the minimum of participants. Neither the media nor the public would be allowed into the courtroom. Meier-Göring made just one exception, for Dey's immediate family.

The hearing was indeed brief, and devoted to just two items. One involved reading out Dey's criminal record, which everyone in the room knew to be clean. It was a formality, but it allowed the court to claim that it had done a piece of official business and bought more time—at least another three weeks—until the next hearing. The other was the reading of the court's decision on Waterkamp's application to have Meier-Göring removed from her role on grounds of bias. It was, to the surprise of no one, rejected. The task of reading the decision fell to the presiding judge herself. It started by noting that the key fact underpinning his claim was simply wrong. Contrary to Waterkamp's allegations, the medical expert present in the courtroom had not signaled to the judge that Dey was incapable of carrying on (which was confirmed by the doctor himself). The decision also pointed out that the two-hour time frame for individual hearings was a recommendation rather than a hard limit. Dey had, in sum, not been "degraded to a mere object," as the defense had claimed. Meier-Göring would remain in charge of the case.

Closing the hearing, she did her best to sound upbeat: "Stay well, and keep your distance, especially you, Herr Dey," she told the court, before adding: "Everything will be fine."

Stefan Waterkamp, the Hamburg lawyer who
took on the defense of Bruno Dey.

Waterkamp accepted the decision to leave Meier-Göring in charge. This, too, was no surprise. The COVID pandemic had, after all, just presented the defense with a far more significant—and entirely legitimate—opportunity to put an end to the trial, and save Dey from a guilty verdict. In fact, Waterkamp had already made a formal request to the court asking for a suspension of the trial, on the grounds that continuing the hearings put his client at risk of infection. Suspending the trial would have much the same effect as removing the judge: the case could eventually be restarted but it would have to be treated like an entirely new trial. All the procedural steps, all the witness statements, all the expert testimony would have to be repeated. The duration of the suspension, of course, was unknowable, as was a potential date for the restart. In light of Dey's age, it seemed at the very least doubtful that he would face another day in court if the suspension went ahead. Waterkamp himself had told the judge in an email the day before the March 20 hearing that "as things stand now the trial cannot be saved without risking the defendant's life over and over again." He cited expert opinions predicting it would take at least a year for a COVID vaccine to be discovered and rolled out. "This means that the trial, even on optimistic assumptions, could be continued only a year from now. That would presume that a tolerable vaccine exists and works reliably. Until then there is an extreme risk that the defendant will die in the case of infection." Even under the new court rule rushed through by German authorities, a trial could only be interrupted by a maximum of three months. One way or the other, Waterkamp argued, the case against his client was doomed to fail.

Meier-Göring, however, was not willing to give up so easily. Nor was she prepared to make use of the new provisions and agree to a three-month interruption. She had set the date for the next hearing for April 14, and was determined to hold it.

In the days since the March 20 hearing, Meier-Göring had worked feverishly to secure an FFP2 face mask for the defendant, an exceedingly rare commodity at this early stage in the pandemic, and one that at the time was reserved exclusively for medical personnel. The judge imposed special social distancing rules inside the courtroom: everyone present had to sit at least two meters apart. Meier-Göring also ordered the construction of a custom plexiglass screen to shield Dey from infection. Every forty-five minutes, courtroom 200, the largest by far in the criminal justice building, would be aired for twenty minutes. As a final safety measure, the judge imposed a sharp reduction in the number of participants: spectators would not be admitted until the end of April, and journalists were told to follow the trial via audio transmission from a separate room. Taken together, these measures would lower the infection risk for the defendant "almost to nil," she argued. The trial would go on—at least for now.

It was an agonizing decision. Meier-Göring was clearly determined to bring the case against Dey to a conclusion. But she also knew the risk. Should Dey indeed contract the virus in the courtroom it would be a disaster—first and foremost for the defendant and his family. But it would also deal a heavy blow to the court. She would be exposing herself to accusations that securing a conviction against a former SS camp guard had been more important than protecting the life of a vulnerable old man. It was a decision, moreover, that she had to take at a time when the world's understanding of COVID-19 was still limited. Barely a month into the pandemic, who really knew how big the risk was of continuing with the trial?

The next hearing went ahead, despite Waterkamp's formal protestations, on April 14. This was scheduled to be another short hearing, without witnesses or expert testimony. It was called, much like the previous hearing in March, mainly to satisfy the strictures of procedural law and keep the trial alive. But it was not without drama. Within minutes it was obvious that Dey was in distress. He struggled to breathe under his tight-fitting FFP2 mask—the very piece of protective equipment that court officials had scrambled for weeks to obtain. Meier-Göring ordered a break in the proceedings to give Dey time to recover. When the court reconvened twenty minutes later, he was without his mask—but everyone else wore theirs (all had come with standard surgical masks). Meier-Göring went speedily through the day's business, notably by denying a request made by a group of lawyers representing survivors for the court to travel to Stutthof and inspect the camp. The idea was for the judges and other participants to gain a better understanding of its precise layout, and the physical distance and sightlines between the watchtowers and the gas chamber and crematorium. The value of such an excursion would have been debateable even in normal times. In the midst of a global pandemic, it made no sense at all. The hearing was brought to a swift conclusion.

The court reconvened nine days later, on April 23, to hear from another Stutthof survivor, via video link from Israel. The plexiglass screen had finally been completed, offering additional protection to the defendant. Outside the courtroom, too, there was better news: after an early spike in March, the number of confirmed COVID cases was now falling across Germany. As the world would learn over the next two years, the ebb and flow of case numbers was the result of a complex interplay between public health measures, the behavior of the population, and the sporadic emergence of new virus variants. The worst was very much yet to come, both in terms of infections and deaths. But at the time it was not unreasonable to feel cautious optimism, and many—including key policymakers in Hamburg and elsewhere in Germany—did. Case numbers, which in any case had been lower in the city state than other parts of Germany, were falling fast, and the local government was preparing to loosen some of the lockdown measures pushed through the previous months. Within a month, the first bars and restaurants were allowed to open again.

The outbreak of the COVID pandemic was a make-or-break moment for the Stutthof trial. Amid the panic and fear of the first wave, it would have been an easy decision for the court to abandon the case in March or April 2020, scuppering the chance to bring one of the last Holocaust cases in history to an end. That it didn't was largely the result of Meier-Göring's determination and nerve. At a time when much of the world was frozen in fear of the virus, she cooly assessed the risk, worked hard to make the courtroom as safe as possible for the defendant, and plowed on. For Waterkamp and Dey, this was clearly a missed opportunity. The outbreak of the COVID crisis offered them the best—and perhaps the only—chance to bring the trial to an end without a conviction. The weeks that followed showed the cost, in legal terms, of their failure to do so: they would deliver some of the most damaging evidence yet heard.

The pandemic had erupted in the midst of a trial phase that was dominated by expert witnesses: historians, medical experts, police investigators, and psychologists. The court still heard from survivors on an occasional basis, but for much of April, May, and early June the tone inside the courtroom was set by the dispassionate presentations of professionals and academics. The first to appear in court after the COVID interruptions were Dennis Tappe and Sven Anders, two professors of medicine from the University of Hamburg who had the grim task of explaining to the court the nature of the typhus epidemic that broke out in Stutthof in late 1944, as well as the lethal impact of the poison gas Zyklon B on the human body. A few weeks later the court heard from Stefanos Hotamanidis, a child and youth psychiatrist who had been asked to examine the defendant and assess his relative state of maturity when a teenager, more than seventy-five years ago. At stake was the crucial question of what German lawyers call *Schuldfähigkeit*, the ability to bear guilt. Only if this ability is confirmed can a defendant be found guilty in a court of law. Hotamanidis had appeared twice before the court, and was subjected to intense questioning both from the judge and from Waterkamp. His assessment was by its very nature lacking in certainty: Hotamanidis had essentially been asked to analyze the mind of a teenager based on conversations with his nonagenarian later self. There were interesting insights all the same. The expert noted that Dey had shown a "tendency toward obedience" and a general disposition "to avoid any kind of conflict." These were not traits that would have helped him take a stand against his superiors in Stutthof, but neither did they mean that Dey was unable to differentiate between right and wrong.

By far the most important expert witness, however, was a young, bespectacled historian named Stefan Hördler, who appeared in front of the court on no fewer than nine occasions. Hördler's day job was at the memorial site of Mittelbau-Dora, a former concentration camp in central Germany that became notorious for using slave labor to manufacture V2 rockets, Hitler's vaunted wonder weapon, toward the end of the war. He was the director of the site, an expert both on the concentration camp system and on slave labor, and had provided historical testimony already in an earlier trial related to Stutthof. Over the course of multiple hearing days, Hördler described the layout of the camp, its history, command structure, and personnel. One important fact that he established early on was that Stutthof suffered from an extremely poor personnel situation: in January 1945, for example, while other concentration camps on average had one SS guard for seventeen prisoners, the ratio in Stutthof was one to forty-nine—the worst in the entire concentration camp network. This suggested that Dey would have likely been deployed in all sections of the camp and in all manner of functions, and undermined his claim that he had little understanding of what happened at Stutthof. There were simply not enough guards around to assume otherwise. Nor was it at all plausible that the defendant would not have known about the gas chamber and other methods of killings, Hördler argued, pointing to surveys of SS men in Auschwitz. "Almost all guard companies stated uniformly that within two weeks they knew what was happening inside the camp," he added.

Hördler also provided a detailed account of how the causes of death—and the types of murder—changed over time: with the outbreak of the typhus epidemic at Stutthof in late 1944, he explained, it no longer became necessary to send inmates into the gas chamber or to gun them down. Instead, the camp commandant ordered entire sections of Stutthof sealed off, and left the infected prisoners inside to die. And they did, in their thousands.

This historical background information was relevant, and in parts deeply problematic for the defense. But the most damning testimony from Hördler came on May 15, when the expert tackled two of the key questions facing the court: did Bruno Dey have the option of removing himself from Stutthof? And if he had refused his duty, what would have happened? Both were central to the defense. Dey had insisted from the first day of the trial that he saw no alternative to doing his guard duty—and that any refusal to follow orders would have put his own life at risk. It was, on the face of it, a plausible argument to make. The SS was not an organization noted for its tolerance of ill discipline, and with the front line moving closer by the day the need for strict obedience would have been plain to all. In the case of Dey, moreover, there was an added complication: due to his heart condition he had been classified as unfit to serve in combat duty. Surely that meant that the most obvious path out of Stutthof—volunteering for the front line—was barred to the defendant?

Armed with a trove of archival material and a detailed understanding of the camp's command structures, Hördler began chipping away at these assumptions little by little. His first target was the notion that SS men had no choice to opt out of the gruesome task of killing innocent civilians. He cited statements made by Hermann Pister, the commandant of the Buchenwald concentration camp, who was tried and sentenced to death by an American tribunal after the war (but died of a heart attack before the sentence could be carried out). Ahead of his trial, Pister had been questioned in detail about the SS men who formed the execution squads at Buchenwald, and whether they had been volunteers or not. His answer was unequivocal: participation in this murderous task was entirely voluntary. Those who refused to take part were not punished—"under no circumstance," the interrogation protocol noted.

The same practice, Hördler said, was applied in Stutthof and other camps.

The historian then moved on to the question of whether an SS guard like Dey could have requested a transfer from the camp. The answer that emerged from his trawl through personnel files was clear: yes. Hördler had in fact found numerous examples of SS guards who requested such a transfer, and whose wish was granted. He provided their names and ranks, as well as a sketch of their circumstances. In some cases, the men were simply sent back to their original Wehrmacht units (including the one that Dey had first joined in spring 1944). In others they requested a transfer to combat units on the front. Such transfers, too, had taken place on numerous occasions. Perhaps the most striking piece of evidence Hördler presented in the hearing was a *Sonderbefehl,* or special order, from the Stutthof commandant dated August 22, 1944. It ordered the drawing up of lists with the names of all SS guards who were ready to volunteer for combat duty on the front. This order would have been made public inside the camp and transmitted to all guard companies: "Everyone knew that the possibility existed to move out of the guard duty," the historian told the court. Hördler had been able to track down the list of one of the three guard companies in Stutthof, and found that thirty-five men from this company alone had volunteered for the front. Crucially, at least two of them were accepted despite having been classified previously —like Dey—as unfit for combat duty. The need for soldiers in the summer of 1944 had evidently become so desperate that the Wehrmacht felt compelled to broaden its intake. Indeed, only a few months later the regime ordered the creation of the *Volkssturm*, drafting male Germans as young as sixteen and as old as sixty to defend the Fatherland.

The existence of the *Sonderbefehl* from August 22 delivered a significant—and potentially fatal—blow to one of the central arguments of the defense: it showed not only that it was possible to achieve a transfer from the camp, but that such a transfer was also available to men who had previously been deemed unfit for combat duty. What is more, the document showed that such transfers were—at least at this point in the war—actively encouraged by the Wehrmacht and by the SS. As Hördler remarked, the order had "opened a window." And that window remained open until the bitter end.

That left the question of what happened to SS personnel in concentration camps who refused to follow orders or who showed their distaste for the task they had been ordered to fulfill. Here again, Hördler was able to point to examples from Stutthof and other camps that undermined the claims made by the defense.

As it happened, some of the men who had been transferred out of Stutthof were moved precisely because they showed signs of disapproval. Their personnel files made reference to an apparent absence of *Dienstfreudigkeit*, a strange term that is perhaps best translated as "joyfulness in service." Another SS man was moved from guard duty to administrative tasks after he was found to be lacking in "ideological firmness." These were not the kind of qualities the SS was looking for in a concentration camp guard —and the commandant had a strong incentive to move such men on as quickly as possible. "The SS had no interest whatsoever in having men with such moral qualms inside their companies," Hördler told the court. They were seen as "risk factors," and as potential subversives who would undermine the group dynamic.

The SS did punish its own men for disobedience and—in the very rare cases where this happened—for providing assistance to concentration camp inmates. But the punishments were not nearly as severe as might have been imagined. In extreme cases, these men were sentenced to be incarcerated in a concentration camp themselves for three to six months, albeit in separate sections of the camp. There was no case in which an SS member had been sentenced to death or sent to a concentration camp indefinitely for such behavior, Hördler said.

But that, in any case, was not the central question facing Dey at the time; nor was it central to the work of the court seventy-five years later. He was on trial not for the failure to help the inmates at Stutthof, but for his decision to stay at the camp when it would have been possible—difficult, but possible—to find a way out. And pursuing that path would, according to Hördler, almost certainly not have exposed the defendant to any risk of punishment. "There is no provable case in which men who had problems with fulfilling their guard duty and who asked for a transfer either to their former army unit or to the front suffered personal harm," he said.

The defense was given ample opportunity to question Hördler, beginning on May 25, ten days after the historian's damaging assessment on the possibility of transfers from Stutthof. Waterkamp knew he faced an uphill battle. He told me after the trial that Hördler's testimony on this matter had been a "drastic" moment for the trial, and one that "significantly worsened the prospects for the defense." Hördler's examples of SS men who had managed to leave Stutthof had been well documented and numerous, leaving the defense lawyer precious little to work with as he tried to poke holes in his testimony. He tried nonetheless. Dey had previously told the court about an incident in which he fell asleep while on guard duty, and had been warned by a superior officer that he might be shot if this happened again. Was it possible, Waterkamp asked, that the severity of this threat had convinced the young guard that any further sign of disobedience would indeed be punished very severely? Hördler demurred. This was a subjective recollection, he responded, and as such he could neither prove nor disprove its veracity.

As hard as he tried, Waterkamp's attempts to land a blow on the expert missed their mark. Was it possible that the appeal for camp personnel to join the war effort was directed mainly at older SS guards? Was it conceivable that the order had not been circulated as widely as suggested? Was there evidence of similar orders going out after August 22, 1944, or was this an isolated event? The questions from the defense rained down over the course of several hearing days, but they mostly amounted to hopeful speculation. Hördler had spent long years studying and researching the minutiae of Nazi concentration camps, and many months examining Stutthof in particular. His confidence was hard to shake, and so were his facts. When the questions from the defense finally subsided, the historian's testimony was still standing.

Amid the wealth of evidence that Hördler presented in court, there was one small remark that stuck in my mind. It came on June 5, 2020, the thirty-fourth day of the trial, and marked the historian's last appearance in court. He was facing questions from Waterkamp once again, this time on Dey's youth and the political atmosphere that would have surrounded a boy growing up under Hitler. This was not Hördler's core area of expertise (and did not seem directly relevant to the trial), but he engaged with the question nonetheless. There was, he responded, a fundamental truth that had to be grasped to understand Nazi rule: the Third Reich had to be seen as a *Zustimmungsdiktatur*, literally a "consensual dictatorship." I had not heard this paradoxical term previously, but it instantly made sense. The regime was brutally repressive, and determined to crush even the slightest show of opposition and dissent. But it was not, at least until the final years of the war, fundamentally unpopular. There were small pockets of opposition and resistance but even these became mostly manifest only toward the end. "National Socialism was a consensual dictatorship. Most of German society did not have a problem [with Nazi rule]; they identified with it, and also shared the view that different people have a different value," Hördler explained.

Whether Bruno Dey shared that world view was, of course, impossible to demonstrate in court today. The defendant himself had insisted throughout the trial that he did not support the Nazis, and that he did not approve of the cruel and murderous treatment meted out to the prisoners at Stutthof. But Hördler's emphasis on the nature of the Zustimmungsdiktatur seemed important and relevant nonetheless. What happened in Germany between 1933 and 1945—all the policies, measures, and speeches that led to the gates of Stutthof and Auschwitz and the other camps—was not done against the wishes of the German people. Hitler had had, almost until the very end, their consent.

CHAPTER FIFTEEN

The culture of memory

Was the Holocaust a singular event? Until recently, the universal answer in Germany—and much of the rest of the world—would have been: yes, of course. The industrial murder of millions of Jews in concentration camp gas chambers, and the death of millions more through bullets, starvation, disease, and forced labor, has long been seen as a uniquely terrible crime. It took place as a result of unique historical circumstances, based on a unique ideology, and it imposed on the nation that committed this crime a unique historical responsibility. Over time, those tenets have become etched deeply into Germany's collective consciousness. So deeply, in fact, that they are fundamental not just to the country's approach to history but to the very idea of what it means to be German. In the words of Joachim Gauck, the former German president, "there is no German identity without Auschwitz."[1]

The centrality of the Holocaust in German society and politics today is linked inescapably to the notion that it was a singular, unprecedented event. That notion has been challenged on occasions, most notably during the *Historikerstreit*, the so-called "historians' dispute," in the late 1980s. That dispute was prompted by a newspaper article written by the prominent conservative historian Ernst Nolte, who argued that the Holocaust was not only comparable to the crimes of Stalinism but that the Nazi genocide was in some ways a response to those crimes. The article's very title—"The Past That Will Not Pass"—suggested to many readers that the ultimate goal of Nolte and his supporters was to indeed make Germany's past fade from view. It provoked widespread condemnation, as well as a fierce intellectual controversy that raged on for months, and that ultimately led to a hardening of the historical consensus: the Holocaust was indeed singular, as was Germany's responsibility and guilt. In the years since, that consensus view has come under attack again from the nationalist far right, as part of a broader assault on the nation's memory culture. As we saw in an earlier chapter, influential voices inside the far-right Alternative for Germany party have repeatedly called for a new German approach to history: they want Germans to feel pride rather than remorse when they look back in time. They regard the Nazi period as a minor stain on the country's record at most, and they take umbrage in particular at physical manifestations of national remorse, notably the Holocaust memorial in the heart of Berlin. Those attacks have resonated, though mainly along the political and intellectual fringes of German society.

More recently, however, the singularity of the Holocaust and other core principles of Germany's memory culture have faced scrutiny—and critique—also from a very different direction. Intellectuals and historians who can be broadly classified as belonging to the progressive left have started questioning those same tenets, albeit with an intention and with arguments that are distinct from those employed by the far right. The debate they have provoked is lively, contentious, often bitter, always serious—and deeply consequential. At the core of the clash, occasionally dubbed the Historikerstreit 2.0, is the question of how Germany relates to its past, and what lessons the country should draw for its future. The fact that it has played out at a time when the very last witnesses of the Holocaust—perpet-rators and victims alike—are leaving the stage, has given the controversy a particularly sharp edge.

Capturing what exactly this debate is about is not straight-forward. There is no clear or unified ideology at work, and much disagreement even within the opposing camps. At the most basic level, what brings together progressive critics of Germany's memory culture is a feeling of unease at the rituals and dogmas that surround that culture—and a growing sense that they are no longer fit for purpose.

One notable critique focuses on Germany's colonial legacy. It seeks to draw a historical connection between the Holocaust and earlier instances of colonial violence, notably the genocide of the Herero and Nama tribes in what was then known as German South-West Africa and is now Namibia. If the latter was indeed a precursor to the Nazi genocide four decades later, does that not cast a shadow over the singularity thesis? Others highlight the sweeping demographic changes in German society in recent decades and ask what meaning the Holocaust can have to the fast-growing number of German citizens who trace their ancestry not to the perpetrators, but to parents and grandparents from Turkey, Syria, or Ethiopia. If there really is no German identity without Auschwitz, can they ever become truly German? Another critique centers on the forms and rit-uals of German memory culture: how sincere, how effective and how meaningful are those rituals today? Why is the nation of perpetrators expending so much emotional and intellectual effort on identifying with the victims? And are the endless invocations of German guilt and responsibility an expression of genuine remorse, or merely a performative political gesture?

As arcane as some strands of this debate may appear, they resonate deeply in Germany today. The struggle over national identity always matters. But there is also the more immediate question of what a reassessment of the Nazi legacy might mean for German politics today. After all, the Holocaust bequeathed to the country's decision-makers a simple yet powerful moral compass: do whatever needs to be done to ensure that Auschwitz is not repeated. The malleability of that imperative—it has guided Berlin toward pacifism on some occasions and military conflict at other times—does not detract from its force, or its centrality. Indeed, the Holocaust and the legacy of the Nazi period has at times felt almost oppressively omnipresent in public life. When critics of the government's pandemic measures went out into the streets to demonstrate in 2020 and 2021, some showed up wearing yellow stars, inviting comparison with the persecution of Jews under Hitler's rule. When the far-right Alternative for Germany party entered parliament in 2017, warnings about the rise of Nazism two generations earlier were a constant refrain. When Germany agreed to supply Ukraine with weapons to defend itself against Russia's invasion in 2022, it did so only after agonized debates in which both supporters and detractors invoked the country's special historical responsibility in the region. German tanks must never again point their barrels at Russian forces, one side argued. Germany cannot remain on the sidelines when a powerful aggressor seeks to invade a peaceful nation in central Europe once again, the other side countered. The underlying argument was ultimately the same: because of Hitler and Auschwitz, Germany must.

My attempt to understand the new historians' clash began, appropriately enough, with a historian: Jürgen Zimmerer, a professor of history at the University of Hamburg and the director of an institute dedicated to studying German colonialism and its legacy, had long been one of the leading combatants.

An expert both on African colonial history and on genocide studies, Zimmerer had argued for years that Germany was failing to pay sufficient attention to a lesser-known stain on the country's twentieth-century history—the mass slaughter of the Herero and Nama tribes by colonial forces in German South-West Africa between 1904 and 1908. Faced with a rebellion against colonial rule by the two tribes, the German military unleashed a brutal campaign of subjugation, forcing parts of the population into the desert without supplies and herding others into concentration camps. The German commander, Lothar von Trotta, issued a notorious decree stating that "any Herero found inside the German frontier, with or without a gun or cattle, will be executed. I shall spare neither women nor children." As many as 100,000 Herero and Nama were killed, in what is now widely seen as the first genocide of the twentieth century.

It took Germany until 2021 to formally recognize its responsibility for the crimes against the Herero and Nama. After years of drawn-out negotiations with both the Namibian government and tribal representatives, Berlin agreed to pay €1.1bn as a "gesture of recognition of the immeasurable suffering inflicted on the victims."[2] Germany also returned skulls, bones, and other human remains taken from its former colony more than a century ago, as well as artifacts like a Bible and whip that once belonged to a leader of the Nama tribe. Zimmerer was a vocal supporter of Germany's belated attempt to recognize its colonial crimes. But he was also keen for the country to understand and acknowledge the connection between the German genocide in south-west Africa and the German genocide in central and eastern Europe less than four decades later. His thesis is summed up in the title of his best-known book, *From Windhoek to Auschwitz*.

What exactly, I asked Zimmerer in his spartan office at the Hamburg institute, was the connection between the two events? "The German military conducted a war of annihilation in Namibia, a genocidal war of annihilation," he responded. "And this principle of a genocidal war of annihilation we find repeated in the war against the Soviet Union. That is the argument." The Holocaust itself, Zimmerer continued, could not be detached from that war. And neither could it be detached from the Nazis' endeavor to create a *Rassestaat*, a state based on racial purity and racial distinctions, that split the German population into Jews and Aryans and explicitly barred any intermingling between the two. That idea of a German racial state was not a creation of the Nazis, Zimmerer told me. It had been pioneered in colonial German South-West Africa, which imposed, among other things, an official prohibition on interracial marriages.

Looming behind these arguments, however, was a deeper question about German history in the first half of the twentieth century: "Here is a military culture and a bureaucratic culture that within the space of forty years brings forward genocidal solutions on two occasions. I think this merits a closer look," he said. In Zimmerer's mind, ignoring that link was tantamount to minimizing German responsibility for the Holocaust, because it presented the Nazi crimes as an aberration: "It is exculpatory because you are decoupling the Holocaust from German history," he told me.

Zimmerer had been making this and similar arguments for many years, sparking debate in academic circles but not necessarily among the wider public. That changed in April 2021, when he co-authored an article in the weekly newspaper *Die Zeit* with Michael Rothberg, a professor of Holocaust studies at the University of California in Los Angeles. The title of their piece was as succinct as it was provocative, ending with a defiant exclamation mark: "End the comparison taboo!" Zimmerer and Rothberg acknowledged that there were "singular elements" to the Holocaust but insisted that these should not prevent "comparative approaches to the history and memory of the Holocaust."[3] They accused their critics of adopting a "provincial" approach to the Nazi genocide that ignored the global and colonial context in which it took place and left German responsibility for its colonial crimes unacknowledged. German guilt was not an "either/or" in the sense that remembering the Holocaust precluded remembrance of the African genocide, or vice versa. Only by recognizing both—and by understanding the connection between the two—could Germany and the world at large draw the right historical lessons.

In the German context, this was explosive stuff. Zimmerer and Rothberg had taken aim (in a roundabout way) at one of the central pillars of German memory culture. If the Holocaust was indeed part of a wider historical narrative, could it still be described as a singular event? And if it wasn't a singular event, what did that mean for Germany and Germany's historical responsibility today?

The debate around these questions grew more heated still a month later, when Dirk Moses, an Australian professor and genocide scholar at City College, New York, published a sharply worded essay called "The German Catechism."[4] Provocative in tone and content, Moses's piece fired a broadside into the cathedral of Germany's memory culture. German elites, he argued, "use the Holocaust to blend out other historical crimes." It was no wonder, therefore, that "descendants of victims of the German state, whose capacities for development were smashed by genocidal colonial warfare, experience German memory culture as racist." In Germany itself, meanwhile, that culture had hardened into a "catechism…internalized by tens of millions as the path to national redemption from its sinful past." The Holocaust, he added, "is more than an important historical event. It is a sacred

THE CULTURE OF MEMORY

trauma that cannot be contaminated by profane ones—meaning non-Jewish victims and other genocides—that would vitiate its sacrificial function." Moses also linked the debate about the singularity of the Holocaust to Germany's relationship with Israel. In the country's public discourse, anti-Zionism had become widely equated with antisemitism, making any criticism of Israel—notably over its treatment of Palestinians under Israeli occupation—taboo. "The moral hubris leads to the remarkable situation of gentile Germans lecturing American and Israeli Jews with [an] accusing finger about the correct forms of remembrance and loyalty toward Israel," Moses wrote.

His essay invited a backlash from historians of the Holocaust and the Nazi period such as Saul Friedländer and Norbert Frei, who took aim at the new "post-colonial" school of Holocaust studies in a series of articles. Frei accused Moses of writing "crude polemic and an activist agenda" and trying to "relativize the Holocaust in relation to other genocides."[5] Friedländer, meanwhile, insisted that antisemitism, not colonialism, was the animating force behind the Holocaust. Hitler saw the Jews as "evil per se...the triumph of the Jew would mean the death of the Aryan, the triumph of the Aryan would mean his redemption."[6] The Holocaust, he conceded, could not be understood in isolation. "But [the Holocaust's] true context was not colonialism but the millennia-old hatred of Jews and Jewry that determined, along with other factors, the paranoid ideology of the Nazis and their obsessive practices of purification."[7] Friedländer, a Holocaust survivor himself and the author of an important study of the Nazi genocide, also voiced concern at the attempt to redefine what the Holocaust meant for Germany's relationship to Israel. Germany had long been among the strongest supporters of the Jewish state, and German leaders had made clear on numerous occasions that this stance reflected a historical obligation deriving from the Holocaust. When former German chancellor Angela Merkel spoke to the Israeli parliament in 2008, she declared that this historical obligation was part of Germany's *Staatsräson*, its core national interest. "That is why for me as German chancellor the security of Israel will never be negotiable," Merkel added. The post-colonial approach to Holocaust memory was now trying to turn this historic German commitment on its head, Friedländer warned. "The implicit link between German support for Israel's defense and the general thrust of the post-colonial argument about the Holocaust can be summarized like this: the Holocaust is an example of extreme colonial violence. Israel is inflicting violent colonial rule on the Palestinians; German support for Israel means support for a state that is inflicting Nazi-like violence on a subjugated population."[8]

These were just some of the salvos in a debate that was—not unlike the initial historians' dispute in the 1980s—laced with bitterness and grievance. That it played out on the otherwise genteel culture pages of highbrow German newspapers and magazines did not hide the rawness of the emotions. It was underpinned by generational tensions: historians and intellectuals who had worn the progressive mantle in the 1970s and 1980s suddenly found themselves cast as forces of conservatism. Their earlier struggle—aimed at forcing German society to face its responsibility for the Holocaust in the first place—had been superseded by a new conflict aimed at broadening that responsibility in ways they found difficult to accept. On paper, the gap between the two camps often appeared quite small: no one disputed that there were unique and singular aspects to the Holocaust, or the central role of antisemitism in the Nazi world view, or even the legitimacy of drawing historical comparisons. Common ground, however, proved elusive.

The debate over the singularity of the Holocaust and its colonial context was (and remains) particularly fractious. But there were other—less contentious—reasons why a new wave of thinkers and writers felt the time had come to challenge Germany's mainstream memory culture. The most obvious centered on the nation's demographic makeup. According to the government census, more than twenty-two million people living in Germany today have a migrant background, more than a quarter of the total population.[9] Those numbers are the result of mass migration from poorer regions in Europe and beyond to a country that has been safe, prosperous, and in need of workers for many decades. Starting with the arrival of workers from Turkey, Italy, Greece, Spain, and Portugal in the late 1950s, Germany has seen distinct waves of immigration through the years: from Iran following the Islamist revolution in 1979; from Russia and other parts of the former Soviet Union in the early 1990s; from Yugoslavia during the civil wars that followed in the same decade; from Poland and eastern Europe after the enlargement of the European Union; and—finally and perhaps most strikingly—from Syria, Afghanistan, and other countries during the great refugee crisis of 2015 and 2016. These new Germans have brought their customs and culture with them, and often also their own historical traumas. One notable example are Jews from the former Soviet Union, who were invited to settle in Germany *en masse* after the collapse of the USSR. More than 200,000 took up this offer. Or the even larger contingent of Syrian refugees who found asylum—and in many cases a permanent new home—in Germany after the outbreak of civil war in their home country in 2011. For all their obvious differences, both Soviet Jews and Syrian Muslims had at least one thing in common: a sense of guilt and historical responsibility for the Holocaust was obviously not part of their identity. In one case because they were the direct descendants of the victims of the Nazi genocide. In the other because their ancestors had lived far from the killing fields of eastern Europe. Syria itself, meanwhile, had been a fierce enemy of Israel, the Jewish state, for more than half a century. Some Syrians arrived with their own deplorable variant of antisemitism, others with a simple dislike for Israel, but whatever Germans made of those sentiments it was hard to argue that they were comparable to the murderous antisemitism that animated the Nazis eighty years earlier.

The dilemma, in any case, was clear. No matter whether they had arrived from Ukraine, Syria, Portugal, Bosnia, Morocco, Russia, Britain, or Afghanistan, none of these new Germans could or should have felt any guilt or responsibility for the Holocaust. This meant, however, that none of them could truly become German. That was the consequence of the dictum formulated by Gauck, the former president: no German identity without Auschwitz. His words had been particularly stark but the notion behind them was widely shared and accepted. The Holocaust had become inextricably linked not just with German democracy but with the very idea of what it meant to be German.

Navid Kermani, a German novelist and writer of Iranian descent, came to realize this on his first visit to Auschwitz, after registering in advance for a tour in German and being handed a sticker that identified him as German. "Suddenly the sticker, really only a small piece of plastic foil, weighed heavily in my hand," he wrote in an essay afterward.[10] "It weighed heavily. Instinctively I took a deep breath before I attached the sticker to my chest, on which was written, black on white, just one single word: German. That was it, this action, this writing on my chest, like a confession: German. Yes, I was one of them, not by origin, not by blond hair, Aryan blood or such rubbish, but because of the language, and by extension because of the culture. If there

THE CULTURE OF MEMORY

was one single moment in which I became German, without ifs and buts, then it was not my birth in Germany, it was not my naturalization, it was not the first time I went to vote…It was last summer, when I attached the sticker to my chest, in front of me the barracks, behind me the visitor center: German. I went to my group and waited silently for our tour guide. At the gate, where it says '*Arbeit macht frei*,' the groups stood one by one for a bizarre photo. Only we were ashamed."

Kermani's essay is a powerful meditation on the power of culture, language, and literature, how they shape national identities, and German identity in particular. His own approach to German culture, and German memory culture, was both subtle and profound, and ultimately led him to accept that Auschwitz was part of his story, too. Others, he argued, will follow the same path. "Today there are many people in Germany who are not only German, who maybe don't even want to become German in the sense of identifying with the flag, the food, the traditions, who regard the fact that they are strangers and different as something beautiful and self-evident…When they visit Auschwitz, they will also wear the word 'German' on their chest. And finally, when they stand below the gate they will see Auschwitz as their own story."[11]

Kermani's essay was a moving and thoughtful piece of writing, but I was not sure that his readiness to absorb German responsibility for Auschwitz could serve as a model for other migrants. Most had arrived in their new home country carrying their own historical wounds, their own stories of guilt and pride. Why should they assume the legacy of Nazi Germany as well? Why indeed should they make the trip to Auschwitz in the first place?

In this new German clash of intellectuals, there was one voice I found especially intriguing. Per Leo, a Berlin-based novelist, historian, and essayist, set out his views on German memory culture in a 2021 book called *Tränen ohne Trauer,* "Tears without Sadness." The subtitle, *Nach der Erinnerungskultur,* made it clear that this was a book about the end of an era: "After Memory Culture." Leo's approach was idiosyncratic: there was a surprising amount of humor in the book, a willingness to offend and provoke, and originality, as well as a deeply personal approach that was rooted in family history. The cover of the German edition showed a photo of a frying pan with four fish fingers, arranged in a pattern that was reminiscent of a swastika.[12] In the uber-serious world of German public intellectuals, such quirkiness stood out.

I went to visit Leo in his Berlin flat one January morning to find out more. We sat down in his spacious front room, where a book-lined desk stood side by side with a well-equipped woodworking bench, tools hanging neatly from the wall. Leo, it turned out, had a side hustle importing and fixing wooden boxes from Morocco. Woodworking, he once wrote, was the only reputable profession he had ever had. (Boxes aside, Leo had also produced a 700-page doctoral thesis on graphology, the study of handwriting, and its role in Nazi ideology; a critically acclaimed novel; and a battery of essays and non-fiction books.)

Dressed in jeans, a blue woolen jumper, and black Converse, Leo looked every inch the middle-aged Berlin hipster. He was generous with his time, speaking almost without pause for the next three hours. I was curious to hear his origin story, how he had first become interested in the Nazi period, and when he first developed a feeling of unease at the way Germany was approaching its past. A key figure in that story, it turned out, was Leo's own grandfather, a senior SS officer during the Nazi years. While he was alive, he had refused to engage with all questions about his past. On his death, Leo inherited what he called the "poison cupboard," a section of his grandfather's library, separated by a little curtain, that contained his collection of Nazi and SS literature.

"That my grandfather had a Nazi past, an eminent one in fact, was not a secret. Everyone knew. But all the questions that arose from that—what exactly did he do? Why did he do that?—were not raised. I didn't even try. That was the surprising thing. But when he died, all this suddenly acquired a huge relevance for me, in the sense of a fascination for the theme, both politically and personally," Leo told me.

His fascination was channeled into two books: one was his thesis on graphology and antisemitism, an attempt to understand the cultural and intellectual origins of the Nazi obsession with classifying and dividing people. The other was a novel about his grandfather, the senior SS officer, and his grandfather's brother, Leo's great-uncle, who suffered from a hereditary disease and was subjected to the Nazis' forced sterilization program. What Leo discovered long before either work was finished, however, was that confronting your family's Nazi past was no longer an especially daring or conflictive endeavor. On the contrary: it was a well-trodden path to social and cultural recognition. "To confront your own Nazi past no longer meant breaking a norm, as it did in 1968, but it meant upholding a norm. Accordingly, it garnered meaning and it garnered applause," he said.

I had made much the same discovery in my mid-teens, when I first became interested in the Holocaust, traveled to Auschwitz, wrote about it—and won my own modest accolades for those efforts. The Holocaust held a deep fascination for me, too. I remembered wrestling—in the pompous way that teenagers do—with my own feelings of collective guilt and historical responsibility. It seemed like a burden at the time, but looking back I wondered whether a more honest assessment would be that talking and writing about the Holocaust was in fact a naked attempt to show off my moral superiority. *Look at me: I am conscious of my history and sensitive enough to feel its weight on my shoulders even today.* Reading Hannah Arendt many years later, I stumbled on a passage that captured my teenage state of mind with sarcastic precision: "It is quite gratifying to feel guilty if you haven't done anything wrong: how noble!"[13]

Arendt wrote that line in the 1960s, at a time when Germany's approach to the Holocaust was still characterized by repression rather than remembrance. The note of self-congratulatory smugness she detected at the time would become harder still to ignore in the decades that followed. The remorse and shame that many Germans felt and still feel about the Holocaust is without doubt genuine, as is the political impulse to ensure that the crimes of the Nazis are not repeated. But Germany's collective sense of shame is often matched by a collective sense of pride in the fact that the nation feels shame in the first place—and expresses that shame so openly in monuments, speeches, and school curricula on a daily basis. In a remarkable feat of historical jiu-jitsu, Germany managed to turn a negative into a positive: through remembrance and recognition, the terrible crime of the Holocaust became a new source of moral strength and even of moral superiority. Other nations, too, had dark chapters in their histories (not least neighboring Austria, which enthusiastically embraced Nazism after 1938 but later styled itself as Hitler's first victim). Yet none had been so thorough in examining those crimes, and atoning for them. In marketing parlance, Germany's memory culture became a unique selling point, an important part of the national brand, admired abroad like one of those precision-engineered luxury cars.

"A symbol in concrete for the utter incomprehensibility of the crime."
The Holocaust memorial in Berlin

German pride in that culture is validated not least by intellectuals from outside the country, who frequently hold up the
country's Erinnerungskultur (memory culture) as a model
for other countries to follow. Susan Neiman, a Berlin-based
American philosopher and writer, made that case explicitly with
regard to the U.S. and its legacy of racism and slavery. The title of
her book, *Learning from the Germans*, summed up the argument
in a manner most flattering to her adopted home.

Leo had followed all this with customary skepticism.
Germans, he noted in his book, took an almost competitive
approach to memory culture, as if preparing for the *Erinnerungs-
weltmeisterschaft*, the memory world cup.[14] It was a trophy—not
unlike the quadrennial football world championship—that
Germany pursued with single-minded obsessiveness, and,
indeed, great success.

What ultimately pushed Leo toward taking a more critical stance toward memory culture was the rise of the Alternative for Germany. The emergence of a new far-right party was greeted by many Germans with desperation and near-hysteria. Many of its policies and statements were indeed obnoxious. What bothered Leo, however, was the constant use of Nazi imagery and metaphors by the AfD's critics. Such parallels, he thought, were not only historically inaccurate, but ultimately self-defeating. The AfD thrived on them. The political outrage and the Nazi comparisons did not just fail to scare off its supporters, they reinforced a sense—nourished by populist parties everywhere— that the liberal mainstream had a lock on what could be said and what could not be said, and that the AfD was perfectly entitled to challenge that lock. If criticism of Germany's asylum policy made you a Nazi in the eyes of the political establishment, then perhaps it was the establishment that had lost its way. "We have to stop the new Nazi Party so that there is no repeat of a fascist regime—that's bullshit," Leo told me. "It doesn't work. You are just making the AfD stronger than it needs to be."

The response to the AfD was, he concluded, a symptom of a much wider problem. The Nazi period and the Holocaust were so dominant in the public discourse that Germans reached for comparisons constantly and reflexively. "The basic claim that our memory culture and Holocaust remembrance is the foundation of our democracy is utter nonsense. That does not mean we should forget the Holocaust, but it does mean that we need to think very carefully about how we remember it," Leo argued. A new approach was needed, not least, he added, because German society had changed so radically over the past decades. German society today could no longer be seen or understood as the successor of the society that had brought forward Hitler and Auschwitz. "You could make that case in 1978 or in 1988 and maybe even in the early 1990s. But you can't make that case now," Leo said. "There are three dimensions to this. First of all, we now have the fourth generation [after Nazism], the generation my daughter belongs to, which is the first generation that is no longer biographically touched and marked. We also have an immensely complex migration society with a very large Arab and Muslim population, and a small but very outspoken Jewish minority that is itself completely diverse. And then we have the population of the former GDR [Communist East Germany] that has a very different approach to the history of dictatorship and whose memory in many ways runs counter to Holocaust memory."

Germany's memory culture, in other words, was the product of a particular set of circumstances in a particular place and at a particular time. Imposing it on a new generation and on new German citizens whose roots were elsewhere was both misguided and ultimately futile.

Ulrike Jureit, a historian at the Hamburg Institute for Social research, had identified some of the flaws and contradictions in Germany's memory culture earlier than most. Her 2010 book *Gefühlte Opfer*, co-written with Christian Schneider, developed the idea that Germans had over time come to identify with the victims of the Holocaust so strongly that they felt like victims themselves.[15] She saw the Holocaust memorial in Berlin as a particularly striking example—a place where the descendants of the perpetrators went to experience what it felt like to be the victim. That, indeed, was the intention of the design, as the architect himself made clear in an interview: "What we wanted to do was to give people the feeling, maybe only for a brief moment, how it might feel to be in a state of hopelessness, to feel the ground below your feet shift, to feel isolated from your environment."[16] The monument, Jureit argued in her book, was representative of a memory culture that embraced identification with the victims of the Holocaust without examining the more complex and difficult question of who did the killing and why.

"Our society has concentrated on the victims for a very long time. That was the right thing to do. It was necessary. And it took a long time to get there," Jureit told me. "But our challenge is that—unlike in the U.S., in Britain, in France, or in Israel—we cannot have a memory culture that is centered on the victims. We have to examine these crimes as a society that succeeded the society of perpetrators."

What such a memory culture might look like was not easy to say. When societies look back at their history, Jureit said, they tend to commemorate either their triumphs or their victims. From Paris to Moscow and Washington to London, there was a well-established artistic vocabulary—a ready catalog of monuments and sculptures, but also of services, speeches and rituals—that immortalized the heroes and the victims of war. To this day, no such vocabulary exists to keep alive the memory of the murdered victims within a society of perpetrators. To remember without glorification was no easy task, Jureit conceded. "Finding an aesthetic response to a crime and its perpetrators is a challenge that only really arose in response to the Holocaust," she told me.

The concentration on the victim in German memory culture was just one of the problems identified by Jureit. She also took aim at many of the practices and forms of Holocaust commemoration today, which in her view had turned into empty rituals that no longer served their intended purpose. The moral posturing and excessive sentimentality often on display during these occasions were likely to trigger "exhaustion, boredom, and unease" even among those who wanted Germany to engage seriously and honestly with the Holocaust.

Both Jureit and Leo made the case—in many ways convincingly—for why Germany needed a new approach to remembering the Holocaust, and a new way of thinking about the historical lessons that should be drawn from it. What exactly that new approach would be, however, was far from clear. Leo's view was that German democracy was now so strong and so deeply entrenched that it no longer needed to be constantly reinforced and legitimized by referring to the Holocaust. Nor could the Holocaust remain a crucial element of German identity, at least not for the millions of new Germans. The country had to accept that the Holocaust would mean different things for different people, depending not least on when and where they were born. Leo was also keen to banish Nazi comparisons from the everyday political discourse in Germany. The far right in particular had to be defeated on terms and with arguments that were relevant today, not by constantly invoking the ghosts of the Third Reich.

"When I say that the Erinnerungskultur will be gone twenty years from now, that doesn't mean that we hopefully won't still be engaging in many ways, and intelligently, with National Socialism," Leo concluded. That Germany would and should continue to feel responsibility for the victims of the Holocaust was beyond doubt. What flowed from that responsibility in practical and political terms, however, was much less certain. "Of course we need to honor the victims," he said. "But this cannot be the basis for our politics."

The only certainty that emerged from my conversations with Leo, Jureit, Zimmerer, and others was this: nothing was settled about Germany's memory culture. Perhaps nothing ever would be. Over the years, Germans have grown accustomed to the periodic eruption of controversy and debate in this field. To some, there may even be something reassuring about the heat and fury generated by these intellectual clashes. They show that the Holocaust remains a live issue, and one that still has the capacity to make the country stop and think. As long as we argue, we won't forget. That, in essence, was also the conclusion drawn by the U.S. writer and poet Clint Smith, who examined Germany's memory culture in 2022 in an attempt to draw lessons for the struggle to commemorate the legacy of slavery and racism in his own country. "No stone in the ground can make up for a life. No museum can bring back millions of people," he wrote. "It cannot be done, and yet we must try to honor those lives, and to account for this history, as best we can. It is the very act of attempting to remember that becomes the most powerful memorial of all."[17]

CHAPTER SIXTEEN

The final verdict

"The following judgment is entered in the name of the people..."

Shortly after 11 a.m. on Thursday, July 23, 2020, presiding judge Anne Meier-Göring delivered her verdict in the criminal trial against Bruno Dey. It was prefaced, like every verdict in a German court, with the introductory formula "*Im Namen des Volkes*," a phrase so commonly heard that few lawyers pay it any attention. Today, however, it seemed pertinent. What the court was about to say was more than the interpretation of the law by an individual jurist. It was a judgment delivered—quite literally—in the name of the German people, representing a shared moral and legal stance that transcended, or aspired to transcend, the individual defendant and his judge. It was the same formula, of course, that had prefaced the verdicts acquitting Nazi perpetrators in the years after the war, and the minuscule sentences imposed on hardened SS murderers. Those judgments too had been rendered in the name of the people. The formula hadn't changed, and neither had the law. What had changed—suddenly, and ever so late in the day—was the way Germany and its judges viewed the crimes and contributions of men like Bruno Dey.

I was not in the courtroom when the verdict was read out. COVID restrictions meant that the majority of reporters had to follow the final day of the trial through an audio transmission in a separate room a floor below. I was disappointed but had no cause for complaint: the court operated a rotation system and since I had been allowed to sit in the courtroom the previous day, for the final intervention made by Dey himself, it was my turn to stay outside. As had been the case throughout the trial, court rules forbade journalists from making their own audio recording of the final day, which meant I had to write down by hand as much of the judgment as I could.

There had been plenty of time to consider the case, and no shortage of arguments to ponder. The court had heard the last witness statements more than two weeks before the verdict. Meier-Göring had then devoted five entire hearing days to the closing pleas from the prosecution, the defense, and the lawyers representing Stutthof survivors and their descendants. The last person to speak before the verdict was Bruno Dey himself, who read out a personal statement at the end of the forty-fourth hearing day, the penultimate of the trial. He wanted to express his "thoughts and feelings," the defendant told the judge. "That I had to answer in court for my time in Stutthof seventy-five years later has cost me a lot of strength. But it also gave me the chance to confront this time once more," Dey continued. "I am accused of being jointly responsible for the death and the abuse of people because I stood guard, or had to stand guard. I shared my recollections truthfully and answered questions as best I could. I want to emphasize once more that I never volunteered to join the SS or any other unit. And certainly not for a concentration camp. That I had to stand guard in this system weighs on me heavily even today. Had I seen an opportunity to escape from this deployment I would certainly have used it."

Dey's words until here were a repeat of his well-rehearsed lines of defense: I never wanted to be in Stutthof and once there I saw no way of getting out. But the defendant hadn't finished yet. "It was only in this trial, and through the testimonies of the witnesses and historians, that I came to realize the full extent of the cruelties and the suffering," he said. "Today I want to apologize to the people who went through this hell of madness, and to their loved ones and descendants. Something like this must never be repeated. Thank you."

There was nothing redemptive about Dey's last words—no sweeping moment of self-examination or eloquent exposure of late guilt. Having watched him over the course of many months, I doubted that he was capable of developing and expressing such insight. His statement seemed important and valuable all the same. Dey had said what he wanted to say, in his own words, simply and apparently with honesty. It included an apology to the victims, and recognition of the cruelty of the endeavor he was involved in. It stopped far short of a full admission of personal guilt, and it came very late in the trial. But his skeletal acknowledgment of the victim's suffering at least had the benefit of sincerity. This was not a speech ghostwritten by Dey's lawyer. It was a flawed but genuine summary of the defendant's thoughts at the end of a grueling trial. It was all the court could ask for, and all the court was going to get.

Dey's personal statement followed a closing speech by his lawyer, Stefan Waterkamp, that marshaled the case for the defense one last time, and urged the court to acquit the accused. Waterkamp's plea was based on a series of arguments both legal and factual, some of which had already been debated at length during the trial. Perhaps his strongest line of defense concerned the broad definition of the principal crimes—the murders that took place at Stutthof—and how Dey's own responsibility as a guard related to them. Even in the case of Demjanjuk and other late Holocaust trials, the courts had taken care not to stretch the limits of previous jurisprudence too far: John Demjanjuk, for example, had been found guilty as an accessory to sixteen separate instances of killing, each one representing one specific transport of deportees. In the case of Oskar Gröning, the verdict was limited to the (admittedly very large) number of killings that were conducted over a period of only a few months as part of the *Ungarn-Aktion*. Dey, in contrast, had been charged for his role in murders that spanned much of his time in Stutthof, notably the more than five thousand deaths that resulted from neglect, illness, and hunger. In Waterkamp's view, this was a crucial weakness in the prosecution's case. For a start, Germany's highest court had never sanctioned such an expansive definition of the role of the accessory in Holocaust cases. None of the previous cases argued before lower courts had taken a similar line. In the case of Oskar Gröning, Waterkamp told the court, the verdict had been based on a "concrete principal crime…with a concrete contribution from the defendant that was directly related to the mass murder of people." Recent rulings by the *Bundesgerichtshof*, the Federal High Court, had confirmed this jurisdiction, and signaled that "merely belonging to a guard company is not sufficient for the attribution of all the murders" that took place during that time, he added. In the case of Dey, Waterkamp insisted, a "concretely defined principal crime cannot even be intuited." The prosecution had, in other words, taken the new legal doctrine that was established in the Demjanjuk trial, and confirmed in the Gröning case, and pushed it to the extreme. For the Hamburg court to find Dey guilty of all charges, it would have to enter new legal territory, and do so in open defiance of Germany's highest criminal court.

Waterkamp was not wrong in his assessment, but I was not alone in doubting that his line of argument would cut through. Looking back at the Demjanjuk trial and subsequent court decisions, there was a clear pattern: in ruling after ruling, lower courts had consciously and deliberately decided to go beyond the traditional jurisprudence of the high court. Their defiance of the *Bundesgerichtshof* was no accident—it was what these trials were at heart all about. Over the past decade, case by case, they had pushed the legal doctrine ever further toward expanding the area of culpability: from extermination camps like Sobibor to concentration camps like Auschwitz; from individual transports like in the Demjanjuk case to the complete extermination of Hungary's Jews in the Gröning ruling; from the core of the murder machine to the outer zones, where guards like Bruno Dey did their duty. What is more, there was strong evidence that the higher court itself was prepared to rethink its previous stance: on the one occasion it had been asked to review a recent Holocaust verdict—the Gröning case—it ultimately upheld the lower court's ruling. The story of the late Holocaust trials was a dynamic one, and there was every reason to believe that the Hamburg court would try to shift the case law further once more.

Waterkamp was not yet finished, however. For his next argument, he turned to the reality of life in the camp, and the personality of the accused. Was it reasonable, he asked, to expect a young man like Dey to defy his orders and find a way to leave Stutthof? This issue had been debated for hours during the trial, and had been the subject of a forensic analysis by the historian Stefan Hördler in May, two months before the verdict. Waterkamp had voiced skepticism of the historian's conclusions at the time, and saw no reason to shift his view now. "There was no such thing as not following orders at this time, not even in the case of an evidently criminal order," he told the court. "How of all people should an eighteen-year-old living in such a society and in such a place at that time step out of line?"

Dey, he added, saw no alternative to doing his service at

Stutthof. Even if that conclusion was ultimately found to be wrong (as the historical experts had shown), there was still a strong reason for acquittal. Dey, the lawyer argued, had made what is known as a "mistake in law," a term in criminal law that is applied when the offender "lacks the awareness of acting unlawfully." If that error was unavoidable, the court must find the defendant not guilty. For law students and academics, the byzantine doctrinal disputes surrounding mistakes in law are of crucial importance. In the courtroom, however, their practical application is limited, largely because such errors are rarely found to be "unavoidable." Dey was a case in point: had he ever asked his comrades about this? Had he approached a superior officer? Had Dey not noticed that other guards were leaving Stutthof to join the war? Had he not seen the official announcements circulating in Stutthof and other camps asking for volunteers for the front? Dey had been asked these questions over and over again during the trial. Not once did he produce even a shred of evidence to suggest that he made an effort to understand the true nature of his situation.

The truth was that Waterkamp held a weak hand, and he knew it. He had briefed Dey and his family long before the final judgment that a guilty verdict was the most likely outcome. Irrespective of the law and judicial precedent, recent experience had shown that German judges were not inclined to conclude a landmark Holocaust trial with an acquittal. Since Demjanjuk, the only way for former concentration camp guards to avoid a sentence was for a trial to be halted on health grounds. For Waterkamp, therefore, the key objectives at this point in the trial were to ensure that his client stayed out of jail and to avoid financial ruin for the Dey family. In his bid for leniency in sentencing, the lawyer leaned heavily on the character of the defendant, his relative youth and inexperience at the time, and the fact that Dey was by all accounts no fervent supporter of the Nazi regime. "The defendant had no National-Socialist, anti-semitic disposition. He felt sorry for the prisoners, and he realized that, at least as far as the Jewish prisoners were concerned, they were being held there without any justification," Waterkamp told the court. Dey's upbringing and background had made it especially hard for him to confront his superiors and chart an independent course, he added: "He saw no way out of the guard duty. You have to consider that the defendant had been raised by his parents to stay away from trouble. He was told not to take part in confrontations, and when he did, at school, he was blamed and not supported morally."

Waterkamp also returned to a line of argument he had made

Bruno Dey is wheeled toward the Hamburg
courtroom, followed by his daughter.

on the opening day of the trial—that Dey should not be made a scapegoat for the appalling failure of German courts over many decades to punish the perpetrators of the Holocaust. The desire to correct this historic mistake was understandable, he said, but it should not lead to an overly harsh penalty. Adopting a rare tone of sarcasm, the defense lawyer noted: "The signal from the courts that is really at the heart of this trial—'We are different, we have learned from the past'—is, as far as I know, not one that should play a role when it comes to sentencing."

Dey, he concluded, was unlikely to survive a prison term, and neither might his wife. Should the court indeed decide to enter a guilty verdict, a possible prison sentence should be suspended. Waterkamp ended his speech with an appeal he knew had little chance of resonating with the court: "Ultimately I plead for an acquittal."

The defense had the last word. But the interventions by Waterkamp and Dey had been preceded by hours and hours of arguments and appeals from the prosecution and the lawyers representing Stutthof survivors, urging the court to find the defendant guilty. The first to speak was Lars Mahnke, the chief prosecutor, who had been working on the Dey case for the past four years. His plea was, like most of his interventions, brief and to the point—and not without provocation. After a short summary of high-court doctrine on the role of the accessory, the prosecutor noted that recent rulings had included a "certain erosion of the borders" of the concept. It was not necessary, for instance, that the action taken by the helper was in any way causal for the success of the primary crime. It was not even necessary for the helper to be aware of the concrete nature of the mass murder that was at the center of the principal crime. With that in mind, Mahnke continued, one might ask whether "the

SS man who stands on the tower in a SS uniform and carrying a gun is aiding the murder of six million Jews. One could have this thought."

This was a radical idea indeed, and one that would have turned decades of German Holocaust jurisprudence entirely on its head. Mahnke was floating the idea that the Holocaust itself could be treated as one concrete and singular crime, and that all perpetrators and participants should therefore be found guilty of the crime in its entirety—no matter whether they were posted in Auschwitz or Stutthof or at SS headquarters in Berlin, and regardless of when and for how long they were active. Bruno Dey, an accessory to murder in six million cases? There was little time for that thought to sink in, before Mahnke himself dismissed the idea. All criminal law, he continued, was based on the principle of individual guilt. "It cannot be right that someone like [Adolf] Eichmann is punished in the same way as an SS man [who served] as the last link in the chain of these gigantic murders."

As Mahnke himself conceded, the Dey case was almost certainly the wrong case to explore such radical avenues in earnest. But I wondered whether the chief prosecutor should have lingered a little longer on his thought experiment. Defining the Holocaust itself as the principal, indivisible crime did not strike me as absurd at all—it was what most historians had been doing for decades. It was certainly no less absurd than the excruciating efforts by German prosecutors and judges in preceding decades to split the Nazi genocide into tiny bite-sized pieces. I had to think of the Frankfurt Auschwitz trial, in which the court went to strenuous lengths to show that the accused had signed an order for fresh supplies of Zyklon B for use in the gas chambers. Or even the 1955 trial against Paul Werner Hoppe, the commandant of Stutthof, in which the court in Bochum convicted the defendant of murder in just a few hundred cases. That comparison in particular underlined how far the debate had shifted: Dey, the teenage guard on the watchtower, was on trial for aiding the killing of more than five thousand people while the man charged with running the entire camp—from the watchtowers to the gas chamber—had been sentenced for a fraction of that number. Expanding the murders under review by the court to all six million Jewish victims of the Holocaust in the case of Dey would have seemed, on balance, not just disproportionate but grossly unfair.

That Dey acted as an accessory to murder was, Mahnke argued, beyond doubt. By guarding the camp, he had clearly contributed to the functioning of Stutthof, and hence to the killings that took place during his time there. Dey had recognized that what happened before his eyes was wrong. None of the standard justifications or defenses allowed under the German criminal code were applicable. There was, in particular, no ground to assume a case of necessity, which can justify or excuse culprits who act wrongfully because they are desperate to avert a danger to their own life, limb, or liberty. Dey had not felt that desperation, which is why he never even bothered to investigate ways of leaving Stutthof in the first place. "This is not [a person] acting under necessity. This is being an accessory to murder," Mahnke declared.

The prosecutor then turned to the crucial—and, in the eyes of most observers, the only contentious—decision that was left to the court: the sentence. The arithmetic was simple: a prison sentence of two years or less could be suspended, which would allow Dey to live out his final years in freedom. A sentence of more than two years meant sending the 93-year-old defendant to prison. Mahnke weighed the arguments. On the one hand the court had to recognize that the crimes under examination took place seventy-five years ago, and that Dey had led a life free of crime ever since; that he would very likely never have broken the law—let alone been involved in mass murder—had he not lived under the Nazis; and that he himself was not a supporter of the regime. Yet those arguments, Mahnke concluded, were not strong enough to outweigh the severity of the crime. "We are obliged, even after seventy-five years, to send a clear warning to all. Murder does not expire. No one should feel that they can get away with it," he said. This was not a case of an individual who failed to resist a totalitarian dictatorship: "We do not punish the absence of resistance," Mahnke said. "Those who do not resist have to make a reckoning with themselves. But when people become part of the organized mass murder, when they stand on the watchtower in uniform and with a gun in their hand, then things are different. Then everyone must know that it is no longer enough to look away and flee into solitary individualism, to rely on criminal orders, and wait for the end. In such a situation, there must be an end to loyalty toward criminals," Mahnke said.

"In such a situation, everyone should expect the soldier to climb down from the watchtower, to hand over his gun, and to declare that he can no longer go along with this, that he wants to return to the Wehrmacht or go to the front. That was evidently possible. That is not what Bruno Dey did."

The prosecutor ended his plea with his sentencing request: three years.

The question of how to punish—as opposed to whether to punish—had evidently posed a challenge also to the Stutthof survivors and their lawyers. Some backed the prosecutor's call for a three-year sentence, but others stressed that punishment —let alone retribution—was not what their clients were asking for. Several lawyers said they had been instructed specifically by the survivors to ask for Dey to be spared time in prison. Some found deeply personal words at the end of a trial that had clearly left a mark on jurists and survivors alike. Pleading on the forty-second day of the trial, a lawyer called Markus Horstmann recounted a conversation with one of the co-plaintiffs, a Stutthof survivor from Israel, who expressed a remarkable final wish for the defendant: "Maybe this trial will allow the perpetrator to find peace at the end of his life. I want the perpetrator to find his peace. We all want you to find this peace."

Speaking as a German born long after the end of the war, Horstmann also addressed the generational tension underlying the trial. "This is not about pointing the finger at you," he told Dey. "I was born in 1974, and grew up in a time when everything was great. It would be too easy to put you in a corner and say you have done something wrong. How can I presume to say that I would have acted differently as a seventeen-year-old? Looking at the case with humility no one can say how they would have acted as a seventeen-year-old at the time."

Christine Siegrot, another lawyer for Stutthof survivors, told the court her client, the survivor Abraham Korycki, who now lived in Israel, had a personal message for the defendant. She then turned to Dey directly: "Herr Korycki has asked me to tell you that in his whole time in Stutthof he never encountered a guard who was friendly toward him or showed sympathy even in a hidden way. Every day he had to bear the feeling that his life or death depended only on the mood and insanity of his guards. He felt that his life was in danger every minute of the day. He was terribly afraid—terribly afraid of guards like you."

Korycki, she concluded, had testified at the Hamburg trial with a clear sense of purpose: "He said he did not come for revenge, but that he did not forgive: 'I want the world to know what happened. Everyone must know, and especially the next generation.'"

The most substantial plea—and the longest by far from any of the lawyers acting for Stutthof survivors—came from Cornelius Nestler, the law professor from Cologne, who provided a sweeping overview—and condemnation—of Germany's historic failure to prosecute Nazi criminals after the war. Doctrinal disputes and legal arguments were only part of the reason for this failure, he argued. It had ultimately been down to people: to the individual willingness of prosecutors and judges to do the right thing. That was true even today.

What did the survivors want out of this trial, Nestler asked. His own client, Judith Meisel, had a very clear idea. "First of all she wants clarity that the Shoah was not just Auschwitz, or [the killings] of the Einsatzgruppen, or Treblinka and Majdanek, but that almost all the concentration camps inside Germany were places of organized mass destruction, often under the eyes of the local population. Secondly, [she wants] the murders and the inhumanity in Stutthof to serve as a warning to the world of what racism can lead to. And—and this is above all directed at you, Herr Dey—she wants a determination that it was wrong to take part in mass murder. Even as a guard, not even eighteen years old, one should not have taken part."

Meier-Göring and her fellow judges had listened carefully as the arguments and pleas swayed back and forth. Now, finally, the moment had come to give her verdict: guilty or not guilty. The judge's voice, so familiar to everyone in the room after nine months of hearings, rang loud and clear: "The accused is guilty of being an accessory to murder in 5,232 cases and an accessory to attempted murder in one case. He is sentenced to a juvenile prison term of two years. The enforcement of the juvenile sentence is suspended."

It had taken forty-five hearing days to reach this point. Hours and hours of testimony had been heard in court, dozens of witnesses had spoken, and Dey himself had been questioned relentlessly week after week. The world had changed dramatically since the start of this criminal trial, as evidenced by the face masks and plexiglass separation walls on display inside the courtroom. The outbreak of the COVID-19 pandemic in February 2020, at the midpoint of the trial, had come close to putting a premature stop to the proceedings. But the court had persevered, and now it had made its judgment: Dey was an accessory to murder on a scale almost unimaginable. Five thousand, two hundred, and thirty-two lives cut short. I tried to imagine those lives branching out into children and grandchildren and great-grandchildren, along the decades all the way to this day in court. The loss was too immense to take in, and yet it was tiny when set against the totality of the murders. Oskar Gröning, the Bookkeeper of Auschwitz, had been sentenced as an accessory to murder in 300,000 cases. Even that number captured barely one in twenty of the Jewish men, women, and children murdered by the Nazis.

The crime that Bruno Dey was sentenced for was terrible. The sentence itself, however, was far from draconian. Crucially—and controversially, as would soon become clear—Meier-Göring had decided to impose the maximum term that still allowed her to suspend the prison sentence. This meant he would only have to go to jail if he broke the law during that two-year period, or violated the specific conditions of his probation. Given Dey's advanced age and his decades-long record as a law-abiding citizen, this was of course exceedingly unlikely. The defendant would almost certainly never see the inside of a prison cell. Nor was he facing financial ruin. Meier-Göring could have ordered

Dey to bear much of the cost of the trial but she didn't. The defendant would have to pay for his own legal costs but nothing else. Crucially, the legal costs of the forty co-plaintiffs with their phalanx of lawyers, would be borne by the German state.

The guilty verdict did not, in the end, come as a surprise. The sentence, too, was—at least in my mind—in line with expectations. Sending a 93-year-old man to prison would have seemed harsh, particularly given the special circumstances surrounding the case. A three-year sentence, at least part of which Dey would have had to spend in prison, might also have contravened a historic ruling by the German constitutional court demanding that every prisoner, even a murderer, must have at least a chance to live out his final days in freedom. Meier-Göring had agonized over the sentence, all the same, "hour by hour, [for] days and even weeks," as she admitted in her ruling.

It was an exceedingly difficult call to make, and Meier-Göring knew perfectly well that she was certain to cause anger and disappointment either way. (The two-year suspended sentence indeed attracted sharp criticism from some survivor groups, and prompted one set of co-plaintiffs to launch a legal appeal, which was later dropped.) Yet to me, and perhaps also to the judge, the sentence itself was less significant than the words that followed. As the minutes rolled by, and my notepad filled with page after page of shorthand scribbles, I realized that Meier-Göring had written a remarkable—and a remarkably ambitious—judgment. She had pushed the boundaries of criminal responsibility further than previous judges, not least by finding Dey guilty of being an accessory to attempted murder in one case. A seemingly small part of the ruling, it made clear that the mere act of deporting a person to a concentration camp constituted an attempt on their life. In some ways this was a statement of the obvious but Meier-Göring's was the first court to make it part of its verdict.

More consequential still was that she had tried to provide a psychological and moral response to the questions that had drawn me to this trial in the first place, many months ago. She used simple, declarative sentences—almost as if speaking to a child—to capture an impossibly complex theme: how was this possible? What made normal human beings like Bruno Dey become accomplices to the most terrible crime ever committed? And was it right to punish men like him, even after so many decades of peace and stability? This was a historic trial. Her verdict, I realized, would rise to the occasion.

Court etiquette demanded that everyone present in the courtroom stood while the guilty verdict and the sentence—contained in the opening paragraphs of the ruling—were read out. Having pronounced Dey guilty, Meier-Göring asked the court to sit while she continued with her oral justification. Her first words were frank and personal—and set the tone for what was to follow: "This trial was difficult. Both legally and personally. It has been trying for all of us, and it has followed us outside the courtroom. It has not let us go," she said. It had been demanding above all for the survivors of Stutthof, asked to relive the horrors of their youth in the witness stand and to confront their most painful memories in public once again. "They felt it was their duty not to succumb to relief and suppression, not to forget but to tell. Over and over again."

Then she turned to the defendant: "You too, Herr Dey, felt a duty to face this criminal trial. For this you have already had expressions of respect from some co-plaintiffs. We too recognize this. You answered all our questions and the questions of the co-plaintiffs, and so gave us an insight into an unimaginably dark time, the last months inside the concentration camp Stutthof and of National Socialism in Germany."

Where this sense of duty came from, she could not say. "Maybe you simply knew that you could not resist [standing trial] in a state governed by the rule of law. Or maybe you unconsciously wanted to confront your guilt, without ever having to express it? A guilt that you refused to recognize until the end, until your final words, even though you told us that this trial had made you confront your time in Stutthof once again, which you now recognized as a 'hell of madness.'"

The defendant's failure, the judge continued, was to not see his own responsibility for the crimes at Stutthof. "You still see yourself as a mere observer of this hell, Herr Dey. Not as one of the people who personally helped to maintain this hell. And yet you were one of the helpers of this man-made hell. That is part of the objective truth that this trial has established." Dey, she added, had not managed to acknowledge his personal guilt, but he had "approached" it.

"In this trial we have examined a period of history that we cannot understand, as much as we try," Meier-Göring said. "Whose cruelties exceed our imagination. But that were inflicted by humans on other humans—by very normal people like the defendant Dey on very normal people like Rosa Bloch, Halina Strnad, Marek Dunin-Wąsowicz, David Ackermann, Adam Koyski, Henri Zajdenwergier, who we all heard here as witnesses. How was this possible? How was it possible that you, Herr Dey, a person who later spent an entire life orderly and free from crime, as a seventeen- and eighteen-year-old young man saw the suffering of these people, but did not suffer yourself? How was it possible that you, who were not even a fervent Nazi, found it so easy to accept that the co-plaintiffs were deprived of their humanity and reduced to a number? How was it possible that putting on an SS uniform and being told to stand guard in a concentration camp was enough to turn you into a diligent guard—and to forget your humanity and your conscience?

285

How could you get used to the horror, and after a short period of time consider it merely boring?"

This was, Meier-Göring suggested, the essential lesson that should be drawn from the Stutthof trial: that the Holocaust was no historical abstraction but the result of individual decisions and actions and omissions. Decisions and actions and omissions like those made by Bruno Dey. "You and we have to understand that you as a human being inflicted this terrible injustice on the co-plaintiffs as human beings. That is why, in a state governed by the rule of law—which Germany thankfully is today—you must be punished. Even at the very end of your life. Because murder does not expire. We all must understand that people were capable of doing such things to other people—and that they are capable still today."

The Holocaust, she continued, was not merely the work of sadists. It was the work of "perfectly normal people" like Bruno Dey. "Thousands, hundreds of thousands, even millions of perfectly normal people in Germany did this to perfectly normal people, thousands, hundreds of thousands, millions of Jews, Poles, Lithuanians, Hungarians, Russians, and dissidents. Just like that. Out of indifference. Out of a sense of duty. Because of an order. Because of an individual and collective failure of conscience."

The courtroom had followed the judge's speech in complete silence. I too was transfixed. Her words cut through the quiet like thunderclap. In a few short phrases Meier-Göring had sketched a typology of guilt that captured not just the moral disaster of Nazi Germany but that seemed painfully relevant today. It was not just Hitler and Himmler and Heydrich and Hoppe who did this. They did this, they could only do this, because they had the support—sometimes enthusiastic, sometimes reluctant, but support nonetheless—of millions of ordinary Germans.

The Holocaust was possible not because millions of Germans delighted in the crime, but because millions of Germans failed, often in small ways, to do the right thing at the right time. This great evil was the sum of countless moral failings, small and large, and of countless decisions made not by monsters but by perfectly normal human beings. It was that human, individual aspect of the Holocaust that Meier-Göring was determined to bring to the fore—and it was the reason why she firmly rejected the metaphor of the concentration camp as a killing machine. "The SS guards are supposed to be 'small cogs' that kept the 'killing machine' running. No. The defendant Dey was not a small cog, he was a human being and one of hundreds of thousands of people in Germany that furthered and supported the crimes of Hitler and Himmler, Glücks, and Hoppe.[1] And this was no killing machine but mass murder invented by people, organized by people, and implemented with the help of a multitude of people. We believe the metaphor of the killing machine obscures this perspective, and depersonalizes once more the victims and the perpetrators. And this metaphor also allows us to push the monstrosity of the crimes of National Socialism away from us and from our time today. As if to say that the killing machine has been switched off. That it belongs to the past and has nothing to do with us and our society today."

The longing to create a distance between past and present was understandable, the judge added. But it was beside the point. "The decisive questions raised by this trial were: what crimes against humanity are humans capable of, and what brings people to commit cruelties like those at Stutthof concentration camp, or to take part in them? Because it is only from the answers to these questions that we as humans can learn for the future. That is why the warning is not: do not allow another Nazi killing machine. It is rather—and this was shown also in this trial and especially in the personality of the defendant: resist the beginnings, when people are being degraded, excluded, humiliated, and deprived of their rights. Resist the beginnings, when racism and injustice become acceptable in society. Don't look away, but take note when people are robbed of their dignity. Be compassionate, and be mindful of your own indifference, your selfishness, your comfort of obedience and your ability to live with injustice! Think for yourself and question what you are being asked to do. Don't obey orders when they call for inhumanity, injustice, and murder. Respect human dignity—at all costs. And yes, even when that cost is your own safety. That is the message of this trial," she declared. "Only then can you say: 'I have not made myself guilty.'"

That this was a hard imperative to follow, especially for a young man like Dey, was clear, not least to the judge. But there was, she insisted, no alternative. "Of course this is asking a lot—especially from someone who was only seventeen or eighteen at the time like yourself, Herr Dey. And of course none of us knows how we would have behaved if we had been in your place. But precisely because of that the message has to be: whoever behaves like the accused Dey is guilty and has to answer for it until the end of his life. That is the just response to the unjust Nazi state and the crimes against humanity committed by human beings under this regime."

The judgment was not finished, but this was all I could take in for the moment. I would return to the ruling in the weeks and months that followed, and read certain passages over and over again. But the essence of Meier-Göring's message had been impossible to miss at the time, even with a newspaper deadline looming a few hours away and a pile of barely legible notes spread out on the table in front of me. Here was an answer—perhaps the only answer—to the question that had vexed me since the first day of the Stutthof trial. Was it right to punish a man for failing to do the right thing, when the right thing was so hard to do? When no one—not even the judge handing down the guilty verdict—could say with confidence they would have acted differently?

Meier-Göring acknowledged the dilemma, but her response was clear. We must punish regardless. Her conclusion was above all the result of sound legal deductions: like any good jurist, she had worked her way through a thicket of factual and legal problems, guided by law and precedent and common sense, and emerged with a verdict that seemed—with hindsight at least—inescapable. Bruno Dey was an accessory to murder. He had objectively helped the SS murder thousands of people at Stutthof. Subjectively, he knew what was happening, he knew what he was doing, and he knew that what he was doing was wrong. Despite his protestations, there was no basis for exculpation. In this sense, the trial of Bruno Dey was not so different from any other criminal trial. Meier-Göring had simply applied the tools of her trade, with rigor and clarity of thought.

But there was more to her verdict than legal mechanics. By convicting Bruno Dey she had extended the sphere of criminal guilt to include the lowest rungs of the concentration camp hierarchy, and to a perpetrator who for decades was thought to be too insignificant to prosecute. Mahnke's thought experiment in his final plea, asking whether Dey should not have been charged for aiding the murder of all six million Jewish victims of the Holocaust, had been largely speculative. But together with the verdict it pointed toward a profound insight, one that German courts and jurists had been able to internalize only too late: that the Holocaust was, directly or indirectly, indeed the work of millions; that the guilt of German society as a whole went far deeper than those court rulings in the 1950s and 1960s implied;

that these crimes ought to have been punished much earlier. Dey was, by dint of his proximity to the killing and his specific role, much closer to the sphere of guilt than most of his compatriots. But if that sphere could be widened to include him, why not enlarge it further? What about the railway schedulers ensuring the deportation train made its way swiftly to its final destination? What about the policeman back in Berlin or Cologne or Darmstadt who helped round up the Jewish population? What about the neighbors who denounced the Jewish family hiding in the attic? What about the nurses who were on hand when SS medics gassed the disabled? What about the millions of ordinary soldiers fighting on the Eastern Front who observed—and at times more than observed—the mass killings that took place in the lands they conquered? What about the very ordinary men and women back home, who voted for the Nazi Party, saluted the Führer, sent their children to the Hitler Youth, and looked the other way as their country descended into criminal madness? Would the Holocaust have been possible without them? Are they not guilty as well?

We cannot know what we would have done in Bruno Dey's position. I know I can't. But, to all of us, the trial of Bruno Dey ended with a message, and with a warning: *Don't look away. Be compassionate. Resist the beginnings. Respect human dignity—at all costs.* Meier-Göring's words applied not just to Dey and his fellow SS men, but to everyone at the time, and to everyone today. Hard as they may be to follow, they must be followed. And they must be followed even in the most difficult and most dangerous of circumstances—precisely because the stakes are so high. That is not just what our conscience demands. That is what the law demands. Meier-Göring said it in her judgment: Resist. *Only then can you say: I have not made myself guilty.*

290

Epilogue

The trial of Bruno Dey was not the last Holocaust trial to take place in Germany. It was not even the last trial to examine the crimes at Stutthof. In December 2022, more than two years after the Hamburg verdict, a criminal court in Itzehoe sentenced a 97-year-old woman as an accessory to murder in more than 10,500 cases. She had worked not as a guard but as a secretary in the office of the Stutthof commandant, from June 1943 to April 1945. The punishment was identical to the one imposed on Bruno Dey—a two-year suspended prison sentence—but it was striking all the same: as a lowly office worker she was even further removed from the killings than Dey had been on his watchtower. Her case showed again just how far German justice had traveled since the Demjanjuk ruling.

A few months earlier, a court in Neuruppin had handed down a significantly harsher sentence—five years in jail—to a former guard at the Sachsenhausen concentration camp. The defendant was 101 years old at the time of the verdict, making him the oldest man to be convicted for a crime relating to the Holocaust.

A handful of similar cases was still making its way through the system at the time of writing, though with every month that passed their chances of reaching a verdict grew fainter. The head of the Central Office in Ludwigsburg told me at the time of the Dey trial that it was official practice not to initiate new cases against suspects who were older than ninety-nine. The arithmetic is clear. The story of Germany's late struggle for Holocaust justice is coming to an end, and soon the greatest crime in human history will be left, finally, to the historians alone.

For those who were involved in the Dey trial, it was not easy to let go. When I spoke to Meier-Göring a few years after the verdict, she had just completed an essay, co-written with one of her fellow judges, that analyzed the case and sought to draw lessons for future proceedings. She remembered the case, the man at the center of it, the witnesses, and key exchanges as if they had happened the previous day. It was clear that she had agonized over the verdict at the time, and that she was wrestling with the guilt of Bruno Dey even years later. The case had stayed with her, as it had with Lars Mahnke, the chief prosecutor, who still kept the vast wall chart detailing the murders at Stutthof in his office. It was positioned in a way that his gaze landed on it every time he looked up from his files, every time a visitor entered, every time he left the office for a lunch break. Both Mahnke and Meier-Göring told me they had children who, at the time of the trial, were not so different in age from Bruno Dey in August 1944, when he first set foot inside Stutthof. The trial had made them think: had they raised their children to be strong enough to say no?

I also met again with Stefan Waterkamp, Dey's lawyer. We spoke for hours in a Hamburg coffee shop, going over his defense strategy and revisiting key moments in the trial. He had done what he could for his client, but I sensed a lingering feeling of unease on his part. The questions Waterkamp had raised at the beginning of the trial—why now and why him?—had not been answered entirely to his satisfaction: if Bruno Dey was guilty, should German prosecutors and judges not be consistent and track down the thousands of men and women, civilians and soldiers, police officers and bureaucrats who also played their part in the Holocaust? Had Dey really been judged solely on the merits of the case, or was this an instance of German judges in the present atoning for the sins of German judges in the past?

Looking back at the case, my own view never changed: it was right to prosecute and sentence Bruno Dey. The trial was fair. The court applied the law correctly. Justice was done. But it was important, too, that the final verdict had been handed down with a sense of humanity and in a spirit of humility. The court did not make an example of Dey, nor did it seek to load more responsibility onto his shoulders than he deserved. The verdict recognized that, in the end, the men who were most responsible for the killings at Stutthof were no longer among us. That void could not be filled by Dey simply because he was the only man left to prosecute.

I had been keen to ask Dey himself about the trial, but despite repeated requests neither he nor his family were prepared to speak to me. I was disappointed but not surprised. He had spent nine months explaining himself, over and over again, in courtroom 200 of Hamburg's criminal justice building. Perhaps there was—at least for him—really nothing more left to say.

The trial of Bruno Dey—and Meier-Göring's verdict at the end of it—went a long way toward answering the questions that had sparked my initial fascination with the case. But there were some that defied, and would likely always defy, resolution. What had made seemingly ordinary men like Dey take part in an enterprise of unsurpassed evil? The judge had given an important part of that response in her ruling: out of a failure of conscience, out of indifference, as a result of succumbing to the comfort of obedience. I found another part of the answer in Christopher Browning's seminal study of a German reserve police battalion that killed tens of thousands of Jewish civilians in Poland in 1942 and 1943. Browning examined how a group of "ordinary men" (the title of the book) turned into mass murderers—and why so few of them were able to resist that transformation. His findings are both complex and concerning, but at least in part the key factors he identified sounded surprisingly mundane. Among them was the influence of peer pressure, or "conformity to the group," as he put it. "The battalion had orders to kill Jews, but each individual did not. Yet 80 to 90 percent of the men proceeded to kill, though almost all of them—at least initially—were horrified and disgusted by what they were doing. To break ranks and step out, to adopt overtly nonconformist behavior, was simply beyond most of the men. It was easier for them to shoot."[1]

As much as the men hated the thought of killing civilians, they hated the idea of social reproach from their peers even more. "Those who did not shoot risked isolation, rejection, ostracism—a very uncomfortable prospect within the framework of a tightly knit unit stationed abroad among a hostile population, so that the individual had virtually nowhere else to turn for support and social contact."[2]

That description rings true also for Bruno Dey, a young man who by his own account struggled to stand up for himself, and who had been taught to always keep his head down. As Browning himself makes clear, highlighting such seemingly quotidian factors must not be understood as an attempt to diminish individual guilt: "This story of ordinary men is not the story of all men," he writes. "The reserve policemen faced choices, and most of them committed terrible deeds."[3] Browning concludes his study into the ordinary men who became mass murderers with a simple yet deeply unsettling question: "If the men of

Reserve Police Battalion 101 could become killers under such circumstances, what group of men cannot?"[4]

Bruno Dey, too, faced choices. As do we today. We, too, know the pressure to conform, the reluctance to stand out, the fear of ostracism, and the comfort of obedience. We, too, succumb to them at times. The consequences and costs of our moral failures today are obviously different. The stakes are lower, at least for those of us lucky enough to live in democratic societies governed by the rule of law. Not many see their moral fiber tested in the same way that Bruno Dey's was in the summer and autumn of 1944. But that should not blind us to the fact that our human frailties are always and forever the same. What changes are the times and the circumstances in which those frailties are exposed.

Helmut Kohl, the former German chancellor, described himself on a state visit to Israel in 1984 as part of a generation that had benefited from the "mercy of late birth." The phrase met with controversy at the time. It was understood as a clumsy attempt by the conservative leader to draw a line under the Nazi legacy, and push for a normalization of modern, democratic Germany. But there was truth in that phrase all the same: of course it was a mercy to have been born after 1945, or, like Kohl, who was born in 1930, to have been young enough not to have faced the existential choice between resistance and complicity under Nazi rule.

The idea that our moral status is shaped by conditions and circumstances outside our control is known in philosophy as moral luck. A much-cited example to illustrate the point is that of two drivers who steer their cars home after a heavy night of drinking. The first arrives home safely, parks his car, and goes to bed. The second driver, just as drunk as the first, runs over and kills a child on his way home. Both men are guilty of the same behavior. Their ethical lapse is identical. Yet one of them

295

is able to live the rest of his life unencumbered while the other has killed an innocent human being, and inflicted personal tragedy on another family, as well as his own. He will most likely spend a considerable time in prison—and the rest of his life weighed down by guilt and remorse. Society, too, will judge both men differently. Yet the only difference between them is an element—the presence of a child in the wrong place at the wrong time—that neither man had any influence over.

Bruno Dey was not merely unlucky to find himself in court in October 2019. His failure to make the right choice all those years ago was a genuine failure. More than that, it was a crime. But his story is one that is freighted with moral luck—or the absence of such luck—all the same. Had he lived in a different time, and a different place, his obedience, his weakness, and his inability to say no would have carried less weight. The consequences of his actions and inactions would have been far less terrible. Had he been born, like I was, in democratic Germany in 1975, would he have become an accomplice to murder? The answer, almost certainly, is no. To say so is not to minimize his responsibility, or relativize his guilt. It is a warning. Thinking back to Bruno Dey, the old man in the dock and the young man on the watchtower, I ponder the same question raised by Browning: if Bruno Dey could become an accomplice to murder, which of us cannot?

Acknowledgments

I wrote this book, one chapter at a time, over the course of several years. It was a slow and arduous process, but the lack of haste was probably for the best. Much happened between the opening of the Stutthof trial and the book's completion, both in the world at large and in my own life, and some events have certainly helped to enrich this book. Most importantly, two years after the verdict, I was finally able to access the recordings of the Hamburg trial that Anne Meier-Göring had wisely ordered made at the start of the proceedings. Those tapes, which I transcribed over a series of visits to the Hamburg state archive between August 2022 and January 2023, gave me the chance to bring to life the key exchanges and interventions of the trial, and to understand the process that led to its conclusion in full. My first thanks therefore goes to the staff of the Hamburg state archive for supporting my research.

I am grateful, too, to the people who agreed to speak to me about the Stutthof trial and the key cases and prosecutions leading up to it. They include Lars Mahnke, Anne Meier-Göring, Cornelius Nestler, Jens Rommel, Thomas Walther, Kai Wantzen, and Stefan Waterkamp. My conversation with Éva Pusztai-Fahidi, the Holocaust survivor from Budapest, will stay with me long after this book is out of print.

The starting point for this book was an article I wrote for the

Financial Times Weekend magazine, which appeared in February 2020. I also drew on an interview with Charlotte Knobloch that was published in the *FT* in December 2018. I would like to thank Alec Russell and Alice Fishburn for commissioning those pieces, and Roula Khalaf for granting me permission to reuse passages from both pieces here. At the *FT*, I am also deeply grateful to my two closest colleagues, Abbie Scott and Oksana Rondel, who tolerated my book-related absences and distractions with grace and generosity.

My colleague and friend Daniel Dombey read the manuscript of *Final Verdict*, and offered countless suggestions, corrections, and improvements. My first reader, as ever, was Ana Carbajosa, whose judgment is second to none, and whose kindness and support have meant the world to me for sixteen years and counting.

I would like to thank Jenny Lord, my editor in London, and Mollie Weisenfeld, her counterpart in the U.S., for their guidance. Toby Mundy, my agent, will always have my gratitude for encouraging me to write this book in the first place, and for his support at crucial moments in the process.

My parents, Helmut and Lyn Buck, helped me in myriad ways, as did my sister Alexy. I am especially grateful to my father for allowing me to tell the story of Rupert, my grandfather and the man in the wedding photo.

Bibliography

Arendt, Hannah, *Eichmann in Jerusalem: A Report on the Banality of Evil* (London: Penguin, 2006).

Bauer, Fritz, "Ideal- oder Realkonkurrenz bei nationalsozialistischen Gewaltverbrechen?" *JuristenZeitung*, vol. 22, no. 20 (October 20, 1967), pp. 625–628.

Baumann, Jürgen, "Beihilfe bei eigenhändiger voller Tatbestandserfüllung," *Neue Juristische Wochenschrift*, 1963, pp. 561–565.

Bazyler, Michael J. & Tuerkheimer, Frank M., *Forgotten Trials of the Holocaust* (New York: New York University Press, 2014).

Bode, Sabine, *Die vergessene Generation: Die Kriegskinder brechen ihr Schweigen* (Munich: Piper, 2006).

Brechtken, Magnus (ed.), *Aufarbeitung des Nationalsozialismus: Ein Kompendium* (Göttingen: Wallstein, 2021).

Browning, Christopher R., *Ordinary Men: Reserve Police Battalion 101 and the Final Solution in Poland* (London: Penguin, 2001).

Craig, Edward (ed.), *Routledge Encyclopedia of Philosophy* (London: Routledge, 1998).

Douglas, Lawrence, *The Right Wrong Man: John Demjanjuk and the Last Great Nazi War Crimes Trial* (Princeton: Princeton University Press, 2016).

Eichmüller, Andreas, "Die Strafverfolgung von NS-Verbrechen durch westdeutsche Justizbehörden seit 1945," *Vierteljahrshefte für Zeitgeschichte*, vol. 56, no. 4 (2008), pp. 621–640.

Frei, Norbert (ed.), *Hitlers Eliten nach 1945* (Munich: DTV, 2003).

Friedländer, Saul; Frei, Norbert; Steinbacher, Sybille; Diner, Dan, *Ein Verbrechen ohne Namen: Anmerkungen zum neuen Streit über den Holocaust* (Munich: C. H. Beck, 2022).

Freudiger, Kerstin, *Die juristische Aufarbeitung von NS-Verbrechen* (Tübingen: Mohr Siebeck, 2002).

Fulbrook, Mary, *German National Identity after the Holocaust* (Cambridge: Polity Press, 1999).

—*Reckonings: Legacies of Nazi Persecution and the Quest for Justice* (Oxford: Oxford University Press, 2018).

Giordano, Ralph, *Die zweite Schuld oder von der Last Deutscher zu sein* (Munich: Knaur, 1990).

Goldhagen, Daniel Jonah, *Hitler's Willing Executioners: Ordinary Germans and the Holocaust* (London: Abacus, 1997).

Greenberg, Daniel (ed.), *Jowitt's Dictionary of English Law*, third edition (London: Sweet & Maxwell, 2010).

Gryglewski, Dr. Elke; Jasch, Dr. Hans-Christian; Zolldan, David (eds), *The Meeting at Wannsee and the Murder of the European Jews—Exhibition Catalogue* (Berlin: House of the Wannsee Conference, 2018).

Hilberg, Raul, *Anatomie des Holocaust: Essays und Erinnerungen* (Frankfurt: Fischer, 2016).

Hoffmann, Friedrich, *Die Verfolgung der nationalsozialistischen Gewaltverbrechen in Hessen* (Baden-Baden: Nomos, 2001).

Hofmann, Kerstin, *"Ein Versuch nur—immerhin ein Versuch": Die Zentrale Stelle in Ludwigsburg unter der Leitung von*

Erwin Schüle und Adalbert Rückerl (1958–1984) (Berlin: Metropol, 2018).

Horstmann, Thomas & Litzinger, Heike, *An den Grenzen des Rechts: Gespräche mit Juristen über die Verfolgung von NS-Verbrechen* (Frankfurt: Campus, 2006).

Huth, Peter (ed.), *Die letzten Zeugen: Der Auschwitz-Prozess von Lüneburg 2015, Eine Dokumentation* (Stuttgart: Reclam, 2015).

Jasch, Hans-Christian & Kaiser, Wolf, *Der Holocaust vor deutschen Gerichten: Amnestieren, Verdrängen, Bestrafen* (Stuttgart: Reclam, 2017).

Jasch, Hans-Christian & Kreutzmüller, Christoph, *The Participants: The Men of the Wannsee Conference* (New York: Berghahn, 2017).

Jureit, Ulrike & Schneider, Christian, *Gefühlte Opfer: Illusionen der Vergangenheitsbewältigung* (Stuttgart: Klett-Cotta, 2010).

Keldungs, Karl-Heinz, *NS-Prozesse 1945–2015: Eine Bilanz aus juristischer Sicht* (Düsseldorf: Edition Virgines, 2019).

Klee, Ernst, *Das Personenlexikon zum Dritten Reich: Wer war was vor und nach 1945* (Frankfurt: Fischer, 2009).

Klüger, Ruth, *Weiter Leben: Eine Jugend* (Göttingen: Wallstein, 1992).

Kuhn, Hermann (ed.), *Stutthof: Ein Konzentrationslager vor den Toren Danzigs* (Bremen: Edition Temmen, 2016).

Küper, Wilfried, "Erinnerungsarbeit: Das Urteil des BGH vom 20.5.1969 zur Verjährung der Mordbeihilfe—ein Fehlurteil?" *JuristenZeitung*, vol. 72, no. 5 (2017), pp. 229–236.

Kurz, Thilo, "Paradigmenwechsel bei der Strafverfolgung des Personals in den deutschen Vernichtungslagern?" *Zeitschrift für internationale Strafrechtsdogmatik* (2013), pp. 122–129.

Leo, Per, *Tränen ohne Trauer: Nach der Erinnerungskultur* (Stuttgart: Klett-Cotta, 2021).

Longerich, Peter, *Wannseekonferenz: Der Weg zur "Endlösung,"* (Munich: Pantheon, 2016).

Lüttig, Frank & Lehmann, Jens (eds), *Die letzten NS-Verfahren* (Baden-Baden: Nomos, 2017).

Mächler, Stefan, *The Wilkomirski Affair: A Study in Biographical Truth* (New York: Schocken Books, 2001).

Mitscherlich, Alexander & Margarete, *Die Unfähigkeit zu trauern: Grundlagen kollektiven Verhaltens* (Munich: Piper, 2020).

Moses, Dirk, "The German Catechism," Geschichte der Gegenwart blog (2021).

Nehmer, Bettina, *Das Problem der Ahndung von Einsatzgruppenverbrechen durch die bundesdeutsche Strafjustiz* (Frankfurt: Peter Lang Edition, 2015).

Nestler, Cornelius, "Der 2. Strafsenat des Bundesgerichtshofs und die Strafverfolgung von NS-Verbrechern" in *Festschrift für Thomas Fischer* (Munich: C. H. Beck, 2018).

Pendas, Devin O., *The Frankfurt Auschwitz Trial, 1963–1965* (New York: Cambridge University Press, 2006).

Renz, Werner, *Auschwitz vor Gericht: Fritz Bauers Vermächtnis und seine Missachtung* (Hamburg: Europäische Verlagsanstalt, 2018).

Rothberg, Michael, "Lived Multidirectionality: 'Historikerstreit 2.0' and the Politics of Holocaust Memory," *Memory Studies*, vol. 15, no. 6 (2022), pp. 1316–1329.

Rückerl, Adalbert, *NS-Verbrechen vor Gericht: Versuch einer Vergangenheitsbewältigung* (Heidelberg: C. F. Müller, 1984).

Rüter, Christiaan F. & De Mildt, Dick W. (eds), *Justiz und NS-Verbrechen: Sammlung deutscher Strafurteile wegen nationalsozialistischer Tötungsverbrechen 1945–2012*, 49 volumes (Amsterdam: Amsterdam University Press).

Salzborn, Samuel, *Kollektive Unschuld: Die Abwehr der Shoah im deutschen Erinnern* (Leipzig: Hentrich & Hentrich, 2020).

Sereny, Gitta, *The German Trauma: Experiences and Reflections 1938–2001* (London: Penguin, 2000).

Steinke, Ronen, *Fritz Bauer oder Auschwitz vor Gericht* (Munich: Piper, 2018).

Stone, Dan, *The Holocaust: An Unfinished History* (London: Pelican, 2023).

Ustorf, Anne-Ev, *Wir Kinder der Kriegskinder: Die Generation im Schatten des Zweiten Weltkriegs* (Freiburg: Herder, 2016).

Wachsmann, Nikolaus, *KL: A History of the Nazi Concentration Camps* (New York: Farrar, Straus & Giroux, 2015).

Wandres, Thomas & Werle, Gerhard, *Auschwitz vor Gericht: Völkermord und bundesdeutsche Strafjustiz* (Munich: C. H. Beck, 1995).

Weinke, Annette, *Die Verfolgung von NS-Tätern im geteilten Deutschland* (Paderborn: Schöningh, 2002).

Werle, Gerhard, "Der Holocaust als Gegenstand der bundesdeutschen Strafjustiz," *Neue Juristische Wochenschrift* (1992), pp. 2529–2535.

Wistrich, Robert S., *Who's Who in Nazi Germany* (London: Routledge, 2002).

Notes

Chapter One: The man behind the red folder

1 All direct quotes from the hearings are derived from the author's transcript of the official recordings of the trial preserved in the Hamburg state archive. This opening exchange is the exception, as the recording of the first day of the trial started only later. It is based on the author's contemporaneous notes.

2 The court operated a "pool" system for the media. Only one photographer and one cameraman were allowed to take pictures and film inside the courtroom, and only during the opening minutes of each hearing. The images were then shared with other media.

Chapter Two: The second disgrace

1 Renz, *Auschwitz vor Gericht*, p. 188.
2 Eichmüller, *Die Strafverfolgung von NS-Verbrechen*, p. 639.
3 *Ibid.*
4 Renz, p. 188.
5 *Ibid.*
6 Kuhn, *Stutthof*, p. 93.
7 Miriam Hollstein, "SPD-Politikerin fordert KZ-Pflichtbesuch für Deutsche und Migranten," *Bild am Sonntag* (January 7, 2018), accessible online, www.bild.de/politik/inland/konzentrationslager/pflichtbesuch-fuer-fluechtlinge-54396060.bild.html
8 Theodor Adorno, in *Prismen, Kulturkritik und Gesellschaft* (Munich:

DTV, 1963), p. 26. The famous appeal was almost certainly not intended to be taken literally, but "Adorno's dictum" became a touchpoint for German intellectuals and writers after the war all the same. See also Klaus Hoffmann, "Poetry after Auschwitz—Adorno's Dictum," in *German Life and Letters*, vol. 58, no. 2 (April 2004), pp. 182–194.

9   Jasch & Kaiser, *Der Holocaust vor deutschen Gerichten*, p. 85.
10 *Ibid.*, p. 51.
11 *Ibid.*, p. 52.
12 *Ibid.*, p. 53.
13 Baumann, "*Beihilfe bei eigenhändiger voller Tatbestandserfüllung*," p. 561.
14 Douglas Martin, "A Nazi Past, a Queens Home Life, an Overlooked Death," *New York Times* (December 2, 2005), accessible online, www.nytimes.com/2005/12/02/world/europe/a-nazi-past-a-queens-home-life-an-overlooked-death.html
15 "West Germany: The Monster," *Time* magazine (July 14, 1958), accessible online, http://content.time.com/time/subscriber/article/0,33009,868574-2,00.html
16 *Ibid.*
17 Jasch & Kaiser, p. 34.
18 Longerich, *Wannseekonferenz*, p. 129ff.
19 Jasch & Kreutzmüller, *The Participants*, p. 196.
20 *Ibid.*, p. 198.
21 Gryglewski et al. (eds), *The Meeting at Wannsee and the Murder of the European Jews*, p. 154.
22 Mitscherlich & Mitscherlich, *Die Unfähigkeit zu trauern*, p. 25.
23 *Ibid.*, p. 27.
24 Jasch & Kaiser, p. 91.
25 Eichmüller, p. 626.
26 *Ibid.*
27 *Ibid.*

Chapter Three: Factories of death

1 Walther was admitted to the Hamburg trial as the lawyer for one of the private accessory prosecutors, but he asked a colleague to appear for him in court.
2 Jasch & Kaiser, p. 96.
3 *Ibid.*, p. 97.
4 The judgment can be found at https://openjur.de/u/2130562.html
5 *Ibid.*
6 Douglas, *The Right Wrong Man*, p. 149.
7 Weinke, *Die Verfolgung von NS-Tätern*, p. 76.
8 Hofmann, *"Ein Versuch nur—immerhin ein Versuch,"* p. 450.
9 *Ibid.*
10 After his resignation from the Zentrale Stelle, Schüle returned to his previous position as a senior public prosecutor. He retired in 1978, and that same year was awarded one of Germany's highest honors—the Grosses Bundesverdienstkreuz—for his work bringing Nazi perpetrators to justice. He died in Stuttgart in 1993, aged eighty.
11 Lüttig & Lehmann, *Die letzten NS-Verfahren*, p. 86.
12 Douglas, p. 218.
13 Rüter, *Justiz und NS-Verbrechen*, vol. 49, p. 362.
14 Kurz, *"Paradigmenwechsel bei der Strafverfolgung des Personals,"* p. 122.

Chapter Five: The wedding photo

1 Suzanne Grindel, *Bildungsgeschichte Deutschlands*, 2018, http://worldviews.gei.de/open/B_2018_Grindel_Deutschland/ger/
2 Figures taken from the *Sozialgesetzbuch (SGB) Sechstes Buch (VI)—Gesetzliche Rentenversicherung—(Artikel 1 des Gesetzes v. 18. Dezember 1989, BGBl. I S. 2261, 1990 I S. 1337)*, annex 1, accessible online, www.gesetze-im-internet.de/sgb_6/anlage_1.html
3 The evidence itself may in any case have been only partial. Among the documents I found a letter of confirmation from 1938, signed by a senior SS officer, noting that Rupert Buck left the organization at the end of 1935 due to a "transfer to the Reichsarbeitsdienst." There is no mention of mutiny.

Chapter Six: "The only route to freedom is through the chimneys"

1   Kuhn, p. 41.
2   Klüger, *Weiter Leben—Eine Jugend*, p. 139.
3   *Ibid.*
4   The number of deaths cited here is higher than most estimates, which are usually in the range of 60,000–65,000. In his 2015 study of the concentration-camp system, *KL—A History of the Nazi Concentration Camps*, Nikolaus Wachsmann estimates that 61,500 prisoners perished at Stutthof.

Chapter Seven: Bullets and birdshit

1   "Der Täter schoss mehrfach auf die Tür," *Der Spiegel* (October 9, 2019), accessible online, www.spiegel.de/panorama/justiz/halle-saale-augenzeuge-der-taeter-schoss-mehrfach-auf-die-tuer-a-1290726.html
2   Friederike Haupt & Berthold Kohler, "Es ist richtig, dass das jetzt ein anderer übernimmt," *Frankfurter Allgemeine Zeitung* (October 30, 2021), accessible online, www.faz.net/aktuell/politik/inland/merkel-im-interview-ueber-fluechtlinge-die-csu-den-zustand-der-welt-und-ihr-blick-aufs-aelterwerden-17609086.html
3   Guy Chazan, "Nationalist AfD makes breakthrough in German election," *Financial Times* (September 24, 2017), accessible online, www.ft.com/content/d18213e0-a105-11e7-b797-b61809486fe2
4   *Frankfurter Allgemeine Zeitung*, "Gauland: Hitler nur ein 'Vogelschiss' in deutscher Geschichte" (June 2, 2018), accessible online, www.faz.net/aktuell/politik/inland/gauland-hitler-nur-vogelschiss-in-deutscher-geschichte-15619502.html
5   *Die Welt*, "Gauland fordert Recht, stolz zu sein auf 'Leistungen' in beiden Weltkriegen" (September 14, 2017), accessible online, www.welt.de/politik/deutschland/article168663338/Gauland-fordert-Recht-stolz-zu-sein-auf-Leistungen-in-beiden-Weltkriegen.html
6   *Ibid.*
7   Anton Troianovski, "The German Right Believes It's Time to Discard the Country's Historical Guilt," *Wall Street Journal* (March 2, 2017),

accessible online, www.wsj.com/articles/the-german-right-believes-its-time-to-discard-their-countrys-historical-guilt-1488467995

8 *Ibid.*

9 *Die Zeit*, "Die Höcke-Rede von Dresden in Auszügen" (January 18, 2017), accessible online, www.zeit.de/news/2017-01/18/parteien-die-hoecke-rede-von-dresden-in-wortlaut-auszuegen-18171207

10 *Ibid.*

11 Figures taken from the Federal Ministry of the Interior publication "Politisch motivierte Kriminalität im Jahr 2021, Bundesweite Fallzahlen" ("Statistics on politically motivated crime in 2021: nationwide case numbers"), accessible online, www.bmi.bund.de/SharedDocs/downloads/DE/veroeffentlichungen/nachrichten/2022/pmk2021-factsheets.pdf

Chapter Eight: The subjective problem

1 Greenberg (ed.), *Jowitt's Dictionary of English Law*, p. 1502.

2 *Ibid.*, p. 1313.

3 Nehmer, *Das Problem der Ahndung von Einsatzgruppenverbrechen*, p. 88.

4 Jasch & Kaiser, p. 102.

5 Freudiger, *Die juristische Aufarbeitung von NS-Verbrechen*, p. 183.

6 Jasch & Kaiser, p. 103.

7 Information provided by the German Peace Society—United War Opponents (DFG–VK), Darmstadt branch, accessible online, https://dfg-vk-darmstadt.de/Lexikon_Auflage_2/MohrRobert.htm

8 BGH ruling October 19, 1962, 9 StE 4/62, https://openjur.de/u/55500.html

9 *Ibid.*

10 Stiller, Alexa, "The Mass Murder of the European Jews and the Concept of 'Genocide' in the Nuremberg Trials: Reassessing Raphaël Lemkin's Impact," *Genocide Studies and Prevention: An International Journal*, vol. 13, no. 1 (2019), pp. 144–172.

11 *Nuremberg Trial Proceedings*, vol. 1, "Indictment: Count Three," accessible online, https://avalon.law.yale.edu/imt/count3.asp

Chapter Nine: "May I embrace you?"

1   *Die Welt*, "Wie kann ein KZ-Überlebender einen SS-Wachmann umarmen?" (November 19, 2019), accessible online, www.welt.de/regionales/hamburg/plus203636192/Kunst-des-Vergebens-Wie-kann-ein-KZ-Ueberlebender-einen-SS-Wachmann-umarmen.html

2   Moritz Gerlach, "Die leider falsche Geschichte von der grossen Vergebung," *Der Spiegel* (December 27, 2019), published in English on January 14, 2020, and accessible online, www.spiegel.de/international/germany/the-concentration-camp-victim-who-never-was-a-a7c50dd3-773f-4697-b9c0-e40618a62e9e

3   Helen Lewis, "The Identity Hoaxers," *The Atlantic* (March 16, 2021), accessible online, www.theatlantic.com/international/archive/2021/03/krug-carrillo-dolezal-social-munchausen-syndrome/618289/

4   Robert M. Kaplan, "Holocaust Deception in Australia: A Review," *Forensic Research & Criminology International Journal*, vol. 2, no. 5 (2016), p. 186.

5   Fiachra Gibbons & Stephen Moss, "Fragments of a Fraud," the *Guardian*, October 15, 1999, accessible online, www.theguardian.com/theguardian/1999/oct/15/features11.g24

6   Elena Lappin, "The Man with Two Heads," *Granta* (June 4, 1999), accessible online, https://granta.com/the-man-with-two-heads/

7   Stefan Mächler, *The Wilkomirski Affair*, p. 149.

8   *Ibid.*, p. 268.

9   *Ibid.*, p. 269.

Chapter Ten: Auschwitz on trial

1   Pendas, *The Frankfurt Auschwitz Trial*, p. 122.

2   Wandres & Werle, *Auschwitz vor Gericht*, p. 42.

3   Pendas, p. 24.

4   Steinke, *Fritz Bauer*, p. 95.

5   *Ibid.*

6   *Ibid.*, p. 97.

7   *Ibid.*, p. 13.

8 Wandres & Werle, p. 43.

9 Death and ill health reduced the number of defendants to twenty-two by the time of the opening of the trial, and to twenty by the time of the verdict.

10 Richard Baer, who succeeded Höss as commandant of Auschwitz, was also due to stand trial in Frankfurt, but died of heart failure six months before it opened.

11 Wandres & Werle, p. 168.

12 Jasch & Kaiser, p. 141.

13 Pendas, p. 85.

14 *Ibid.*

15 Wandres & Werle, p. 55.

16 *Ibid.*

17 Pendas, p. 134 ff142.

18 Pendas, p. 135.

19 Steinke, p. 195.

20 The Fritz Bauer Institute has published key documents, transcripts and biographies relating to the Frankfurt Auschwitz trial at www.auschwitz-prozess.de/zeugenaussagen/Weis-Jan/

21 Wandres & Werle, p. 31.

22 www.auschwitz-prozess.de/zeugenaussagen/Schlussworte_der_Angeklagten/

23 *Ibid.*

24 *Ibid.*

25 *Ibid.*

26 *Ibid.*

27 Pendas, p. 215.

28 www.auschwitz-prozess.de/zeugenaussagen/Urteilsbegru endung_1/

29 Pendas, p. 246.

30 Rüter & De Mildt, *Justiz und NS-Verbrechen*, volume 20, p. 450.

31 *Ibid.*, p. 448.

32 *Ibid.*

33 *Ibid.*

34 Bauer, "Ideal- oder Realkonkurrenz," p. 627.

35 Nestler, "Der 2," p. 1182.

36 Renz, p. 169.
37 *Ibid.*
38 *Ibid.*
39 Nestler, p. 1182.
40 *Ibid.*, p. 1187.
41 Wandres & Werle, p. 215.
42 Pendas, p. 263.
43 *Ibid.*, p. 287.
44 Bauer, p. 628.
45 Steinke, p. 177.

Chapter Eleven: The dancer and the bookkeeper

1   Huth, *Die letzten Zeugen*, p. 10.
2   *Ibid.*, p. 13.
3   *Ibid.*
4   Gröning offered a contrasting view on this subject later in the trial, saying that it "would have been just as terrible if the baby had been shot."
5   Matthias Geyer, "Der Buchhalter von Auschwitz," *Der Spiegel* (May 8, 2005), published in English on May 9, 2005, and accessible online, www.spiegel.de/international/spiegel/an-ss-officer-remembers-the-bookkeeper-from-auschwitz-a-355188.html
6   *Ibid.*
7   Huth, p. 15.
8   Renz, p. 188.
9   Huth, p. 12.
10 Geyer, "Der Buchhalter von Auschwitz."
11 *Ibid.*
12 Huth, p. 43.
13 *Ibid.*, p. 94ff.
14 *Ibid.*, p. 135.
15 *Ibid.*
16 *Ibid.*, p. 239. The phrase had actually been coined by Cornelius Nestler, the law professor who served as a lawyer in all the key late Holocaust trials, including those against Demjanjuk, Gröning, and Dey.

17 *Ibid.*, p. 31.
18 *Ibid.*, p. 30.
19 *Ibid.*, p. 34.
20 Lüttig & Lehmann, p. 175.

Chapter Thirteen: A legacy of stones

1   Bundeszentrale für politische Bildung (Federal Agency for Civic Education), *Gedenkstätten für die Opfer des Nationalsozialismus*, two volumes (1995 and 2000).
2   Florian Dierl, "Historische Orte und Erinnerungspolitik," in *Aufarbeitung des Nationalsozialismus:Ein Kompendium* (Göttingen: Wallstein Verlag, 2021), p. 249.
3   Jürgen Hohmeyer, "Mutter im Regen," *Der Spiegel* (November 14, 1993), accessible online, www.spiegel.de/kultur/mutter-im-regen-a-5f07305e-0002-0001-0000-000013681887
4   Fulbrook, *Reckonings*, p. 497.
5   *Ibid.*
6   Speech by Wolfgang Thierse, May 10, 2005, accessible online, www.stiftung-denkmal.de/wp-content/uploads/flyer_10thmay.pdf
7   *Ibid.*
8   Richard Brody, "The Inadequacy of Berlin's 'Memorial to the Murdered Jews of Europe'," *New Yorker* (July 12, 2012), accessible online, www.newyorker.com/culture/richard-brody/the-inadequacy-of-berlins-memorial-to-the-murdered-jews-of-europe
9   Speech by Lea Rosh, May 10, 2005, accessible online, www.stiftung-denkmal.de/wp-content/uploads/flyer_10thmay.pdf
10 Kirsten Grieshaber, "Plaques for Nazi Victims Offer a Personal Impact," *New York Times*, November 29, 2003, www.nytimes.com/2003/11/29/arts/plaques-for-nazi-victims-offer-a-personal-impact.html

Chapter Fourteen: A trial on the edge

1   *Allgemeinverfügung* (General Decree), March 15, 2020, accessible online, www.hamburg.de/coronavirus/13721232/allgemeinverfuegung-zur-eindaemmung-des-coronavirus-in-hamburg/

2   Wilhem Bühner & Anni Rank, "The Effects of SARS-CoV-2 on Criminal Procedure in Germany," *German Law Journal*, vol. 23, no. 4 (May 26, 2022), accessible online, www.cambridge.org/core/journals/german-law-journal/article/effects-of-sarscov2-on-criminal-procedure-in-germany/ADBED72F66FD7306BD57C975ACA45A2A

Chapter Fifteen: The culture of memory

1   Joachim Gauck, speech in front of the Bundestag on the day of remembrance of the victims of National Socialism, January 27, 2015, accessible online, www.bundespraesident.de/SharedDocs/Downloads/DE/Reden/2015/01/150127-Gedenken-Holocaust-englisch.pdf?__blob=publicationFile

2   Speech by Heiko Maas, German foreign minister, on May 28, 2021, accessible online, www.auswaertiges-amt.de/en/newsroom/news/-/2463598. At the time of writing the reconciliation agreement had yet to be ratified by the Namibian parliament. Representatives of the Nama and Herero rejected it as insufficient.

3   Jürgen Zimmerer & Michael Rothberg, "Enttabuisiert den Vergleich!" *Die Zeit* (April 4, 2021), accessible online, www.zeit.de/2021/14/erinnerungskultur-gedenken-pluralisieren-holocaust-vergleich-globalisierung-geschichte/komplettansicht

4   Moses, "The German Catechism."

5   Norbert Frei, "Deutsche Vergangenheit und postkoloniale Katechese," in Friedländer et al., *Ein Verbrechen ohne Namen*, p. 47.

6   Saul Friedländer, "Ein Genozid wie jeder andere?" *Ibid.*, p. 19.

7   *Ibid.*, p. 24.

8   *Ibid.*, p. 28.

9   Federal Ministry of the Interior, Building and Community, "Migration Report 2021," p. 15, accessible online, www.bamf.de/SharedDocs/

Anlagen/EN/Forschung/Migrationsberichte/migrationsbericht-2021-zentrale-ergebnisse.html?view=renderPdfViewer&nn=447198

10 Navid Kermani, "Auschwitz morgen," *Frankfurter Allgemeine Zeitung* (July 7, 2017), accessible online, www.faz.net/aktuell/feuilleton/debatten/auschwitz-morgen-navid-kermani-ueber-die-zukunft-der-erinnerung-15094667.html

11 *Ibid.*

12 The fish finger photo is a work by the German conceptual artist Ruppe Koselleck.

13 Arendt, *Eichmann in Jerusalem*, p. 251.

14 Leo, *Tränen ohne Trauer*, p. 237.

15 The German title of her book is a wordplay that is perhaps best translated as "Feeling Like Victims."

16 Jureit & Schneider, *Gefühlte Opfer*, p. 28.

17 Clint Smith, "Monuments to the Unthinkable," *The Atlantic* (November 14, 2022), accessible online, www.theatlantic.com/magazine/archive/2022/12/holocaust-remembrance-lessons-america/671893

Chapter Sixteen: The final verdict

1 Richard Glücks served as the head of the SS concentration camp inspectorate. He committed suicide following the capitulation of Nazi Germany in May 1945.

Epilogue

1 Browning, *Ordinary Men*, p. 184.

2 *Ibid.*, p. 185.

3 *Ibid.*, p. 188.

4 *Ibid.*, p. 189.

Index

Page numbers for illustrations are in *italics*, notes by the use of "n."

319